THE POWER OF
STRATEGIC
INFLUENCE!

10 SUCCESS FACTORS OF
HIGHLY INFLUENTIAL LEADERS

GARY C. LANEY

The Power of Strategic Influence!
10 Success Factors of Highly Influential Leaders
Copyright © 2021 Gary C. Laney
All rights reserved

MINDSTIR MEDIA

Published by Mindstir Media, LLC
45 Lafayette Rd | Suite 181| North Hampton, NH 03862 | USA
1.800.767.0531 | www.mindstirmedia.com

Printed in the United States of America
ISBN: 978-1-7370915-9-2

The information presented herein represents the views
of the author as of the date of publication.

This book is presented for informational purposes only. Due to the rate at which
conditions change, the author reserves the right to alter and update his opinions at any
time. While every attempt has been made to verify the information in this book, the
author does not assume any responsibility for errors, inaccuracies, or omissions.

CONTENTS

PART THREE: INFLUENCE EXPANSION AND THE END GAME

SPHERE OF LEADERSHIP

SPHERE OF OPPORTUNITY

SPHERE OF STRATEGIC INFLUENCE

PRAISE FOR
THE POWER OF STRATEGIC INFLUENCE!

"In *The Power of Strategic Influence!*, Gary C. Laney distills a career's worth of wisdom into a relatable guidebook that walks you through each of the critical spheres of influence. You reap the benefits of his influence through the inside advice from other business and entrepreneurial heavyweights. His positive, proactive tone makes this a great read. No matter where you are in your career, pick up a copy and start your own journey to becoming a person of greater influence. You won't regret it."

—J.J. Hebert, #1 bestselling author featured in
Forbes, Entrepreneur and *Business Insider*

"Gary has created a fascinating look at what makes people happy and successful. Most important is the concept of building and using influence to achieve your goals. A positive mental outlook and accepting personal responsibility should ring true for all of us. What you think and believe shapes your attitude and your future. Gary has found a very real and impactful way of delivering that message through national leaders and bringing that forward to allow readers to imagine themselves in a role to which they will aspire."

—John T. Hewitt, American entrepreneur, CEO at Loyalty Brands,
Co-Founder of Jackson Hewitt, and Sole Founder of
Liberty Tax Service, author of *iCompete*

"Gary's superb new book will become a classic in how to build and use influence for power and profit. It captures our need to depend on each other and become more self-aware."

—Tom Kuczmarski, President – Kuczmarski Innovation,
Co-Founder -Chicago Innovation, Senior Lecturer, Kellogg
School of Management, author of 8 books

"In his powerful new book, *The Power of Strategic Influence!*, Gary Laney shares how you can cultivate and create highly effective and strategic business spheres of influence. Gary is a pro! He knows what he is talking about. Follow his proven example!"

—Kyle Wilson, Founder of Jim Rohn International
& KyleWilson.com and a multiple #1 bestselling author including
*Success Habits of Super Achievers, Chicken Soup for the Entrepreneurs
Soul* and *52 Lessons I Learned from Jim Rohn and Other Legends*

"Gary Laney has done his homework to stir up a whole new field of thinking! Everything we do is through our own influence or the influence of others. Gary helps you understand how to build a mega influence that helps you maximize your success. *The Power of Strategic Influence!* is jammed full of creative ways to build powerful relationships, combine your efforts with the best of others and have fun doing it. This is a must-read book and you will never be the same again after reading it."

—Steven R. Shallenberger, Author of the national bestselling book,
Becoming Your Best, The 12 Principles of Highly Successful Leaders.
Founder of Eagle Systems International and Synergy Co's

"The Power of Strategic Influence! has more heart than what we're seeing today with "Influencers." There's a shift happening—people are beginning to see through these inauthentic ways, and I believe it will be leaders like Gary who will hold a space for the wholeness and community to come back and lead into the future. Like, actual life skills that evolves the being, not a quick-fix to get somewhere higher."

—Sarah Woods, Author, business coach, and previous contributing
writer for Mountain Life Media, *The Huffington Post,* and Liftopia

FOREWORD

Gary Laney is an accomplished executive and entrepreneur. In his book, *The Power of Strategic Influence!*, Gary breaks down how to build influence, maximize it, and share it … to achieve true success in life.

All of us start at the bottom, on the lowest rung of the ladder, but none of us want to stay there. The trick is figuring out how to take that next step. But there's more to it than that. You have to take the next step in the right direction. Now imagine how much easier that would be and how much more confident you would be if you had your own personal coach directing you. You don't have to imagine. You're holding it in your hands.

You can read Gary's bio for yourself and see that he knows what he is talking about. He has used everything he outlines in this book to develop and leverage his own sphere of influence. Not only that, but he also warns you about outdated methods, time-wasters, and energy-stealers so you can focus on actions you can take starting today to deliver results.

After pioneering the "As Seen On TV" business, I'm no stranger to industry leadership. I have spent decades building my network, my reputation, and my wealth of experience, then passing that wisdom on to my followers. I even published a bestselling book called *Key Person of Influence*, so I can say Gary's book truly hits the nail on the head. I wholeheartedly agree with him. Your sphere of influence is the essential ingredient in your recipe for success, respect, and a lasting legacy. Even today, my Rolodex is one of the most powerful resources I have, and that's all because of years of building my network.

As each chapter builds on the previous one, you'll learn how to move into the next sphere, gaining more influence, growing your network, and positioning yourself when opportunities develop. Gary shows you how to become a master in your field and add real value in your career and relationships. Let's face it, you can have great technical expertise, but if no one knows that, it loses value. Likewise, you can have worldwide connections, but if you don't know what you're talking about, that phone will quit ringing. However, with a substantial foundation and strong network, opportunities begin to flow in with less and less effort.

The Power of Strategic Influence! is a playbook for resourcefully rising to the top by purposefully utilizing tactics such as understanding the marketplace, specializing in your field, differentiating yourself, achieving competitive leadership competencies, and how to make strategic, game-changing connections, just to name a few. Gary imparts all of this with engaging stories and examples that will help the information take root. Graphics and tables summarize the key takeaways and make it easy to refer to them again and again. He demonstrates how universal theories, such as the law of attraction, help you connect with the right people in the right situations. Gary taps into his own sphere of influence, which includes some of history's greatest minds. In these pages, he shares inside secrets gleaned from today's top executives and entrepreneurs in a variety of industries and with a range of specialties, illustrating how these legends utilized the very tactics in this book.

Gary doesn't just teach you how to build your sphere of influence and how to seize the opportunities that it brings, he encourages you to give back at every step on your journey. Each one of the influencers he enlists for insight also models that for you.

Every spring at colleges and universities across the country, thousands of people graduate with business degrees, and yet, only a handful distinguish themselves from the masses. Thousands of people have ideas for new businesses or new products, but they don't all find success. What makes the difference? Harnessing the power of influence. Never underestimate the importance of influence in achieving life's most essential objectives and learn the strategy for building your influence throughout these pages.

If your goal is to rise to the top in your company or industry, pick up a copy of *The Power of Strategic Influence!* by Gary Laney and learn from his powerful insight. Take it from a Shark…you'll be glad you did.

Kevin Harrington,
Original Shark from
ABC's *Shark Tank* and
Bestselling Author

This book is dedicated to my best friend and love of my life Carla, to our four daughters Leisa, Kylie, Morgan, Alexandra, and our two sons Nicholas and Joshua. I love you all!

ACKNOWLEDGMENTS

I will forever be grateful to my family, friends, research staff and publisher who encouraged me and provided welcomed support during this book-writing process. I thank my mother who has since passed on, who was my biggest fan and the prime example of positive influence.

Thank you to my wife, Carla. I don't know what I did to deserve this amazing woman in my life, but something extraordinary happened when we met at a New Year's dance in 1979 and were married under a year later. Life has been wonderful ever since. She has been by my side through thick and thin. Her love, support, and belief in me is why I am a happy man today. I owe any success I have to her. Writing this book was no exception. I'll spend the rest of my life trying to repay her.

Thank you to Kevin Harrington for his interest, valuable feedback, and support of my book. He is the epitome of a strategic influencer and a selfless Center of Influence that I teach about in my book.

Thank you to Steven Shallenberger, one of my first employers and, for the past forty-two years, a loyal friend, role model, and confidant. I thank him for his willingness to be interviewed, for his mentorship, and for the time, attention and guidance he freely gave during my book-writing experience. I greatly value our meaningful relationship.

Thank you to John Hewitt, who from the moment he learned I was writing a book, offered to endorse it and to be interviewed. John and I were first introduced in 2019 at a dinner in San Jose, California, with a group of other CEOs where I had the honor to sit next to him and learn firsthand why people follow him. He is an industry icon and a Center of Influence, because he has vision, competitiveness, and because he has the uncanny ability to make people feel comfortable in his presence.

Thank you to Brian Esposito for being one of my featured CEOs. He offered continual support during the writing of my book and connected me to some key business leaders who are included in this book. Brian was first a client of mine nearly twenty years ago and has always had a positive influence on me. He is an exceptional business leader who spends the bulk of his time helping business leaders solve their problems.

To the other nine truly remarkable and inspiring CEOs who accepted the invitation to be interviewed, I say thank you! They are Larry Namer, Anu Shukla, Tom Ziglar, Christal Bemont, Gary Kennedy, Glo Gordon, Somdutta Singh, Kimberly Carney, and Daniela Ciocan. You each exemplify unending work ethic, vision, and my favorite—you all do what you do because you actually care about the people who depend on you and follow you. The true measure of leadership is positive influence.

INTRODUCTION BY GARY C. LANEY

MY FATHER WAS MY FIRST influencer and a successful entrepreneur. He owned and operated a chain of mercantile department stores and a first-run movie theater. Though I'm proud of my MBA achieved from Northwestern's Kellogg School of Management, I have always said that I earned my first MBA from my dad, growing up in the family business. I learned every aspect of business from him by starting at the bottom: stocking shelves, then progressing to delivery boy, next to bookkeeper, to sales, and on up the ladder to marketing and advertising, then as a manager for one of his stores and ultimately as a store owner, buying his last store so he could retire. I admired and respected my dad. His influence greatly impacted my life. His example of discipline, strong work ethic, and mentorship groomed me to become the successful entrepreneur I am today.

This book is about positive and strategic influence and aptly named *The Power of Strategic Influence!*. I wrote this book because I'm passionate about positive forms of influence that stem from meaningful relationships, built upon trust. This book is about learning how to cultivate relationships with influential business people from your industry who can be strategic to your business and marketing plan. Developing relationships with these types of influencers can have an enormous impact on your business because of the potential sustaining relationships you can experience with them. Unlike social media influencers, who are very transactional, and seldom make a real connection with their clients, business influencers are more open to developing an actual business working relationship, and a strategic long-term relationship. I'm referring to experts who have vested interest in the industry, influential connections, and who have similar values that relate to your company's mission and vision. These strategic business influencers can get involved in your business planning and marketing strategy, can share their personal value of knowledge, expertise and experience, and facilitate important business introductions.

The Power of Strategic Influence! will provide you with the necessary perspective, as well as tools, called Success Factors, to help you advance through the Six Spheres of Influence. Sphere One is Perspective. This is a preparatory sphere, providing Two Points of Perspective which will paint a mental picture of the journey you are about to embark on. Spheres Two through Six will teach you about the Ten Success Factors that will guide you step-by-step through the development process of acquiring, expanding, and ultimately sharing your personal sphere of influence.

BRIEF OVERVIEW

The six spheres are Perspective, Accountability, Relationships, Leadership, Opportunity, and Strategic Influence.

PERSPECTIVE

The first two chapters are about getting a mental perspective of the journey you are about to begin and to also prepare you for the exciting experience of influence development.

In the first chapter, *Perspective Point One*, we will dive into foundational criteria for "Establishing a Survival Mindset" (committing to the idea that you can handle anything life throws at you) and a critical understanding that developing a powerful and personal sphere of influence is a worthy goal. We will have a discussion about exchanges of value (what value each party brings to the table), then begin a dialogue about the importance of trust, followed by the concept of personal value (your knowledge, expertise, and experience), and finally learning the criteria for meeting the right people with potential reciprocal value.

This is followed by *Perspective Point Two*, gaining the mental understanding and perspective of the importance of "Developing a Networking Focus" for building your personal sphere of influence.

INTRODUCING THE TEN SUCCESS FACTORS

ACCOUNTABILITY

Success Factor One is "Accept Personal Responsibility" or looking at problems with a solution-oriented approach, being adaptable, and recognizing what you can and cannot control.

This is followed by *Success Factor Two*, "Be Self-Reliant." To effectively interact with other people and build your network of influence, you must start with a solid personal foundation, by knowing your strengths and capabilities and be willing to face your fears.

RELATIONSHIPS

Success Factor Three is "Develop a Network of Influential Connections." This is where influence begins, that of taking connections to the next level by exhibiting a giver attitude to attract influential relationships, and by locating and joining business networking groups. You need to make yourself indispensable by being a fountain of knowledge, a resource, and a people-connection expert.

Success Factor Four is "Form Trusted Partnerships." Advance special relationships by selectively cultivating connections that can turn into trusted partnerships. You have graduated from self-reliance and are now entering the realm of inter-reliance. Make sure that trust is the key component of your partnerships.

LEADERSHIP

Having built a network of influential connections, along with a handful of trusted partnerships, you are now ready to advance to *Success Factor five*, "Assume the Role of Influencer." To broaden your influence, align yourself with other influencers who can help expand your personal reach.

Success Factor Six is "Prepare and Plan for the Ultimate Journey." As you assume the role of leader and influencer, you need to raise your sights, and envision new opportunities to expand your influence.

OPPORTUNITY

Success Factor Seven is "Assess Your Personal Driving Forces." These are elements of purpose and motivation that drive you and keep you moving forward when challenges arise. To create staying power in your career and/or business, you must determine what motivates you.

The companion to assessing your driving forces is *Success Factor Eight*, "Identifying and Leveraging Your Competitive Competencies." Competencies are those skill sets you have mastered that allow you to compete effectively as a leader. In this chapter, you will learn the ten competencies that can elevate you as a leader and influencer. Combined with motivation and competencies, there will be no stopping you.

STRATEGIC INFLUENCE

Success Factor Nine is "Become a Center of Influence." Now, that you are armed with motivation and competitive competencies, you are eligible to enter the sixth and final level of influence, the Sphere of Strategic Influence. At this stage, you will have a powerful and mature level of personal influence. This is the highest level of influence you can attain, where, if you maintain your influence integrity, genuine leadership style, and a giving spirit, others will consider you to be a Center of Influence.

Success Factor Ten is "Give Back." As a Center of Influence, others look to you for inspiration, guidance and leadership. Your successes, industry authority, and connections give you powerful influence and the opportunity to positively impact people, businesses, and communities.

No matter what level of success you achieve, everyone has the ability to give back, whether it be time, money, resources, or even a smile to someone who desperately needs a lift. Be that person!

May the winds of influence ever compel you to do
good in this world. Enjoy the journey!

THE SIX SPHERES OF STRATEGIC INFLUENCE

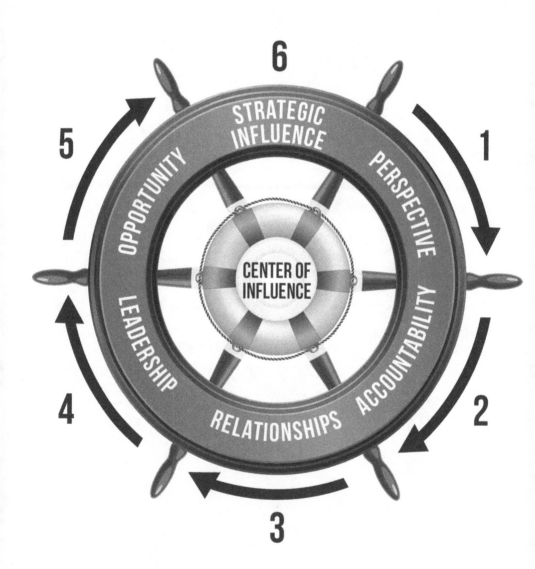

PLAN YOUR JOURNEY

PERSPECTIVE

PERSPECTIVE POINTS:
- ESTABLISH A SURVIVAL MINDSET
- DEVELOP AND MAINTAIN A NETWORKING FOCUS

10 SUCCESS FACTORS:

ACCOUNTABILITY
1. ACCEPT PERSONAL RESPONSIBILITY
2. BE SELF-RELIANT

RELATIONSHIPS
3. DEVELOP A NETWORK OF INFLUENTIAL CONNECTIONS
4. FORM TRUSTED PARTNERSHIPS

LEADERSHIP
5. ASSUME THE ROLE OF INFLUENCER
6. PREPARE AND PLAN FOR THE ULTIMATE JOURNEY

OPPORTUNITY
7. ASSESS YOUR PERSONAL DRIVING FORCES
8. IDENTIFY AND LEVERAGLE YOUR COMPETENCIES

STRATEGIC INFLUENCE
9. BECOME A CENTER OF INFLUENCE
10. GIVE BACK!

PART ONE:
THE INFLUENCE PERSPECTIVE

SPHERE OF PERSPECTIVE

POINT 1: ESTABLISH A SURVIVAL MINDSET

A STRANGER IN A NEW LAND

"Unexpected events can set you back or set you up.
It's all a matter of perspective."
— *Mary Anne Radmacher*

MAGINE, IF YOU WILL, YOU'RE a traveler on an old-fashioned sailing ship. Your voyage takes you across the wide ocean. One day, the lookout cries, "Land, ho!" A port comes into view with its tall lighthouse. As your ship draws closer, you can see a bustling city with people engaged in commerce. The ship ties up at the wharf, and you—the only passenger—disembark.

You arrive as a stranger in this city we'll call Metropolis. You know no one here, and no one knows you. Fortunately, you speak the local language. In your pocket you have a few dollars, and in your suitcase a change of clothes. They are just enough to sustain you—but not for long.

At this point, we say that your sphere of influence—the circle of people and organizations in which you can command attention—is zero. You have no influence because no one *personally* knows you. You may have a big presence on social media, but that does not always transform into real influence over real people.

As you read the book and make progress through each chapter, you should ask yourself three questions:

"What sphere of influence am I in currently?"
"What is my potential sphere of influence?"
"What is my plan for getting there?"

There is no time to waste. The clock is ticking. You need to figure out how to enter into the daily commerce of the people in Metropolis and participate to the extent that you can make some money and support yourself. Eventually, you don't want to merely survive; you want to succeed. You want to become a respected and influential member of the community.

You realize that your first task is to provide the basic necessities for yourself. If you can do that, then you'll concern yourself with achieving a level of safety and stability in your life. As your position in your newly adopted city becomes more secure, you'll start thinking about ways to participate in civic life and maybe even add to the common discourse and influence political decisions. Eventually, you'll enjoy the status and esteem that comes with being a leading citizen.

MASLOW'S HIERARCHY OF NEEDS

As you work your way up through the ranks of the city, you may think about your situation in terms of Maslow's hierarchy of needs (*Figure 1.1*). Proposed by Abraham Maslow in his 1943 paper "A Theory of Human Motivation" in *Psychological Review*, it's a simple pyramid with six levels.

Figure 1.1 Hierarchy of Needs
by Abraham Maslow including Self-Transcendence

His concept sprung from this line of reasoning:

> "It is quite true that man lives by bread alone—when there is no bread. But what happens to man's desires when there is plenty of bread and when his belly is chronically filled? At once, other (and "higher") needs emerge, and these, rather than physiological hungers, dominate the organism. And when these, in turn, are satisfied, again new (and still "higher") needs emerge and so on. This is what we mean by saying that the basic human needs are organized into a hierarchy of relative prepotency."

With a few exceptions, every human being exists at one of the six levels. They are:

1. PHYSIOLOGICAL NEEDS

At this most basic, ground-floor level, the survival of the organism is at stake. Until a person's physiological needs are met, the individual cannot hope to achieve anything else. Physiological needs include homeostasis (a stable set point of physiology), health, food and water, sleep, clothing, and shelter. If a level existed below physiological needs, it would be illness, suffering, and death.

2. SAFETY NEEDS

Having satisfied the basic physiological needs for survival, the next highest need is for safety. This means safety in the "big picture"—freedom from war, natural disaster, family violence, and childhood abuse. It also refers to economic safety, which includes job security, protection from abusive authority, the right to own personal property, and access to banks and insurance policies. Maslow proposed that if a person does not feel safe in an environment, then before attempting to meet any higher level of survival, he or she will seek safety.

3. SOCIAL BELONGING

Having fulfilled the requirements for survival and safety, then the person will seek to become a recognized member of a social, family, or another human group. Humans are susceptible to feelings of loneliness and isolation, and to solve that problem, we pursue a sense of belonging and acceptance among social groups, including our neighborhood friends, clubs, religious groups, professional organizations, sports teams, and online communities. Smaller, more one-to-one groups include the family, intimate partners, colleagues, mentors, and confidants. We instinctively feel there is psychological safety in numbers, and in fact, research studies show that people with strong social connections tend to live longer and healthier lives.

4. SELF-ESTEEM

We can have social belonging and yet feel as though we're just "one of the herd." On the next highest level, self-esteem means we feel valued and special and enjoy recognition, status, importance, and respect from others. We also have influence, whether it's political, economic, or social. What we do and say matters to other people. They may even pay us for our advice.

Maslow classified self-esteem into two categories: Esteem for oneself (dignity, achievement, mastery, independence) and the desire for reputation or respect from others (such as status and prestige).

To gain recognition, people often engage in a profession or hobby that gives the person a sense of contribution or personal value. Becoming a leader in business is an obvious route, but there are others. For example, a person may work a fairly boring job as a cab driver or assembly line worker, but their participation in a championship amateur bowling team may give them the self-esteem they need. Accomplishing something, such as publishing a novel or acting as a business mentor to a younger colleague, can also be a source of esteem for oneself.

5. SELF-ACTUALIZATION

According to Maslow, this was the top level of the pyramid and the highest manifestation of human life. In his 1954 book *Motivation and Personality*, Maslow summed it up as, "What a man can be, he must be." (This of course, applies to women as well!) It expresses the realization of your full potential, the ability to accomplish everything that you can and to become the most that you can be. To achieve this level of need, a person must not only succeed in the previous needs but master them.

People tend to perceive or focus on this need with great specificity. For example, one person may have a strong desire to become the CEO of their company. In another, the desire may be to amass great wealth for its own sake or to enter politics and aspire to the highest level you can reach in the United States—becoming President. Others may be driven to excel in music, sports, or even to be the very best parent to their child.

6. TRANSCENDENCE

Years after his 1943 theory—which he kept refining—Maslow proposed a sixth dimension of motivation. Here one finds the ultimate fulfillment in giving oneself to something beyond oneself, such as altruism. As he wrote in *The Further Reaches of Human Nature* (1971), "Transcendence refers to the very highest and most inclusive or holistic levels of human consciousness, behaving and relating, as ends rather than means, to oneself, to significant others, to human beings in general, to other species, to nature, and to the cosmos."

For the purposes of this book, we'll leave considerations of Level #6 to the discretion of the reader.

To be sure, there are exceptions to the linear progression proposed by Maslow. Consider the artist Vincent van Gogh. During his short life—he lived only until the age of thirty-seven—he never had a steady job. He was supported by his younger brother Theo, a successful art dealer, but it wasn't much, and his living conditions were squalid. As an artist, Van Gogh was commercially unsuccessful during his lifetime, and most people thought he was a crazy eccentric.

On the Maslow pyramid, during his lifetime Van Gogh barely made it to

Level #2—Safety needs. Social belonging and self-esteem were far beyond his reach. Influence? Zero. Most respectable people avoided him.

But spectacularly, near the end of his life, Van Gogh shot straight to Level #5—Self-actualization. (Some people would even say he reached Level #6— Transcendence.) The focus of his life was painting. Nothing else mattered. In just over a decade as an active artist, he created about 2,100 artworks, including around 860 oil paintings, with his most productive period being the final two years of his life. Today, we regard his finest pieces as among the most influential works of art ever created. Art collectors pay huge prices for them. In 1990, at auction at Christie's in New York, his 1890 painting *The Portrait of Doctor Gachet* was sold for $82.5 million to a Japanese collector.

I include the example of Van Gogh not because I expect you to emulate him—please don't cut off your own ear!—but to illustrate the vast range of human experience. While Van Gogh became one of the world's most influential artists long after his death, my goal is to help you become influential, and to reap its benefits, while you're still young enough to enjoy it.

EXCHANGES OF VALUE

If there was one thing that Van Gogh was lousy at, it was getting paid for his work. In his lifetime, he sold only one painting that experts have confirmed, a landscape called *The Red Vineyard,* which was bought for 400 francs by Anna Boch, a fellow artist. Imagine how his life might have been different if he had sold enough of his artwork to enjoy a comfortable lifestyle, like so many of his artist contemporaries!

In order to survive and thrive, people need a wide range of physical items. We need food, transportation, shelter, clothing, amusements—the list is long. There are two important things about the items on this list.

1. They are of value to us because they help to preserve and enhance life.

2. Without exception, no human being is capable of making all of them alone.

No one can grow their own food, design their own car, make their own clothing, build their own house, and make their own movies to watch on the TV set they built. Even hermits who live far off in the deep forest need that once-a-year trip to the general store to buy stuff they can't make, grow, or forage. Therefore, whatever we cannot produce for ourselves, we need to acquire from other people.

Unlike solitary hunters such as leopards, humans survive and prosper only by working in collaboration with each other. The key to successful collaboration is specialization. Within a defined group of people, some will be hunters, some will be farmers, some will make clothing, some will be doctors, and so on. Each person produces something of value—that is, something that people need to survive and thrive. If enough people produce the proper variety of goods and services needed by each individual in the group, then the group will collectively prosper. (The problem faced by Vincent van Gogh was that he dedicated his life to producing objects that, at the time, no one wanted. They were worthless, with no value. That's why his brother Theo had to regularly send him cash.)

With individuals each creating specific goods and services, the next question becomes how to distribute those goods and services to the other people who need them. If John is the only guy who grows potatoes, then there must be a mechanism for distributing his potatoes to the other members of the community.

In a "communist" economy, all the goods and services produced by the group would be pooled together and then doled out to each member of the group. If the system worked perfectly (which it never does), you wouldn't need to "pay" for anything. You would submit your contribution—say, your potatoes—and in return receive clothing, an apartment, a TV set, and all the other stuff you need to survive.

In the real world, we don't do that. Instead, we depend on individual localized exchanges of value. In the caveman days, it was a stone axe for furs. Today, except for a few Luddite barterers, we exchange money for goods and services. The free-market system is self-regulating in the sense that items in short supply have more value, while surplus items have less value. Since people, by nature, seek to acquire wealth, they are incentivized to produce goods and services that are in short supply while cutting back on the production of surplus items.

THE 5 REQUIRED CONDITIONS

To successfully engage in exchanges of value—whether it's axes for furs or money for a new car—certain conditions must be met.

1. KNOWLEDGE OF THE MARKETPLACE

A marketplace needs to be open, transparent, and well defined. The stock market is a good example of this. All the investment opportunities are visible to everyone, and the prices are listed. In other markets, that's not always the case. Sellers who want to dispose of an item quickly—such as a house—will often make a deal on the side without exposure to the marketplace. People who are buying often need to do research to uncover potential purchases or investments. For example, if you land in a strange city and you need to provide for yourself, it may take you months to learn the best venues to make purchases and get the most value for your money.

2. SUPPLY AND DEMAND

If everyone had everything they needed, there would be no commerce and no exchanges of value. But in human society, with specialized producers (and also specialized consumers, such as the Japanese art collector who plunked down $82.5 million to buy *The Portrait of Doctor Gachet*), commerce is necessary. Goods and services flow from the points of supply to the points of demand.

In addition to the mere existence of a state of supply and demand, the person who has the goods must be willing to sell them, and the person who needs the goods must be able to buy them. It does no good to open a Rolls-Royce dealership in a small rural town with no millionaires. While the product will be in supply to those who don't have it, and they would probably be thrilled to own it, there will be no demand, and sales are not going to happen.

Likewise, we've seen examples where people who have a product refuse to sell it because the best price is too low or for political reasons. In October 1973, the Organization of the Petroleum Exporting Countries (OPEC), which at that time was a global leader in oil production, announced a cessation of oil shipments from the Middle East to the United States and the Netherlands. The reason was political: the US and the Dutch supported Israel during the Yom Kippur War. The embargo was lifted in March 1974. This was the first "oil crisis," leading to a worldwide energy shortage and major price increases. For OPEC, the embargo had unintended consequences because it caused the United States and western European countries to examine their dependence upon Middle Eastern oil. The United States ramped up domestic oil production and put a greater emphasis on improving energy efficiency.

3. TRUST

For any exchange of value to take place, a level of trust must exist between the two parties. The biggest risk for the seller is that the buyer either won't pay or will pay with some sort of fraudulent money, such as a stolen credit card. The biggest risk for the buyer is that the goods or services sold to him will be defective or fake, or that they won't be delivered on time or at all.

People who transact one on one with other people, such as diamond merchants or those involved in private lending, demand a high level of personal trust. This can take years to develop. In human culture, we've used various devices to "fast-track" the development of trust in commerce. One of the most interesting was the idea of the market cross. Developed in the British Isles in the early medieval period, a market cross was a structure used to designate a market square, where the monarch, bishop, or local baron had granted the town the right to hold a regular market or fair. They often resembled gazebos or other roofed structures that you could stand under. As time went on, they became used for any sort of public business. Presumably, because it was a sort of miniature church, and therefore under the ever-watchful eye of God, a typical provision of a market cross was that you could make deals with a handshake on the honor system without writing formal contracts.

Figure 1.2 Medieval market cross in Chichester, England circa 1501

Many market crosses are still standing. The one in Chichester, England, is believed to have been built in 1501 by Bishop Edward Story (*Figure 1.2*). He paid ten pounds to the mayor of Chichester for the ground on which it is built. The bishop intended that poor peasants could stand under the cross and sell their meager farm produce—a few eggs or vegetables—without paying the usual fee.

When building trust, a useful motto to follow is, "I trust you before you trust me." This means that when approaching an exchange of value, you behave with such transparency and goodwill that your customer has inherent trust in you. If you give your customer every opportunity to satisfy his or her objections, then you make him more comfortable, and trust can be built.

4. GOODS AND SERVICES TO EXCHANGE

This applies to you, the person who has landed in the strange new city by the sea.

If you hope to earn a living and move up the Maslow pyramid to a state of self-actualization, then you need to be able to offer something of value in the marketplace. You must be able to satisfy a demand for something.

If you have a particular skill or product, it needs to align with the requirements of the marketplace. If you enter Metropolis and your sole marketable skill is playing the accordion, unless you've happened into a place where polkas are popular, your service will have very little value because no one wants to pay for it. Or, if you discover the city is full of accordion players and there is a surplus, your service will have little value because it's a ubiquitous commodity. What you want is a city where 1) People love accordion music, and 2) There are too few accordion players to satisfy the demand.

The traditional way to ensure your services have value is to have highly specialized knowledge that most people don't have but need. Specialized knowledge comes in endless forms.

For example, you can be a neurosurgeon. In the United States, the average neurosurgeon earns up to a million dollars a year.

You can write amazing novels. Stephen King, the former high school English teacher, has a net worth of $400 million, and in the world of entertainment, he's highly influential.

You can sell potato peelers on the street. (Really.) Joe Ades made a small fortune selling five-dollar potato peelers on the streets of Manhattan. He enjoyed café society at the Pierre Hotel on the Upper East Side and lived with his wife, Estelle Pascoe, in her three-bedroom apartment on Park Avenue. He also sent his daughter to college. He is remembered for saying, "Never underestimate a small amount of money gathered by hand for sixty years."

You can influence the buying habits of millions of consumers. Kylie Jenner has parlayed her role in the reality TV show *Keeping Up with the Kardashians* into an influence empire. In 2017, Jenner made the Forbes Celebrity 100 list. In November 2018, the *New York Post* pegged her as the most influential celebrity in the fashion industry. According to *Forbes,* in 2019, Jenner's net worth reached $1 billion, making her, at age twenty-one, the world's youngest self-made billionaire.

5. A METHOD OF REDRESS

Let's face it—even the most promising of transactions can go south. The product you buy may arrive late or damaged. It may not perform the way it was advertised. Or the person you hire for a job may perform poorly or rip you off.

To increase the level of trust in a transaction, you need to be confident that if there's a problem, you can either negotiate with the other party or use an impartial third party to settle the issue. In underdeveloped or corrupt nations where civil mechanisms for settling disputes either do not exist or are tainted by graft, doing business is much more difficult and costly than in well-functioning nations. With no rules other than "might is right," every transaction becomes riskier and more expensive. This was starkly demonstrated off the coast of Somalia, where, at its peak in 2008, piracy was a serious problem. Teams of impoverished Somali pirates would board a commercial vessel and hold it for ransom. The Somali government in Mogadishu, weakened by civil war, had no influence over them. The strategy proved profitable. In 2009, pirate income derived from ransoms was estimated to be 42.1 million euros (about $58 million), increasing to $238 million in 2010. Eventually, international countermeasures suppressed the pirate activities, but for several years the region was the source of major headaches for international shippers.

While the goal of this book is to help you develop and leverage influence, in this special case, what you want is a court system that is *free* from influence, even from you. You don't want to be able to bribe or influence a judge because you don't want anybody else to be able to do that to you.

PERSONAL VALUE

Assess your personal value. Whatever you do, make sure that what you offer in the marketplace is something that consumers and/or businesses value and will pay for. Your journey towards developing influence and your value in society begins with understanding the value you can offer in the marketplace. Ask yourself what value can I offer to others? This personal value can include education, knowledge, expertise and experience. The ability to facilitate strategic introductions to influential leaders in your personal sphere of influence, will also become an essential part of personal value as your reputation and influence grows over time.

MEET THE RIGHT PEOPLE

This brings us back to your arrival in Metropolis. Your goal is to make your way up through Maslow's hierarchy of needs. You need to provide for your own sustenance, then safety, then social belonging, then self-esteem, and finally, self-actualization.

In order to do this, you need to engage in exchanges of value that go in both directions.

The first direction is that you'll need to acquire the necessary goods and services to sustain your life and, eventually, make it better than it was before. As we saw in the first chapter, you cannot personally create all the things you need. You can't make your own clothing, build your own house, grow or gather your own food, and heal yourself when you become ill. You need to buy these things or trade for them. You need to make an exchange of value. You can call it "incoming value" because you're acquiring things of value that you need.

The second direction is that to receive something, you must either pay money or provide something else of value to your trading partner. You can call this "outgoing value."

For example, if you trade one of your cows for a new tractor, the cow is "outgoing value," while the tractor is "incoming value." You lose the cow and gain the tractor. If money is the stuff being traded, it's the same. Money you pay is outgoing value, while money paid to you is incoming value.

But you've arrived in the city with no cow, no money. You have nothing to trade. Or do you?

At the bare minimum, if you're reasonably healthy, thanks to your basic capabilities as a human being, you can provide a simple service (a form of outgoing value) to someone in exchange for incoming value, which is usually money. You can sweep the floors, pick fruit and vegetables on a farm, move stock in a warehouse, flip burgers in a fast-food joint. These are entry-level jobs that often require no prior experience. You walk into the business or agency, and if you ask for a job, you can get one.

If you have professional training, an advanced degree, or you can demonstrate a higher-level skill, then you'll have a wider range of employment options.

And as we'll see in the pages ahead, if you're really audacious and you're starring in a popular reality TV show, you can become influential through sheer force of will.

THE FIRST INFLUENCER

When you go out to look for your first entry-level job in order to generate a flow of incoming value, your most important task is to identify people who can and will hire you for a job that both exists and pays. You want someone with legitimate influence over hiring for legitimate jobs. I call this person the first influencer.

This may sound like a minor concern, but it's not, and for two reasons.

First, for millions of people living on the edge, including refugees and immigrants, there are scam artists, pimps, and predators who would make you into a slave and are real threats. While slavery is illegal across the globe, the SumAll Foundation has found there are twenty-seven million slaves worldwide. Their 2013 report says that most are held in bonded servitude, into which they are forced by taking loans they cannot repay.[1] And everyone knows the scenario of the runaway teenage girl who gets off the bus in a strange city and is greeted by a pimp who offers to protect her, or the refugee who's promised a good job but

---

1   *NYT.* https://bits.blogs.nytimes.com/2013/03/06/global-slavery-by-the-numbers

quickly finds that after he's paid for his room and board, he owes his employer money.

Second, this problem exists at the higher levels of the employment ladder, where it's not so much that you're deceived by someone who cannot hire you—it's easy to determine if someone has hiring authority—but that you'll deal with someone who's not being straightforward. They will try to sell you on the desirability of working for the organization while glossing over the negative stuff. If you're a woman, for example, the hiring manager might extol the fairness of the company's pay scales, and then after you've been hired, you discover you're being paid half of what the men are.

Or you're brought on board a prestigious law firm with promises of eventual partnership, only to discover the place is a snake pit and that the really powerful partners all hate the guy who hired you, and you will forever be identified with this particular pariah.

Or you've been hired by a company that looks healthy but, on the inside, is rotten and ready to collapse. On December 2, 2001, the energy giant Enron suddenly filed for bankruptcy, and the very next day, the company fired 4,500 of the 7,500 employees at its showcase fifty-story headquarters in downtown Houston. Enron management sent Houston police officers into the building, and just before lunchtime, all nonessential employees were kicked out. Others were called at home and terminated. The vast majority of these were honest, hardworking people who had no part in the corruption at the top.

How do you assess the first influencers—the people who can actually hire you? This is not easy. It's why ethnic groups rely on networks of established immigrants to guide and support the newcomers. If you have a family member—say, an uncle—who arrived in Metropolis years earlier and has gotten established, then you head for your uncle's house. He may hire you directly, perhaps to work in his restaurant or dry-cleaning business, or he may know someone who will. If you are literally fresh off the boat and don't know a soul and have no marketable skills, you'd probably head straight for a global fast-food chain, like McDonald's or KFC. You know they have strict employment systems, and if you get hired, you'll be treated fairly.

In fact, no small number of influential people got their very first paying jobs at McDonald's.

Comedian and *Tonight Show* host Jay Leno worked at the McDonald's in his hometown of Andover, Massachusetts. "I worked at a restaurant on Main Street for two years, from 1966 to 1968," Leno told author Cody Teets in *Golden Opportunity: Remarkable Careers That Began at McDonald's*. From his experiences there, Leno was impressed by the company's dedication to quality control and their efforts to produce a winning product. "That was very impressive to me," Leno told Teets. "The standards for quality were quite high. It was one of those life lessons I never forgot."[2]

Jeff Bezos, founder of Amazon.com and currently the wealthiest person in the world, got his start at age sixteen, working the grill at the back of a McDonald's. This summer job not only gave him an early insight into customer service and working under pressure, but it also taught him the value of being a good manager.

"The most challenging thing was keeping everything going at the right pace during a rush," he told Teets. "The manager at my McDonald's was excellent. He had a lot of teenagers working for him, and he kept us focused even while we had fun. You can learn responsibility in any job if you take it seriously. You learn a lot as a teenager working at McDonald's. It's different from what you learn in school. Don't underestimate the value of that!"[3]

There are two lessons to be learned from these stories.

1. TAKE THE OPPORTUNITY YOU HAVE

If you survey the landscape of opportunities in front of you, and you see just one, then that's the one you take. It may seem insignificant, but insignificant is better than nothing, and you never know where it might lead. Just ask Mary Barra, the first female CEO of a Big Three automaker. She began her career at General Motors in 1980, at age eighteen, as a lowly co-op student, checking fender panels and inspecting hoods to pay for her college tuition. She then earned a succession of engineering and administrative positions and eventually managed the Detroit/Hamtramck assembly plant. She continued to rise through the ranks, serving as vice president of Global Manufacturing Engineering, vice president of Global Human Resources, and executive vice president of Global Product Development, to which was added Global Purchasing and Supply Chain. In January 2014—thirty-four years after accepting her student co-op job—Barra took over as chief executive of General Motors, becoming the first female head of an automobile manufacturer.

2. YOU CAN LEARN FROM EVERY SITUATION AND EXPERIENCE

It's not unusual to hear Jay Leno and Jeff Bezos talk about the lessons they learned at McDonald's. They retained that knowledge because of two things.

2   CNBC. https://cnb.cx/3uoRtbW

3   https://www.businessinsider.com/amazons-jeff-bezos-worked-at-mcdonalds-2018-4

First, their situations provided opportunities for learning. But then again, when you think about it, *every* situation is an opportunity for learning. Every interaction you have with coworkers, managers, and customers is a chance to learn something new.

Second, they were *receptive* to learning. How many people do you know who trudge through life, dutifully putting in their hours at their paycheck job, and who never appreciate the lessons—both about the job and about life itself—that they could be absorbing? How many people do you know who have met someone influential, someone who could have changed their life, and they failed to follow through? They say, "Oh, Jones gets all the breaks. He's so lucky!" Really? Perhaps the reality is that Jones is more perceptive to opportunity and seizes it when it presents itself.

BE SELECTIVE

While you need to take the opportunities that are presented to you, the fact remains that none of us has an unlimited amount of time. In fact, most of us live on tight schedules, particularly in business and at business meetings. If you step off a ship and enter a city with a population of 100,000 people—not to mention a place like New York City, with 8.4 million—there's no way you can meet and get to know every person. It's simply impossible.

You cannot connect with every person, and you cannot form relationships with everybody. There are various levels of meeting people and forming relationships. In fact, there are five levels, and I'll discuss them in much more detail in the chapters ahead. As a stranger in a strange city, you need to start meeting people as quickly as possible while at the same time quickly filtering out the people who will either have no impact or a negative impact on your life. It may seem calculating, but with the clock ticking, you need to focus on success.

In forming your personal sphere of influence for success, take note of the three categories of people you will meet.

1. GRIFTERS

These are people who are negative and are either engaged in criminal or unethical conduct or seek to take advantage of you.

Most grifters promise an exchange of value but provide nothing in return. A grifter could be anyone—a lawyer, a broker, a contractor, a self-help guru. The most notorious grifter in the modern era was Bernie Madoff, who was sentenced to a federal prison for offenses related to a massive Ponzi scheme. Madoff possessed the rare combination of three personal characteristics that made his scheme so powerful: He was a respected and influential figure in high-echelon financial circles, he was knowledgeable and intelligent, and—for some reason—he chose to fleece people who entrusted him with their money, which in many cases represented their life savings.

His scheme was breathtakingly simple. He told investors that he controlled an investment fund that, thanks to his brilliant stewardship, generated spectacular returns. Using his influence and the trust his clients had in him, according to the Securities Investor Protection Corporation (SIPC), over several decades, he took in an estimated $18 billion. To convince his clients, he and his staff created fake client account statements based on nonexistent purchases and sales of the best-performing stocks on the S&P 100.

Madoff is a clear example of the fact that influence is power, and that the misuse of influence for purely personal gain is not only unethical, but it can be illegal.

Sometimes you have no choice but to deal with a grifter, such as the government official who demands a bribe in exchange for a project permit you must have. In that case, the outgoing value you are compelled to provide—the cash for the bribe—raises the cost of the project, thus lowering its anticipated incoming value. Thankfully, in the United States, we enjoy a low level of government corruption, but in many other nations, not only will you encounter grifters, but you'd better know them and be willing to play the game. According to World Population Review, if your business took you to Somalia, South Sudan, Nigeria, Colombia, or Syria—the five most corrupt nations on earth—you'd better be ready to make nice with rotten officials. On the other hand, if you stepped off the boat and onto the shores of Denmark, New Zealand, Sweden, Singapore, Finland, or any other nation ranked low in corruption, you'd rarely encounter a government grifter.

2. PEOPLE WHO HAVE POTENTIAL VALUE

The vast majority of people with whom you interact will be perfectly pleasant, and you may engage in exchanges of value with them on a regular basis, such as the nice barista at Starbucks who actually spells your name correctly. You can contribute to the overall quality of human society by always being polite and empathetic towards everyone with whom you interact. Say their name, provide your name when appropriate, smile, and then move on. This may sound harsh, but because time is short and you cannot possibly have a relationship with everyone, you need to prioritize.

You will find that the vast numbers of perfectly pleasant people comprise what I call *potential relationships*. These are relationships that hover in the background, filed away in your memory, that provide no immediate opportunities for influence, but in the future, they may blossom into kinetic relationships, which, as the name suggests, are active and beneficial for both parties. In the pages ahead, I'll discuss these relationships in much more depth.

3. INFLUENCERS WITH POSITIVE VALUE

Ideally, you want to meet and get to know people who are capable of either making exchanges of value with you or helping you to make exchanges with third parties. This encompasses a wide range:

- Buyers of your goods or services
- Bankers and lenders who can provide financing
- Facilitators, such as brokers and lawyers
- People who offer protection – insurance agents, politicians, police
- People who help you make or produce your product (suppliers)
- People who can advise you and guide you (mentors and coaches)
- People whom you could hire to work as employees

Make a list of the types of people you want to meet.
Then, train your mind to:

1. Identify and avoid grifters.
2. Meet people with potential value and develop a good relationship.
3. Focus on getting to know influencers and people who can help you with meaningful exchanges of value.

When you encounter and interact with people in your community, ask them about business networking groups that exist in the area. At a minimum you should be able to find a local Chamber of Commerce and request an invitation to attend their next monthly meeting. This can be a good starting place for making initial business connections.

As you meet business owners, ask about upcoming business events, but, be certain to do your research and some pre-planning prior to attending an event. Arriving at an event without a plan and with no objectives can make for a very unproductive use of your time. Take time to learn what the discussion topics will be, who will be speaking, what types of business people will be attending and who will be sponsoring the event. Ask for a list of attendees along with their titles, business names and contact information. Create a target list of influential people you want to meet and make contact with as many as possible prior to the event and schedule meetings. With a plan in hand, and meetings scheduled, you can feel confident that the day will be a success. If you do find yourself with free time, having done your pre-planning and research, you will know what booths you want to visit and which presentations you want to attend. Your time needs to be productive!

How you further broaden your networking perspective will be revealed in the next chapter.

SUCCESS ACTION ITEMS – ESTABLISH A SURVIVAL MINDSET

- Determine what sphere you are in. As you read and make progress through the success factors of the book, ask yourself three questions:
  - ◦ "What sphere of influence am I in currently?"
  - ◦ "What is my potential sphere of influence?"
  - ◦ "What is my plan for getting there?"
- Have a survival mindset with a clear vision of who you are and what you can become. This will allow you to gain a reputation as a person who knows how to overcome challenges and solve problems.
- Think about your current situation in terms of Maslow's Hierarchy of Needs and determine what level you are on.
- Assess your personal value. Your journey toward developing influence, your value in society begins with understanding what value you can offer in the marketplace. Ask yourself what value can I offer to others? This personal value can include knowledge, expertise, experience or even introductions to special connections you have to other influential people.
- Strive to understand the five required conditions for optimal market exchanges.
  1. Study the marketplace to gain knowledge and to uncover potential opportunities.
  2. Confirm that there is a good balance between supply and demand for the product or services you want to market.
  3. Establish trust. A strong basis of trust must exist between you and the people you want to do business with.
  4. Offer specialized goods and services to exchange. You must be able to satisfy the demand for the product or service you want to promote.
  5. Have confidence that when problems arise, you are working with systems and people who will act responsibly and be willing to work through the issues.
- Be receptive to learning. You can learn from every situation and experience.
- Develop a strong personal sphere of influence but be selective. Here are the three different categories of people you will meet.
  - ◦ Grifters. Beware, these are people who promise an exchange of value but provide nothing in return.
  - ◦ People with potential value. Time is short and you cannot have a relationship with everyone. You need to prioritize.
  - ◦ Influencers with positive value. These are people who are capable of either making exchanges of value with you or helping you to make exchanges with third parties.

CHRISTAL BEMONT
CEO TALEND

"Success Started from Humble Beginnings"

MY SUCCESS STORY

I GREW UP ON A FARM in the Midwest. We were quite poor, with little food, water, or electricity, and no indoor plumbing. My mom was a single mom. A kind person, she was not really cut out to be a parent, so I found myself trying to be the adult in the situation.

When I was eleven, we moved from Kansas City to the small farming town of Cameron, Missouri, which was about five thousand people. We took a trailer, put it on a plot of land of about thirty acres, and stayed there for five years until I moved out on my own when I was sixteen. We lived there with kerosene lamps and a wood burning stove, and everything that we did was with our hands.

There was a neighbor named Kay, and to provide money for the family I used to clean her house. At one point my mom decided to leave, and she took a couple of my brothers and sisters, and left me on the farm. My mom was always a very selfless person, but she made poor choices.

Kay said, "I'm going to take you in. I want you to come live with me." It was the very first time in my life that someone offered me a selfless act of kindness and generosity. She made a very important impression on me. I was raised with kindness, which was really important to me.

At that moment, I made a commitment to myself. I remember this moment as if it were yesterday. I was by myself, and I was lying in a pasture, and I was looking up, and I said, "I will never again be in this situation. I'm going to make sure that I have the best life and help as many people as I can along the way." I made that commitment to myself.

I went to college at Missouri Western, home of Pony Express, and was the first one from my family to graduate from college. I didn't have the best grades. I'm a great student, I just wasn't a great test-taker, and I learned in different ways than what school offered. I'm a doer. I learn more from experience than I do from books.

When I graduated in 1992, I moved to Chicago, and thought I wanted to be a buyer for a clothing retailer. I've always believed in working my way up.

I walked into Marshall Fields In Schaumburg IL, Woodfield Mall, and got a job on the sales floor, at seven dollars an hour. It's the only job I have ever applied for. I started talking to people about what I wanted to do. I took the job that I thought would put me in a situation to both make money and to understand, learn, and show my skills. I talked to every person I could about what I did want to do.

Someone called me and said there was a job opening to work at Motorola. So I went to work for Motorola, and then someone at Motorola gave me a job in software. And it became this perpetuating thing where when someone I knew went somewhere they would say, "Will you come with me?"

So fast forward, for every role I've ever had, someone has tapped me on the shoulder to offer me opportunities, including the one that I'm in today.

I would say there were a few inflection points at my time at Concur. I learned I'm an observer of people. That's because there's so much to learn from people who I think have a lot to offer.

For example, I was a solutions consultant for a long time. At first, I had no idea how to be a solutions consultant. A vendor at Motorola had asked, "Do you want to be a technical consultant?"

And I replied, "I have no idea how to be a technical consultant." So I picked up a book and learned how to code. I learned it because I had to.

That sales consultant job was amazing because I worked with hundreds of salespeople, and I would watch them and I would go, "Oh, I hate that they do it that way. Why do they talk to the customer that way?" I got so frustrated with a sales rep that my leader said, "You have to go into sales, because you're running the deal."

I've never been particular about titles or roles. Many years ago, I got to the point where I started defining my own brand, and I was really clear about it. I didn't want people to put me in a box, and people do this generally. People would say, "Well, you've been in this role, so you must do this." I've observed this my entire life. People would tell me what was going to happen to me, such as, "It's unlikely you're ever going to leave this little town." I got to the point in my career where I said, "There isn't a single role or title that I'm interested in per se."

I would say to the head of a company, "Identify the biggest problem or the biggest opportunity you want someone to work on for you. I can help you. I don't care what the role is. I don't care what the title is. I don't care what I'd be doing. I want to work on the things that you need people to help you with."

It became very important to not define myself as one thing and not to get backed into a corner. Those elements have brought me to the point where I'm extremely open. I like to be athletic and diverse, and be aligned with the biggest problem you need solved.

If I were dropped off in a strange city, with no connections, I would apply the same skills that I've applied so far in my life, which is to go and meet as many people as I can, and understand what problems need to be solved and the people who are in need of help.

I would ask around. I think it's about observing and seeing what I would be attracted to, especially things that are on the positive side. I'd try to perform a service or activity that I could at least make a minimum wage and get by. I believe in learning about your surroundings and about yourself in a new environment. By doing things that are a little bit more on the ground floor, I get my sea legs. That's where I get my stability. I think sometimes at different levels you lose perspective, and could lose some of that grounding.

I'll give an example. Go wait tables or go wash dishes, and just talk to people and understand the vibe, what's going on, where things are happening, where's the next opportunity? For me it's not about immediately hitting the ground and getting success, it's about the things that you learn about along the way that bring you to that place.

I've learned that people who are successful want to bring you with them. They want to be surrounded by people they enjoy, but also who contribute in a positive way. They need to know they can have confidence in you, that you're trustworthy, and that they can put things in your hands and everything's going to be okay.

Here's the interesting thing: Everyone's been in a role for the first time, and I was not all that quick to be in the CEO role. I didn't have the first clue about being a CEO. I am not afraid to tell people when I don't know something and when I need help. It's okay to be vulnerable.

The person who has been most instrumental in my life was Steve Singh (Founder and CEO of Concur). He is the epitome of humility. He talks about generational wealth, and I say it's not generational wealth, it's generational *learning*. He has literally passed on to my kids his teachings. You know, teach a man to fish versus give him a fish. He's been a generational giver of what kind of person to be. These are rare individuals, but what a special human he is, so humble, but confident, and the most generous, giving individual. Steve is the person that put me in this role. He is that kind of person, and he's amazing.

INFLUENCE

Influence to me is the ability to create an emotion in someone that brings them to another state, to have an impact on someone emotionally, and elicit a physical response from them. I would say it's what you say to someone, that once you hang up the phone, they're going to get up out of the chair and *do something*. That's what I was taught in sales. When I think about it in my real life, it's how you can connect with someone and create an emotional response that's going to then influence them to believe in something or want to do something. I want to be part of that.

BEING AN INFLUENCER

Yes, I'm an influencer, and I'm very passionate about it. If there is anything I want to do, it is to leave people better and thinking differently than they have thought before.

STRATEGIC INFLUENCER

This is extremely intentional, with a goal in mind of moving people, physically or mentally, from one place to the next, with a very specific intention of where and what you want that outcome to be.

STRATEGIC RELATIONSHIP INFLUENCE

It's about building a connection with someone. It's more personalized and has a deeper meaning. I use this word "emotion" a lot, but it's a deeper emotional connection because it's something that someone can connect with. It's not superficial. It's inspiring at a deeper level. To me, the word "relationship" takes it through another level. It means that you know them well enough, or you've studied them, or you connect with them at a deeper level.

You have to earn people's trust. Trust is a very personal thing. It is based on people's experiences and how they've been impacted.

The different levels of trust start with the initial relationship. I've had experience with people for many years and we're still building trust. That's a human nature thing, but a lot of it has to do with a person's background and the experiences they've had, so they may have a very difficult time learning to trust. This is where the relationships have to do with caring about someone, and getting to know them. It can be a deeply personal thing because of things that may have happened to them or what they've experienced, whether good or bad.

The trust factor is one of the most important things because it can be misunderstood. It's the intent versus the impact, which can be very much misunderstood on both sides; and I think a lot can go awry with the misunderstanding of just someone's need to feel safe.

It's almost like a safe zone. It's where they're protecting themselves, and you need to be able to break down a few walls in order to get there.

I tend to trust immediately, and this is where I want to go talk to everyone, but if I get to a certain point of no trust, then I also will shut someone out, and then there's no return.

I try to expedite trust. I do that by showing. I demonstrate, I show and give, and be as transparent as I possibly can. I say, "I'm going to be vulnerable and tell you all of this because I want you to know you can trust me." You have to build it over time. The only way to impact trust is to say, "I'm going to be as authentic, transparent, and available as I possibly can. I want you to call me." I give every single person in my company my cell phone number, and I tell them to call me. I hope those types of things will bring people to a level of trust faster.

CENTERS OF INFLUENCE

These are the beacons, the people to whom all things and all roads lead. When things are great in your life, when things are bad in your life, or you need some advice, these are the people to whom you want to go. It's a small group, and if you're very lucky, maybe it's a larger group, but these are people that you trust implicitly. These are usually weathered people, who have been through the wringer, and you know they have your best interest in mind. These are typically selfless people, and I'll give you one example.

I've had an ongoing debate with a person who's been an amazing influence on me. He was one of the first people who really believed in me, who brought me in, and told me I actually deserved more, and I should be making more money. He said that I should be surrounding myself with people who make a lot of money. If you surround yourself with really amazing people who think bigger, aspire to drive greater things, then you yourself will be elevated. He was right about the biggest difference between, he believed you should never move or grow beyond that circle. Once you're part of a circle, you never leave that circle.

I believe you should be sincere in putting the other persons best interest first, to not be selfish, and do whatever is best for that individual. If you truly have their best interest in mind, you should support them and elevate them.

It shouldn't be about staying in one spot, but about moving on. He and I had very different views on that. I have had people on my team come to me and say, "I'm thinking about moving to another role," and I would reply, "I have two questions for you: Do you want my support? Or do you want my help figuring out if it's the right thing to do?" I've literally called and given references for other people who report to me. I've helped them get other jobs, and they may come back and work for me again.

I'll tell people in company meetings, "I take very seriously where you spend your time inside and outside this company, and if I'm not doing a good enough job to provide you with the opportunity to get you to live the best life, you call me, and I'll help you get your next job." I have no interest in it just being about me. This is about *you* living a great life. For me, a center of influence is about being selfless.

Steve Singh has been that for me. It's about his actions, not just work, or the roles he's put me in. It's because of his incredible actions, selflessness and humility. He's one of the kindest and smartest people I know.

DEEP DOWN HABITS

A positive mindset is the very first thing. I'm relentless about surrounding myself with reading. I listen to books almost daily. I protect my morning time to listen to people who inspire a mindset. For me, everything is about your mind and what you tell yourself you can do. I have a passion for the study of psychology and your mindset.

I'm also a big communicator. I like to be in constant communication with people. I like asking people to tell me what's going on. Tell me what's happening, what you're seeing, and what you're hearing. How do you feel? The positive mindset and constant communication have been important to create habits around, because I think they're easy to deviate from, especially with COVID-19 this last year.

I'm very clear about setting goals for myself and asking, what is it going to take for me to get there? I'll say, why can't that happen for me? I build a business plan for myself—a personal one and one for the business every year. It's what I learned at Sandler training, and it changed my life. I became much more successful. I literally write it down on these cards from years ago, I mean like since 2001.

I don't expect perfection. I just want progress. I focus on anything that I can do to be better. I have a commitment to learning and to improving. In the past, I would literally start every day and ask, what does success look like today? I'm very maniacally focused on what success looks like for a meeting, or for today. It's easy to follow a schedule, but for me, it's how do I define success? At the end of the day, I ask, was I successful or not? It's important for me to be balanced.

ONE DEFINING MOMENT

The thing that really put me on my trajectory, that put me on this path I'm on now, came when I was at Motorola. I started in customer service and ended up moving into a role that sat between IT and business. I would bring in vendors to help solve problems. This was a defining moment because I had no business experience. In that role as a technology consultant, with zero experience, I had no idea what I was talking about; and when the conversation started coming up, I leaned in. If I could create a mental image, it was like standing on a really tall diving board and deciding whether or not to jump in.

But it was that moment that changed everything for me. I think without getting into technology and getting into software, I would have gone down a very different path in my career.

MY GREATEST INFLUENCER

It's probably apparent by now, but Steve Singh was the greatest influence on me. He's the most humble, kind, and bold person. I feel I've learned all of those attributes under his leadership. To show what kind of a man he is, when my daughter was in college, she called him and asked him to help because she had to interview someone. He turned down paid interviews, but would jump on a call with her. I've never experienced from anyone else his selflessness toward helping other people. I was a sales rep at Concur, and I carried a bag. I made it to club. That year, my daughter was diagnosed with a brain tumor, and I had only been at Concur a few years, but he offered to pay for all her medical expenses. I was one of many sales reps. I was just an individual contributor. There have been many examples, and that's on the personal front; but if you were to walk into a restaurant, you would never know who he is or what he's capable of, and he would never give you that impression. He is the most genuine person.

On a business front, he has the most disruptive mindset. I love the book *The Innovators Dilemma*, by Clayton M. Christensen. Basically, it's about you putting yourself out of business before someone else does. He literally did this, two to three times at Concur, which is the very reason Concur was sold for $8.3 billion. I'm also doing that here at Talend. We are going to put ourselves out of business and create so much value for our customers. It's this idea of being really courageous and bold to think about the problems we face today and also the ones we will face in the future.

Steve Singh is all of that, and he treats everyone the same way. It's not just me—he's just a multiplier of goodness.

Christal is a seasoned executive with a demonstrated track record in defining and leading sales and go-to-market strategies to significantly scale cloud businesses. Currently, she is CEO of Talend, a publicly traded global SaaS data integration platform valued at 2.1B.

Previously, she spent fifteen years at SAP Concur, most recently leading its $2B business organization as Chief Revenue Officer. Prior to her CRO appointment, Christal was Senior Vice President and General Manager of SAP Concur's Small, Midsized and Nationals (SMN) business unit. Early in her career, Christal served in a number of capacities focused on operational and technical roles at Motorola, Extensity, and Clarify.

Website: www.talend.com
LinkedIn: www.linkedin.com/in/christalbemont/

POINT 2: DEVELOP AND MAINTAIN A STRONG NETWORKING FOCUS

"Your network is your networth."
—*Peter Gale*

ACTIVE AND PASSIVE NETWORKING

I N THE BUSINESS WORLD, NETWORKING is a foundational component of building influence. What that means is that in most situations, in order to have a sphere of influence, you build up a personal sphere of influence of human contacts with whom you'd expect to interact at regular intervals to support a given set of activities.

PERSONAL SPHERE OF INFLUENCE

Your personal sphere of influence comprises two groups of people. The first consists of those people who have greater influence upon third parties than you do. To be frank, they are above you on the influence ladder. Sometimes they have specialized knowledge of a particular subject or industry that you do not have. For instance, if your company is building a new headquarters and information technology is not your strong suit, then you'll look for an IT expert who's influential in his field. For legal issues, you look for a reputable and influential lawyer.

The other group consists of people who look to you for influence. When you first begin your career, such people are few and far between. As you get older and become more successful in your field, you'll become a magnet for those who are less experienced, and for them, you may even choose to serve as a mentor.

Having a strong personal sphere of influence means you're connected to a large number of people and resources for mutual development and growth.

Personal spheres of influence consist of relationships with many facets:

- People whom you know, and they know you. (This reciprocity is very important. Just because you've met the president of the bank doesn't mean that he or she knows you and remembers you. Following someone on Twitter does not constitute a relationship.)
- What you know about each other and the depth of your relationship. Does the bank president know where you work or the name of your spouse? Have you ever had lunch together?
- What you are doing together—your shared activities. Are you and the bank president serving on any boards or committees together? Do you play golf at the same club? Do your kids go to the same school?
- Any exchange of value. If you're a retirement financial adviser, lawyer, architect, or business or public relations consultant, then is the bank president one of your clients? Have you volunteered your time on a charitable committee he or she chairs?

Personal spheres of influence are intended to be mutually beneficial, extending the concept of teamwork beyond the immediate peer group. The term is usually encountered in the workplace, though it could apply equally to other pursuits outside work.

When you step off the boat and enter the strange city, your efforts to meet people who would be willing to engage in exchanges of value is called networking. You may have several spheres of influence that are unrelated to each other. Your primary sphere of influence is related to your job and your efforts to satisfy Maslow's first level of needs—physiological. You want to get to know people who will hire you. This will expand to include those who can help you indirectly in your career. Then you'll pursue building a sphere of influence of social friends and possibly seek a life partner. You'll build a sphere of influence of good places to buy food, get your hair done, buy clothing, go to relax. Like a Venn diagram, all these various networks will intersect with you in the middle.

THE POINTLESS BUSINESS CARD NETWORK

As you begin to network, you must beware of a common pitfall, which can be summed up in one phrase: *quantity does not equal quality.*

In the old days—that is, until the advent of the digital age—business cards were ubiquitous. Everyone had one. Your business card had your name, your position, your company, and your contact information. You would go to a business mixer, and everyone would exchange business cards. You'd go back to your office with a fistful of cards, which you'd either dump into a drawer or carefully insert, one by one, into a special business card book, with a clear plastic pocket for each card.

The success quotient for an event would be judged by the stack of new cards you had acquired and the few you had left of your own.

Weeks later, you'd look at them, trying to remember who gave them to you, where you were, why you talked to them, what you talked about, and what was important about that person for you to have their card. And the odds were good that across town, the person you met was looking at their stack of business cards and wondering why they had yours.

The problem with that type of "networking" is that it's far too facile. It requires little effort and even less personal interaction. These days, things are slightly better because when we meet someone, we generally enter their contact information into our smartphone. This takes a bit of effort because you need to have an actual conversation.

No matter how you do it, it's easy to rack up huge lists of names of people who have, at some time or another, crossed your path. Have you looked at your Gmail or Outlook contact list recently? I'll bet it's loaded with hundreds of names you haven't thought about in years. It's harmless—after all, digital information is just a bunch of electrons in your computer. You could store a million names and addresses if you wanted to.

In theory, these are all potential relationships—but in reality, that's not how life works.

In building your sphere of influence, which is the first step or foundation of your productive and positive relationships, you can take a passive approach, an active approach, or a combination of the two.

1. PASSIVE APPROACH

To be passive means to attract influencers to you by virtue of a value that you offer, which they perceive and then respond to. You make no particular effort to "sell" yourself or your service. Instead, you rely on a series of escalating touch-points, with each one being judged favorably by the person whom you're trying to attract.

In the old days, before mass media, your primary method of attracting customers and influencers was through your physical presence. You built or rented a storefront, put up a sign, and waited for people to walk in. It's how most personal injury and other local lawyers got clients in the days before advertising. The theory is that if you offered an outstanding product, word of mouth would attract customers.

Cost of customer acquisition? Zero. Starbucks did this for years. You offer a product that people want, and your customers act as your advertisers. The passive approach works well in seasonal tourist areas too. If you're selling fried dough on the boardwalk in Atlantic City, you don't need to advertise—every day, your customers will stream by your shop by the thousands.

You can build a storefront that's so unusual or bombastic that word will spread organically, and people will come. This is pretty much the marketing strategy of Las Vegas-themed casino hotels. For example, the New York-New York Hotel & Casino looks like a compact version of Manhattan and boasts a grand replica of the Statue of Liberty. The architecture and atmosphere evoke the feel of New York City during the 1940s, with scale replicas of the Empire State Building, Chrysler Building, Whitney Museum of American Art, and Grand Central Terminal. You can even stroll down a fake street in Greenwich Village, minus the colorful crackpots and panhandlers.

You may think, "These are giant, well-funded hotels. I'm just a single person. I could never attract that kind of attention."

Here's the reality: the vast majority of individuals who become powerful passive influencers are entrepreneurs. They start and build their own businesses, and as the business grows, so does their influence and network. People gravitate to them because they are successful, and the more people gravitate to them, the more successful they become.

The most amazing example of conjuring global influence out of thin air is the Kardashian-Jenner family.

Making its debut on October 14, 2007, *Keeping Up with the Kardashians* is a reality television series focusing on the personal and professional lives of the Kardashian-Jenner blended family. The series focuses mainly on sisters Kim, Kourtney, and Khloé Kardashian, their half-sisters Kendall and Kylie Jenner, and other friends and family.

Despite relentlessly negative reviews, *Keeping Up with the Kardashians* quickly attracted high viewership ratings, becoming one of the network's most successful shows and winning many audience awards. To many critics, the show was baffling because the women seemed to have no professional skills and, indeed, no regular jobs. But viewers were enthralled, and the Kardashian empire grew into a branding juggernaut. In 2011, in response to a suggestion that the television series was nothing more than a vehicle to promote their retail stores and endorsement deals, Khloé Kardashian admitted, "These shows are a thirty-minute commercial."

As Gareth Dimelow wrote in *Sabotage Times*, "The Kardashians would be the first to admit that their notoriety has little to do with any discernible talent, beyond an alarming capability for self-promotion."

The reason I classify the Kardashians as taking the passive approach is that they do not ask you, personally, to watch their show. It's available on the network, and you have to choose to tune in. Their strategy has worked. The women have become incredibly influential in the fashion world.

2. ACTIVE APPROACH

When building influence, the passive approach may take too long, and truly wealthy and powerful people may never visit you. To reach them, you need to actively pursue them and enter their world. This book is all about the active approach and how to use it to your best advantage.

In the active approach, you assume that in your normal state, you are invisible, unseen, and unremarkable. What you do goes unnoticed by others. If you had a store, nobody would walk through the door. If you had a website, no one would visit, and your Google ranking would be at the bottom. You exist as an island unto yourself.

If this were truly the case, then, if for your survival you were to rely upon customers to find you and influential people to seek you out, you'd quickly starve to death.

You change this dynamic by being proactive. This means that you *interrupt* the lives of other people. In the world of sales, it's called *interruption marketing*. You interrupt them and get their attention by doing or saying something interesting. To be proactive yet effective, you must send the message that the person should pay attention to you because you have something of value they need to hear.

POSITIVE INTERRUPTIONS

Personal and social interactions can also be intrusive. You go to a chamber of commerce breakfast meeting, and you choose to sit at a table with a bunch of strangers, and you introduce yourself to them. You are inserting yourself into their world. Then you listen to the speaker, and after the presentation, you go to the front of the room and introduce yourself to him or her. You're *taking action* to make connections and expand your sphere of influence.

The key trick to creating a positive interruption and not portraying a feeling of intrusion, is to be friendly and respectful, because you're asking people for their valuable time and attention. Similarly important, you need to have something of value to offer. You can't just be a "taker."

The only people who seem to get a "free pass" for being aggressively engaging are candidates running for public office. During campaign season, they become super-intrusive. They'll come into a roadside diner, walk up to your table in the middle of your meal, stick out their hand, and say, "Hi, I'm Jim/ Jill Jones, and I'm running for mayor. Pleased to meet you." This behavior is not offensive because we understand that a candidate for public office has a finite window of opportunity that extends until election day to wage a massive influence campaign and reach as many potential voters as possible.

DISRUPTIVE MARKETING

A related but more advanced form of interruption marketing is *disruptive marketing*. This goes a step beyond interrupting traditional norms and thinking. Disruptive means changing it up, turning things upside down in terms of how people think about legacy marketing concepts and rethinking the approach to make an old approach more interesting and modern. Here's an example.

The annual Super Bowl TV broadcast is where companies roll out their biggest and most expensive ads. In that sense, it's not only the Super Bowl of football but also of TV ads, as each company vies for the most memorable spot. In 2015, Swedish carmaker Volvo decided to disrupt the rules of the game. Instead of creating an expensive spot, they ran a contest, with the prize being a new Volvo XC 60 automobile. Viewers could enter the contest just one way: by tweeting the company with the hashtag #VolvoContest whenever they saw a commercial *for another car company*. In their tweets, Volvo asked users to make a nomination for one of their loved ones to win the Volvo car.

During the game, six car companies—Mercedes, Toyota, Lexus, Nissan, Kia, and Fiat—each spent $4.5 million on their respective thirty-second Super Bowl commercials. Including the cost of two new cars (one was given away on *Jimmy Kimmel Live* for pre-Super Bowl publicity), Volvo spent a fraction of that amount.

Volvo called the campaign "The Greatest Interception Ever." This highlighted their intention to shift the conversation away from their competitors. Every time viewers saw a commercial for a competing car brand, they instead thought of Volvo and sent their tweet. With this scheme, Volvo sought to draw attention to itself while disrupting the efforts of its competitors.

Did it work? Yes, as MarketingExamples.com pointed out:

- More than 55,000 people used the hashtag #VolvoContest.
- Volvo was the only automobile company to trend globally.
- More than 100 different stories were written about the stunt (this was free publicity!).

- Perhaps most significantly, the result was a 70% increase in Volvo XC 60 sales the following month.

THE THREE RULES FOR BUILDING INFLUENCE

The three fundamental rules of building personal influence are *be proactive, be friendly,* and *offer something of value.* The best way to drive this point home is with the example of television commercials. They are a classic form of intrusive interruption marketing. They often appear in the middle of the show you're watching, at what you think is the worst possible moment. But when you think about it, intrusive television commercials fall into three categories:

1. Obnoxious commercials that make you change the channel. You probably have your own set of TV ads that make your blood boil, and it's likely you will never buy the product or service. As far as enlisting you as a customer, these annoying ads fail. You can compare these commercials to the loudmouth who sits at your table and monopolizes the conversation. Everyone can't wait until he or she leaves.

2. Bland, palatable ads. The vast majority of TV commercials fall into this category. When they appear on the screen, they're pleasant and professional. You may pay attention to them or not. Their message may stick with you subliminally. They are like the nice, quiet person who sits at your table and doesn't say much. The next day you might have some vague memory of them, but the memory is positive. If you saw them again, you wouldn't mind. If they stuck around long enough, they'd become familiar, and you'd find it easy to work them into your circle.

3. The commercials that everyone talks about the next day. Probably the most famous TV commercial in history is the one Apple broadcast during the 1984 Super Bowl. Directed by Ridley Scott, the ad, entitled "1984," played off the George Orwell novel of the same name to introduce its new Macintosh computer. The ad's vivid imagery instantly vaulted Apple into the public consciousness. It was like the person who sits at your table and begins speaking, and what they say is so transfixing that everyone stops and listens.

By the way, there's another lesson here. Apple's board of directors saw an advance copy of the "1984" commercial, and they *hated* it. They did not want Apple to air it.

Despite the board's dislike of the commercial, Steve Wozniak and others at Apple showed copies to friends, and an increasingly confident Wozniak offered to personally pay for half of the spot if Jobs paid the other half. They prevailed, and the spot was aired. Therefore, to our three admonitions for building influence—be proactive, be friendly, and offer something of value—we can add a fourth: Be bold. Don't be afraid to step into situations where you might be out of place. If you are confident you have something important to say, then say it.

This brings to mind one of the most important speeches made by John F. Kennedy, who in 1960 was a candidate for president of the United States. He was a Catholic, and no one of his faith had ever been elected president. It was assumed that Protestant denominations would oppose him, and in fact, his opponent, former vice president Richard Nixon, was quietly fueling that effort. Knowing that he needed to make a bold, disruptive move, on September 12, with less than two months until the election, Kennedy appeared before the Greater Houston Ministerial Association (GHMA), a gathering of Southern Baptist ministers. This event was considered the epicenter of anti-Catholic political rhetoric and even outright bigotry. Before the speech, Ted Sorensen, one of Kennedy's most trusted advisers, worried, "We can win or lose the election right there in Houston on Monday night."

Kennedy took to the podium and addressed the issue head-on, saying, "I am not the Catholic candidate for president. I am the Democratic Party's candidate for president, who happens also to be a Catholic. I do not speak for my church on public matters, and the church does not speak for me."

At the end of his speech, the assembled ministers gave Kennedy a standing ovation.

That night, Kennedy was:

1. Proactive—He went to visit the group on their own turf.
2. Friendly—He was friendly and respectful, and he delivered his message with both confidence and humility.
3. Value—He laid out for his audience how he was going to serve them.
4. Bold—He was bold in his approach, offering much-needed executive-type value by addressing the 900-pound gorilla in the room, and faced an audience that was reputed to be hostile.

Keeping these four qualities always top of mind, starting in Part II, I'll take you step by step through the 10 *Success Factors of Highly Influential Leaders*.

SUCCESS ACTION ITEMS –
DEVELOP AND MAINTAIN A STRONG NETWORKING FOCUS

- Get Connected. Having a strong personal sphere of influence means you're connected to a large number of people and resources for mutual development and growth. Personal spheres of influence are intended to be mutually beneficial.
- Focus on networking! Your efforts to meet and connect with people who are willing to engage in exchanges of value is called networking.
- Focus on getting to know influencers and people who can help you with meaningful exchanges of value.
- As you network, beware of the common pitfall: "quantity equals quality." The success quotient for an event "is not" judged by the stack of new cards you have acquired, and those you handed out.
- Take an active approach to networking. In building your sphere of influence, which is the first step or foundation of your productive relationships, you can take a passive approach, an active approach, or a combination of the two. This book is all about the active approach and how to use it to your best advantage.
- Practice the method of positive interruption when being proactive in personal interactions or social situations.
- Incorporate the four fundamental rules of building personal influence. They are:
  1. Be proactive
  2. Be friendly
  3. Offer something of great value
  4. Be bold

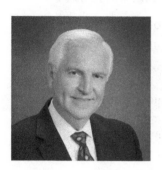

STEVEN R. SHALLENBERGER
CEO BECOMING YOUR BEST

"The End Game is about Relationships"

MY BACKGROUND

I GREW UP IN THE SAN Francisco Bay Area (Vallejo, CA), a place of great cultural diversity. My family consisted of my parents and six siblings, three boys and three girls. I was number three. We grew up in a 900 square foot home. My parents were divorced when I was fourteen. I always liked to work. My jobs included busing dishes at an Italian restaurant, working for the Vallejo Garbage Company, Bruce's Ski Shop, and at sixteen years old, I started my first company, the Shallenberger Maintenance Company. We worked almost exclusively for Dave Conger Realty, one of the top Realty Companies in the Bay Area. Dave Conger was one of my first mentors and became a lifelong friend. He was a former bomber pilot in World War II.

I played baseball from eight years old through college. I was a Student Body President for Solano College. I was actively involved in my church group. My teen years were in the mid and late 1960s, which included the assassinations of John F. Kennedy, Bobby Kennedy, and Martin Luther King. The Vietnam War was raging, with classmates not coming home, the civil rights unrest, and the peace movement. It was in the middle of the Cold War and Neil Armstrong walked on the moon—a great time to grow up.

HOW I WOULD SURVIVE IN A STRANGE LAND

If I were traveling by ship to a distant land, with only the clothes on my back and a few bucks in my pocket, then upon arriving I would first seek to form productive relationships. Everything you do is through relationships.

This reminds me of a quote by Charlie "Tremendous" Jones: "You will be the same person in five years as you are today except for the people you meet and the books you read."

If you're arriving somewhere for the first time—including, say, graduating from college and getting your first full-time job—you'll have to get after it and get going. It's all about the people you meet and putting yourself in a circle of people who can help you and from whom you can learn; and then when you can, you return the favor by helping and supporting them.

INFLUENCERS

Being an influencer is being a force for good. A perfect example of this is an email I recently received. It was from a gentleman by the name of Russell G. Hayden. Three or four weeks earlier I had done a podcast on, "Capturing Your Personal Life Story," and he had heard it.

It just so happens that for a few years, Russell and I had attended the same high school in California. In the email, he explained he had been expelled, and he tried getting into other high schools in the area, and they wouldn't let him in. He finally got into an alternative education school in San Jose, but then he dropped out. He eventually ended up on the streets, and things were not looking good.

This was in 1969. He decided to hitchhike to San Jose. A man in a car stopped and asked where he was headed.

Russell said, "Wherever you want to take me."

The driver said he couldn't take him, and he pulled away, but then he had a change of heart and backed up. The driver then asked him, "What are you doing out here?"

"I've dropped out of school," said Russell, "and I've been trying to get back in."

"Well, hop in," the driver said. "I'm going to give you a ride to Foothill Community College."

During their ride, the man asked, "Have you ever thought of being a firefighter?"

"Heck no. I've never thought of that," Russell responded.

The driver then said, "I'm going to introduce you to the firefighter training program at the Los Altos Fire Station. I'm a professor there and I'm going to help you get in. Would you be interested?"

And Russell said, "Absolutely."

The driver was Irvin Roth, a Jewish professor at Foothill Junior College. He drove the young man to the fire station. Russell had never been in a fire station in his life and had never known a firefighter. He filled out the application to become a student firefighter. The pay rate was $27 a month, with housing.

Russell was offered an interview, and then a position as a student firefighter.

Later he became a summer relief firefighter, and after five years Russell Hayden became the first African American firefighter in the Los Altos Fire Department.

From there, he became a firefighter in the San Jose Fire Department for twenty-nine years. He helped develop diversity in the department, including for men and women and minorities. He founded a national program called Firefighters ABCs, which helps minorities get into firefighting.

So, that's influence. Being an influencer can take many different forms. It can be just that one-hour interaction—driving a kid to a job application—that changes a whole life. That's my definition.

Am I an influencer? You just don't know, but you hope you can be, and you hope whatever you gain from someone else you can pay it forward.

Somewhere along the line, we have to get geared up, and say, "Hold it, let's spend our time and efforts on things that can help other people." And so, hopefully I am trying to put myself in those situations where we can help our own families, our friends, and people with whom we work. A gentleman named Bob Anderson worked for me as an accountant for many years. Bob is ninety-six years old now. He called me a couple of years ago—when he was ninety-four—and told me, "I just wanted you to know you were the best boss I ever had."

I will always want to try and be in a place where I can help people. I think that led to this research that I did and the discovery of the twelve principles of highly successful leaders I teach and wrote about in my book, *Becoming Your Best*. These principles become a foundation, so that as people apply them, they get predictable results. It allows me to be a tool to help people identify what they want in life, and then create a plan and make it happen. Once someone has a positive result, then we encourage them to teach it to others. So they then become the influencer.

STRATEGIC INFLUENCER

Sometimes being an influencer has far more to do with the person being influenced. In other words, their readiness and their desire to learn. Yes, there are definitely two sides of the coin. One where a person needs influence, who needs someone to open doors for them. Hopefully it is a person who has the character, has the willingness, and is prepared to work hard, but they just need a nudge. They need someone to open a door and make some introductions. So there's that side. The other side is the influencer who asks themselves, "Am I a good fit for this person? Can I really add value to this person, and can I do it in a way that's genuine?" When they come together, there's a good compatible story between the two of them.

STRATEGIC RELATIONSHIP INFLUENCER

The end game is about relationships, which gives you something that is more permanent. Referring to my own influencers, most of them started initially as a business relationship. A few started as a friend and then moved into the strategic mode. My business influencers became strategic to me and so I compensated them all to be an influencer and adviser. It was a business relationship, and they had a huge influence on me. Many of them became a deeply felt relationship that turned into a lifelong friendship, and so you become close to them, and something really magical happens. The relationship can become powerful, beyond the money, beyond the strategic part, but it's the friendship and relationship that continues. You continue influencing one another once you get past the strategic part.

This is at a level where there's a deep respect and genuine caring about the outcome of their life. There is an interesting thing that happens. Per the influencer, where does that role end? I'm suggesting it doesn't end when you get to that level. The influence goes on and on.

CENTER OF INFLUENCE

You know, you don't want to be arrogant, you want to be humble. I don't see myself as a center of influence. Perhaps I am, but I don't see it that way. For example, you take my companies. Yes, I'm the president. I can see that, and we have wonderful key leaders and managers and employees. I do have an impact on them, so maybe there's a serious responsibility there. But you know, you have a title or position that puts you there and then you have a responsibility. Your position can have influence on a whole industry because you have the relationships with decision makers, and you have all these people, and so I guess you'd better behave yourself and do good things.

This brings us back to the idea of being dropped in the port, in a new land, coming full circle. The strategy definitely makes sense to want to be involved with centers of influence, where you are the influencer and where you too can influence others. That's a big one.

Another example is the organization YPO. That's been a huge impact on me, but I've also impacted my associates there. I've been our chapter chairman of YPO a couple of times, and so indeed you do put yourself in a place where you can impact others and they can impact you.

Harvard University was the same. From my OPM class, we have a hundred and thirty CEOs from thirty different countries. Talk about an experience where you'll be influenced by them and you can reach out to them for anything! If I need something in Malaysia. I know somebody in Malaysia. If I need to call somebody in Vietnam, I can call them and they will help me, right now.

The very virtue of trying to do good things for people gets back to that strategy of why we spend time with each other in the first place.

IF I COULD START OVER AGAIN...

I would do some things differently. It goes back to being fourteen years old. There was about a five-year dark period there that competed with the good that I knew in life. I'd like to change a lot of things I did back then. Fortunately, there is repentance and another chance to get your life back on track.

Thinking back, it's been a great life. In retrospect, I might change a little bit of how I would do things, but that's what life is about, learning. You can't become who you are today without making mistakes along the way. So I'm not sure you'd want to change some of those things that caused you to change for the better. For example, we had a big financial setback back in 1985. I wouldn't wish that on anyone. Yet from that, it deeply impacted my business philosophy of not having debt, and of having businesses that are self-funded. It changed me fundamentally. So overall we've been blessed, so again I'm not sure I'd change that particular challenge.

HIGH PERFORMANCE HABITS

Here are my four High Performance Habits.

1. PERSONAL VISION

The first one is to have a personal vision. It's inspiring and reaches down to your core to give you direction. And one of the recommendations we have is to create a vision based upon your roles. I'm talking about having a vision for personal, financial, health, mental, and spiritual life, and to include your spouse or significant other. Another one is your role as a parent or grandparent. Another one is your professional role.

It's important to create a vision. Ask yourself, "What do I want from each of those roles?" Interestingly, what happens in the spirit of becoming your best, it's not limited by age. Because every time you ask that question of what your best looks like, you're at a different point in life. When you ask it at age twenty, you're going to get one set of answers. When you ask it at forty, you're going to get another set of answers. When you ask it at sixty, another set, and at eighty, another set. Your vision creates the direction.

2. ANNUAL GOALS

The second is the habit of having annual goals. And similarly, it's the same process, meaning, making goals according to your various roles and sharing them with two or more people you respect and admire.

Why share them with others? Because not only does it create accountability, but there is less chance you will be flaky on your goals when you share them. Your goals each year can be transformational for you. In other words, the New Year is coming up for you. You're never going to have the chance to live this year again. So focus on what are the most important things you can do that'll make a difference.

You are putting focus on what is the best within you, such as your health, your finances, your relationship with your spouse or your children, and also on what you can do professionally. This is a great way to think. I share my goals with all of my influencers every year and have done so for nearly forty years, every single year. That habit is huge.

3. PRE-WEEK PLANNING

A third habit is pre-week planning. Before you start your week, take a few minutes to think about each of those roles and the most important thing you can do this this week coming up for those roles. That is where the rubber meets the road on execution of doing what matters most.

4. HAVE STRONG PRINCIPLES

The fourth habit is to be principle-based, which means you know the principles you'll live by. If someone asks you to be dishonest, then there's not a chance you will do it, because you made that decision long ago.

One of our principle teachings is, "Lead with a vision!" Highly successful leaders lead with a vision. They *create* the vision. They say, "What's the vision? Where do we want to go?"

DEFINING MOMENTS IN LIFE

For me, a defining experience was going on a voluntary service mission. As a young person, the decision to serve as a missionary affected virtually everything else in my life. Because I went on a mission, I was able to get into Brigham Young University.

My mission president was a man named Gardner Russell, a successful businessman. Bill Jones was the previous mission president before I got there, also a successful businessman. He had a huge impact on my life. Because I was attending BYU, I met Stephen Covey, who was my professor of organizational behavior.

Then I met a student who asked me what I was going to do during the summer. I told him I was going to get an accounting internship. He then asked me, "How'd you like to sell Bibles to the Baptists with Southwestern?"

I said, "Okay, yeah, I'm in. Let's go do it."

The student who invited me unfortunately quit; but I decided that since I had committed, I was going to do it. And then the next year I was introduced to Promised Land Publications, which I later acquired. Then I asked Stephen Covey if he'd be on our board, and then I asked Bill Jones if he'd be on our board and an adviser. These associations led to Thomas S. Monson joining our board. One relationship led to another and each was an amazing influence in my life.

Those two decisions led to where we're at today. Sometimes there are turning points in your life.

THE ONE CONNECTION

If I had to name the one connection or most critical relationship who influenced my career the most, although it's hard to narrow it down, I'd say that Stephen R. Covey's impact was enormous.

Steve Shallenberger has more than forty years of experience as a successful business owner, trusted senior executive, professional corporate trainer, and respected community leader. He is a graduate of accounting from Brigham Young and business from Harvard Business School.

Shallenberger is the author of the National Bestselling book Becoming Your Best: The 12 Principles of Highly Successful Leaders. *Steve has co-authored with his son, Rob, their latest books,* Start with The Vision *on creating solutions and* Do

What Matters Most, *a leading authority on productivity, time management and leadership.*

Note from the Author Gary Laney

I've known Steven Shallenberger for over forty years. His bestselling book, Becoming Your Best-The 12 Principles of Highly Successful Leaders, *is a must-read as it represents decades of research from his own experience as a leader and entrepreneur as well as learned observation from hundreds of other leaders he has studied. His book has been an inspiration to me and thousands of others who seek to develop a principles-based leadership style. I highly recommend it.*

Our two books, though completely unique, are very complementary and would be wonderful reading companions. Frequently, individuals and organizations that invest in one book, will also invest in the other book. These two works will provide you with two beneficial perspectives on being successful as a principled leader AND a strategic influencer.

Website: www.becomingyourbest.com
LinkedIn: Becoming Your Best Global Leadership
Facebook: www.facebook.com/BecomingYourBest/
Instagram: Becomingyourbestglobal
Twitter: @BYB

PART TWO:
INFLUENCE DEVELOPMENT & EXECUTION

SPHERE OF ACCOUNTABILITY

SUCCESS FACTOR 1:
ACCEPT PERSONAL RESPONSIBILITY

"Individuals carry their success or their failure with them…
It does not depend on outside conditions."
—*Ralph Waldo Trine*

STARTING THE JOURNEY!

Having landed in Metropolis with no money, no knowledge of the city, and no influence, your task is to shape your life into something meaningful.

You may be in a similar situation right now.

If you've just graduated from college and you have a degree but no job experience, and you know you're starting at the bottom of the career ladder, you need to work your way up to a position of security and influence.

If you're entering politics, or have started a new job, or have joined an influential board of directors, you want to make the journey from the new guy to the respected leader.

Lao Tzu said that a journey of a thousand miles begins with a single step. He was right. Step by step, you can build and expand your sphere of influence, and as a result, create two significant benefits.

1. You will help yourself to a more secure and rewarding life.

2. You will add value to the lives of others and enrich your community.

Please do not think about striving for benefit #1 without also striving for benefit #2. They must go hand in hand. They strengthen each other and justify each other.

The first step is to *accept personal responsibility*.

You have landed in a distant city. You have no friends, no connections, and no knowledge of the local people and their ways. You need to provide for yourself, beginning with the very first level of Maslow's hierarchy, which comprises your physiological needs—homeostasis (a stable set point of physiology), health, food and water, sleep, clothing, and shelter. Then you need to work your way up to your safety, which includes job security, protection from abusive authority, the right to own personal property, and access to banks and insurance policies. Then comes social belonging, self-esteem, and self-actualization.

For the sake of this chapter, let's make your situation even more daunting. Let's say you've been injured on your long voyage, or you have health issues. The residents of Metropolis appear to have no such problems, although you can't be sure because they might be good at concealing them.

And then let's stipulate that you did not choose to come to this city. For some reason, you were put on a ship and sent here. Or perhaps your ship was caught in a storm, and instead of taking you where you wanted to go, it was destroyed on the rocks, and you were forced to come ashore in this strange land, like Odysseus during his epic, twenty-year journey home from Troy.

Your sphere of influence is zero. Nada. You have no influence because no one personally knows you.

In short, you have plenty of reasons to feel sorry for yourself. You have rightful cause to feel abused and mistreated. You look around, and you see all the other people going about their business, looking happy and well-fed, while you stand there, alone and bewildered.

While you would be entitled to have these feelings, they bring with them extreme danger. If you cling to them, you are surrendering your free will. You are acknowledging that external forces are in charge of your life, and that these forces can continue to direct the course of your life.

Your survival depends on your taking clear, decisive action. Your first task is to build your local influence among the people you meet. You must identify opportunities and seize them. You must see the world clearly for what it is and not what you hope it should be.

ACCEPTING PERSONAL RESPONSIBILITY

Perhaps the most daunting and brave act a modern-day business person can muster today is the willingness to accept responsibility for any and all circumstances that occur in one's daily life, both personally and professionally. Let's put this idea to the test as shown in *Figure 3.1*.

For every circumstance that occurs, good or bad, the decision tree below gives you two options, to choose to be a Victim or to choose to be a Victor. For our example, we'll assume that a certain circumstance has a bad outcome. As you can see from the model, the reactions for either choice can vary greatly.

In a challenging circumstance, a *victim* chooses the route of blame, is resistant

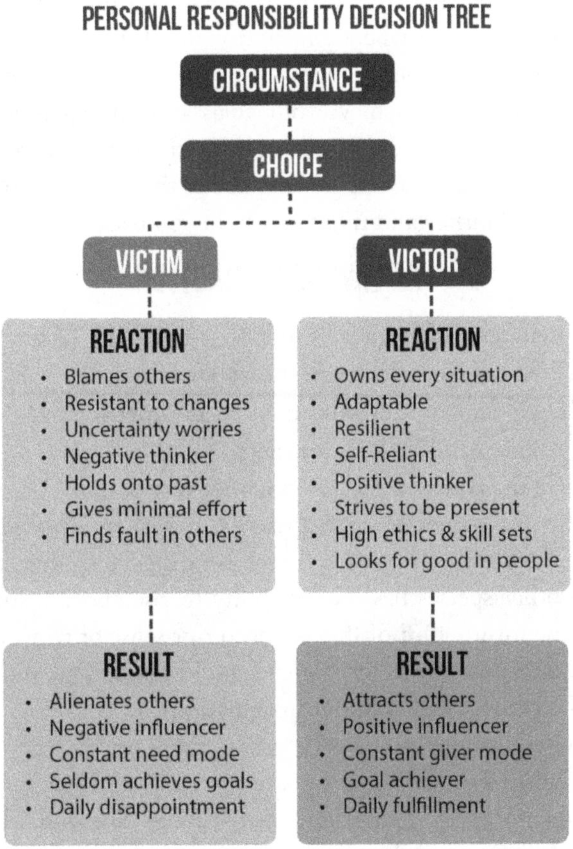

PERSONAL RESPONSIBILITY DECISION TREE

CIRCUMSTANCE

CHOICE

VICTIM

VICTOR

REACTION
- Blames others
- Resistant to changes
- Uncertainty worries
- Negative thinker
- Holds onto past
- Gives minimal effort
- Finds fault in others

REACTION
- Owns every situation
- Adaptable
- Resilient
- Self-Reliant
- Positive thinker
- Strives to be present
- High ethics & skill sets
- Looks for good in people

RESULT
- Alienates others
- Negative influencer
- Constant need mode
- Seldom achieves goals
- Daily disappointment

RESULT
- Attracts others
- Positive influencer
- Constant giver mode
- Goal achiever
- Daily fulfillment

Figure 3.1

to change, worries about things that can't be controlled, is reliant on others to solve a problem, reveals pessimistic negative thinking, has the inability to let go of the past, puts in only the minimally acceptable effort to solve a problem, and places fault of the challenging circumstance on others. On the adjacent side, a *victor*, chooses to own the problem, is willing to be adaptable to new conditions, is resilient in times of change, strives to be self-reliant and not dependent on others for help, has a focus to be ever present in every situation, has a high work ethic, continually works on improving skill sets, and looks for the good in people. To learn whether you are a victim or a victor, take a few minutes to think of the last difficult situation you encountered and compare the two lists of characteristics. Be honest in your assessment about your tendencies, actions, and reactions. Which side do you typically lean towards? Perhaps you are in the middle, having good intentions to follow the path of responsibility but still struggle in situations where you feel you have little control over the circumstance or outcome. Depending on where you find yourself, the results can determine your daily productivity, how effective your interactions are with others, whether or not you can consistently achieve your goals and ultimately your feelings of disappointment or fulfillment. As you read this chapter or success factor about *accepting personal responsibility*, take notes about those characteristics that help you in your success journey and those that hold you back.

THE LAW OF ATTRACTION

If your mind is clouded by negative thoughts—regardless of how justified they are—then you'll be unable to focus on the opportunities that will present themselves to you. The opportunities will exist, but in order to seize them, you need to be tuned in to them and looking for them.

This is where the law of attraction becomes very useful.

The concept has its roots deep in ancient times when *Homo sapiens* acquired the ability to consciously imagine a future condition and then take action to achieve it. No other species has the capability to rise above instinct and make choices about the future. Out of this emerged our sense of connection with the outside world, and that we, as individuals, could manipulate our environment according to the vision we held in our imaginations.

In the modern era, the first person to use the term "law of attraction" was the Russian occultist Helena Blavatsky, who in 1877 wrote in her book *Isis Unveiled* that "attraction" was a universal cosmic force. She said, "By whatsoever name the physicists may call the energizing principle in matter is of no account; it is a subtle something apart from the matter itself, and, as it escapes their detection, it must be something besides matter. If the law of attraction is admitted as governing the one, why should it be excluded from influencing the other?"[4]

In the late nineteenth century, the law of attraction became identified with the New Thought movement. New Thought held that Infinite Intelligence, or God, was everywhere, true human selfhood was divine, sickness originated in the mind, and "right thinking" had a healing effect. Various writers and philosophers explored the concept of thoughts and beliefs being linked to the physical world. Prentice Mulford, a pivotal figure in the development of New Thought thinking, described the law of attraction at length in his 1887 essay, "The Law of Success," in which he wrote, "Your thought is an invisible substance, as real as air, water, or metal…. This is your real power."[5]

---

4   H.P. Blavatsky. https://www.theosociety.org/pasadena/isis/iu1-10.htm
5   Mulford.

Another influential writer was James Allen, author of *As a Man Thinketh*, published in 1903. The opening lines of the book are:

> Mind is the Master power that moulds and makes,
> And Man is Mind, and evermore he takes
> The tool of Thought, and, shaping what he wills,
> Brings forth a thousand joys, a thousand ills: —
> He thinks in secret, and it comes to pass:
> Environment is but his looking-glass.[6]

The twentieth century produced many bestselling books based on the law of attraction, including *How to Win Friends and Influence People* (1936) by Dale Carnegie, *Think and Grow Rich* (1937) by Napoleon Hill, *The Power of Positive Thinking* (1952) by Norman Vincent Peale, *Psycho-Cybernetics* (1960) by Maxwell Maltz, and *The 7 Habits of Highly Effective People* (1989) by Stephen R. Covey.

It was in 2006 that the concept exploded internationally with the release of the film *The Secret*. This Australian documentary and the subsequent publication of the book by the same name re-introduced the law of attraction to the mass market. In three months, the book sold 1.75 million copies, plus 1.5 million DVDs. Executive producer Rhonda Byrne told *Newsweek* that her inspiration for creating *The Secret* came from reading the 1910 book *The Science of Getting Rich* by Wallace D. Wattles. *The Secret* took the law of attraction, which had traditionally focused on personal health and spirituality, to a new level. Byrne didn't merely assert that having a positive viewpoint was good and healthy and would bring you happiness; she claimed that you could manipulate *objective physical reality* through the power of your mind. Other law-of-attraction gurus advocate that just thinking of the things you want and really focusing on them with all of your intention is enough to harness the law of attraction and materialize what you want.

Clearly, most rational people would agree that you cannot make a new Cadillac appear in your driveway simply by willing it to be so. We know that Newton's laws of physics and various other complications would render this notion to be nothing more than a fantasy.

Does it matter if the law of attraction is true or false? In terms of your ability to build and use influence in your life, the answer is something that Martin Luther might agree with: *It doesn't matter, as long as you believe it.*

Think about it this way. If you believe that failure and rejection are your

---

6   *As a Man Thinketh.* http://www.gutenberg.org/ebooks/4507

fate, you'll be looking for them and anticipating them. And since the human mind doesn't want to be wrong, when you see the opportunity for failure and rejection, you'll gravitate toward them.

In contrast, if you believe you are entitled to success and acceptance, you'll look for opportunities to make your belief come true. When you see such opportunities, you'll seize them. You will take responsibility for your future and welcome the chance to better yourself.

Consider this scenario. Susan and Tom attend a social gathering at a local business club. Both Susan and Tom are new in town and don't know many people. They are chatting with John when a man sidles over to their group. John notices the man and then turns to Susan and Tom and says, "Oh, do you know Robert? He's the president of the First National Bank here in town."

Robert extends his hand, and greetings are exchanged.

As we will see, Susan and Tom have different reactions to meeting Robert.

Tom doesn't think much of the introduction. His mind is on a problem he has at work. He half-listens to the conversation and eventually excuses himself.

On the other hand, Susan thinks to herself, "Wow! I've just been introduced to the president of the First National Bank! He's someone I definitely want to know. I don't have a particular goal in mind at this moment, but knowing Robert will be valuable!" She politely engages him in conversation, asks questions about the bank, and tries to find a common interest. She discovers they are both fans of the city's pro baseball team, which gives them a topic to discuss that is a "third party"—that is, it isn't about either one of them personally or their jobs. In the conversation, there is an exchange of value—in this case, it's the pleasure of discovering a peer with a common interest. (Value can take many forms!)

At the end of the evening, Susan has made a new connection, while Tom—who had the *same exact opportunity*—has not. If you like, you can call it the law of attraction. Susan's mind was oriented toward success. She was looking for success, and when she saw an opportunity, she seized it. Poor Tom was consumed by his problems and was not anticipating success, which is why he failed to *recognize* and *act upon* a golden opportunity when it was presented to him.

You need to *believe in success*. As Earl Nightingale said, "Whatever we plant in our subconscious mind and nourish with repetition and emotion will one day become reality."[7]

If you want to win the ball game, you've got to be in the batter's box, swinging at the pitches. If you're sitting on the sidelines, you're guaranteed not to win.

---

7   https://www.awakenthegreatnesswithin.
com/50-inspirational-earl-nightingale-quotes-on-success/

BE ADVENTUROUS AND ADAPTABLE

While it's important to have consistent values, such as honesty and gratitude, the operating conditions of the world around you are always changing, just as you are always changing. Because today's problems require today's solutions, not yesterday's, flexibility in how you solve problems is an asset. Saying, "This is the way we've always done it" is a recipe for failure. Look at each new problem with a fresh eye, and don't be afraid to take responsibility for finding a new solution.

The need to be adaptable is more important every day. This is not just a slogan; it is literally true. The pace of innovation in our society is accelerating. The rate of change is getting faster. Think about it this way. If you lived your entire life between the years 1600 and 1680, how much technological and social change would you have seen? Not very much. The technology you used at birth was pretty much the same as when you turned eighty. Now think about someone whose life spanned the eighty years from 1940 to 2020. How much has changed since his or her birth? An astonishing amount. The entire digital revolution has blossomed just in the last forty years. Do you remember when digital CDs burst onto the music market? In September 1984, Bruce Springsteen's *Born in the U.S.A.* was the first music CD pressed in America. Sales of the new technology exploded, and in the year 2000, a record 942.5 million CDs were sold. Record company executives were ecstatic. They thought they had found the goose laying golden eggs.

Then came digital file sharing. Suddenly CDs were not only old-fashioned but unnecessary. Anyone could buy a single CD and then replicate its songs endlessly and send those replicas to friends for free. To their horror, record company executives saw they no longer controlled the means of distribution. Sales of CDs plummeted, and by 2019, only 46.5 million were sold.

If you don't adapt, you are swept aside.

RECOGNIZE WHAT YOU CAN AND CANNOT CONTROL

This is a foundational axiom. Unless you are able to separate what is under your control and what is not, you will be tormented by your attempts to fight battles you can never win.

Too many people waste precious energy fretting over things they cannot influence. They fume when caught in a traffic jam. They get angry when the weather turns bad. They resent when their boss spends his days on the golf course. As the stranger adapting to the new land, make a rule for yourself: If you cannot change something, put a smile on your face and keep moving forward.

Think about the astonishing resiliency of people who are born with a serious birth defect, such as no arms or no legs. Given what we know about human emotion, it would not be surprising if such people took stock of their lives and said, "This is hopeless. I'm going to end my life." In fact, the opposite often happens, and they become more determined to succeed.

When we begin our life on our journey, we are reliant and dependent on others. Our objective should be to become self-reliant and independent, which is the next stage.

Consider Nicholas James Vujicic, an Australian-American Christian evangelist and motivational speaker. On December 4, 1982, he was born with tetra-amelia syndrome, a rare disorder characterized by the absence of arms and legs. With an astonishingly positive attitude, he and his parents resolved to accept the reality of his condition. He excelled in school and graduated from Griffith University with a bachelor of commerce degree, with a double major in accountancy and financial planning. In 2005, Vujicic founded Life Without Limbs, an international nonprofit organization. Two years later, he founded Attitude is Altitude, a secular motivational speaking company.

In his story, and many others like it, there are two contradictions that are perfectly acceptable. The first contradiction is this: While it's necessary to accept reality as it is without regret or blame, it's also necessary to strive to improve oneself. This is the formulation:

I am perfect the way I am now. I must become better.

These two ideas seem mutually exclusive, but they are not. To say "I am perfect the way I am now" is not a boast or exercise in vanity. It's simply an affirmation that the past is gone, and your condition at this moment is what you have to work with. You may have no arms or legs, but if you say, "I will be forever bitter because I have no arms or legs," the only person you're emotionally torturing is yourself. You will anticipate a miserable life, and it shall be granted to you.

And then to say, "I must become better" is to embrace a fundamental characteristic of human beings, one which separates us from all other species. The desire to make life better is itself a source of great happiness and positive energy and gives us a good reason to get out of bed in the morning. It is not only the actual achievement of a better life that makes people happy; it's also the *hope* of a better life that keeps the human spirit alive.

The second contradiction is this:

As humans, we always rely on each other. I will become self-reliant.

Both statements are true. This is because we depend on each other for skills that each of us, as individuals, lacks. You go to a dentist because he or she has the training and experience to care for your teeth. You buy shoes at a store because you can't make your own. So in that sense, we rely on each other, and no human is literally self-reliant. But the kind of self-reliance I'm talking about is the ability to fend for yourself in today's world. It means having your own home or apartment rather than sleeping on your parents' sofa. It means having an education and an income. It means being able to land in Metropolis and make your way to self-sufficiency in your new community. And the stronger and more self-reliant you are, the more you'll be able to help other people.

As you walk along the path of life, would you rather be the guide of others or the one who is guided? Everyone begins their life as the one who is guided, mostly by parents and teachers. But over time, as your knowledge and experience increase, you no longer need to be guided, and in fact, you become the guide of others. Your self-reliance makes it possible for you to help others.

LEARN TO OBSERVE YOUR NEGATIVE THOUGHTS AND FEELINGS

To take responsibility for your life is to take responsibility for your powers of thinking and feeling because these are the roots of all human experience. Everything you say and do begins with your thoughts, which happen in your brain, and your feelings, which come from your heart (poetically speaking).

But our thoughts and feelings seem to spring up out of nowhere! Images and ideas and emotions wash over us like waves breaking over the rocks on the shore. We cannot stop them, especially if we've suffered from a previous shock like post-traumatic stress disorder (PTSD). How many times have we heard someone say, "I don't know why I did it...? I just couldn't help myself."

In Buddhism, during meditation, practitioners are taught to never try to *suppress* thoughts but to simply *observe* them as they enter the mind. During a bad day at work, do you feel like strangling your boss? Let the violent image pass in and out of your head. Do not judge yourself. Everyone has thoughts and feelings. It's what makes us human.

There's a big difference between *having* negative thoughts and *acting* upon them. There's also the question of how you *interpret* those thoughts. Let's say you're at work and your boss speaks sharply to you for what you think is no reason. Your feelings are aroused. Depending on your mindset, you will respond in two different ways.

1. The negative response will be, "I've done something wrong. The boss is going to fire me. Why does he hate me? I should never have taken this

lousy job. I must be screwing up…" These negative interpretations will lead to an expectation of a bad outcome. They will cloud your thinking.

2. The positive response will be, "The boss just spoke sharply to me. That's interesting. I wonder what it means. Perhaps he's having a bad day or is stressed out. Perhaps he's looking for a reason to fire me. I need to monitor the situation and be prepared to act if necessary. In the meantime, I'll test him by being extra helpful to him. Then I'll see how he responds."

In the second scenario, you're taking notice of information coming to you and rationally processing it. You're acting from a position of self-confidence.

You take responsibility when you accept that *your* thoughts come from *your* mind. The words you speak come from *your* mouth. The actions you take are taken by *you*.

You cannot control the thoughts and actions of others. But with training and discipline, you can control and take responsibility for your own thoughts and actions, and this will enable you to act from a position of strength.

BE PRESENT IN EACH MOMENT

As the old saying goes, "The past is history, the future is a mystery." The only reality is now, at this moment. Take responsibility for this moment and make the best of it to redeem the past and create the future you want.

Persistent thoughts about the past can only clog your brain. Some people dwell on the past because they once experienced a trauma that permanently affected them emotionally. They may have been victims of adverse childhood experiences (ACEs) or PTSD. If you feel this could be the case with you, then you deserve to receive mental health counseling and be free of those memories.

Other people dwell upon the past as being the "golden years" that will never come again. They dream about when they were the high school football star or homecoming queen and lament those glory days. This is so sad because those days are gone, and each new day is a precious gift that must not be squandered.

When you're truly present, you have an awareness of what you are thinking and feeling. This then allows you to discard those intrusive thoughts that do not serve you. Deliberately change them to what you want in that moment to shape your future.

BE FULLY PRESENT

Taking this a step further, when having a one-on-one conversation with another person, you must practice being *fully present*. Being fully present means you are focused only on the person you are speaking with at that moment. It means you are not allowing distractions in the environment around you to interfere with the conversation. It also means not allowing personal thoughts to wander off in another direction such as your daily schedule, your next meeting, concerns of some challenge you may be experiencing, or even the next thing you want to say to the person you are presently with.

When your mind wanders in a two-way conversation, it's no longer a two-way conversation. Rather, wandering can noticeably remove you from the discussion at hand.

To be fully present, you must practice *active listening*, by fully concentrating on what the other person is saying. It is a skill that must be practiced each time you have a conversation, and it requires listening with all of your senses. Active listening, *being fully present*, will indicate to the person with whom you are speaking that you care about the conversation, that the purpose of meeting or speaking is of high importance and priority to you.

Active listening can be sensed through the tone of voice, the momentum of speech, the form of interaction, conversation feedback, through body language, and with eye contact.

When having an engaging conversation, relevant questions will naturally emerge because you are actively listening. The goal of any conversation should be to engage at a level where both you and the other person will feel the conversation at hand is all that matters at that moment in time. You will then experience a level of real engagement. Engaging at a high level will not only enhance the conversation but empower each of you to have a much more meaningful level of discussion.

Furthermore, if the person with whom you are speaking can sense your attentiveness and interest in them, you can potentially take the conversation to an unexpected and elevated level, which can help expedite trust and relationship development. Otherwise, the other person may feel like a bystander who is witnessing you come and go from the conversation.

In summary, make it a goal to be fully present in each one-on-one conversation. It will give you an edge when trying to build strong and meaningful relationships.

DON'T VICTIMIZE YOURSELF – AND QUIT THE BLAME GAME

Let's say your lazy co-worker failed to submit his work on time, and it set back your project, making you look bad. The facts are not in dispute. Your colleague screwed up, and you suffered as a result.

You blame him for your problems. You are factually correct. But "blame" is an open-ended, pointless emotion. It accomplishes nothing. Instead, take responsibility for your response. Ask yourself, "What am I doing to help resolve this problem? How can I keep this situation from happening again?"

In life, blaming your partner, parents, your upbringing, the economy, or the dog for your misfortune does not help you to move forward. Blaming keeps you in victim mode and robs you of the power to proactively change your situation.

When you stop blaming and accept responsibility, you shift from victim to victor. Now you can look at the situation and decide what to do about it.

Rather than blame or victimize, you can and must take the high road. Accept the circumstances you find yourself in. Do not attempt to pass your problems or challenges onto someone else. You alone must resolve and accept the fact that the outcomes of your challenges are determined by your ability to take ownership for them. To succeed in life, simply choose to take responsibility for your decisions, for your actions and results that come. You can follow the example of President Harry S. Truman who kept a sign on his desk in the White House with the phrase, "The buck stops here." (*Figure 3.2*). As president, he wanted everyone to know that he was willing to accept the ultimate responsibility for the position he held and the decisions he made.

Figure 3.2 The buck stops here.
President Harry S. Truman

STOP COMPLAINING

This is the close cousin of the blame game. Complaining is another form of blaming and playing the victim, as if you had no choice. And exactly to whom are you complaining? Your boss, who doesn't want to hear it? Your spouse, who *definitely* doesn't want to hear it? Complaining shows that you're focused on things going wrong and things happening to you.

When everything is not going according to plan, there is always a bigger picture, and an opportunity to *solve the problem*. If something has gone wrong, then there must be a problem, and it can be solved.

Instead of complaining about a situation, ask yourself, "What is the opportunity here? What can I learn from this?" This is the true value of the law of attraction: you always look for the positive energy that can supersede the negative energy.

DON'T TAKE DISAGREEMENTS PERSONALLY

Assuming that everything is about you is a form of narcissism. To take every form of disagreement as a personal attack is vanity.

Be humble. Don't take conflict personally because it's most probably not about you but about the issue at hand. Instead of making assumptions, ask questions. Remember, you have no control over how other people respond, but you have control over how *you* respond. Always look for opportunities, even in rejection.

BE HAPPY

It may sound like a simple, childish thing to say, "Be happy." But the point is that external events don't make you happy, at least not in the long run. Sure, if your team wins the championship game, you're happy—but only for a few minutes or hours. Then you revert back to your baseline level of happiness, or lack thereof.

True happiness, the kind that lasts for a long time, can only come from within. Being happy and taking responsibility for your life goes hand in hand with longevity. Think about the people you see on TV who are celebrating their 100th birthdays. They all seem to have one trait in common, and that is they seem deeply happy. Nothing bothers them. I remember seeing a woman on TV who had turned 105 years old. This woman, the announcer told us, had survived a Nazi concentration camp, family deaths, bouts with cancer, and was nearly blind and deaf—but to hear her speak, you'd think she had lived a charmed life of sunshine and sweetness. She looked not to the past but to the future and what it held in store for her. She blamed no one, and she "owned" her life.

I defy you to find anyone over the age of ninety who's a sour grouch. Such people do not exist.

BEND THE ODDS TO YOUR FAVOR

You have the power to choose. In fact, you are making choices all the time: red dress or black dress, tea or coffee, drive or walk, work or play. Having a life mission will help you make the best choices to increase your chances of success. A vision for your life, your business, your relationship, and your health will provide a roadmap for your decisions, thereby enabling you to align your choices with your best interests.

No outcome is ever guaranteed. Every action or project is a combination of many other actions that together add up to produce a result. Meanwhile, the forces of chaos and entropy, which are constant in the universe, will randomly work to destroy your progress. Therefore you must take the necessary steps to reduce the odds of failure and increase the odds of success.

For example, when you drive your car, even if you're a safe driver, some other guy might be a lousy driver, or be drunk, and hit your car. A car is replaceable; you are not. To increase your chances of surviving an accident, you wear a seat belt, and your car is equipped with airbags. These actions give you a bigger margin of safety and reduce the odds of injury or death.

In business, when building your personal influence, the more people you know, the better. Think back to the story of Susan and Tom, the newcomers in town who attended a social gathering at a local business club. They were both introduced to Robert, the president of the First National Bank. While Tom thought nothing of it and failed to make Robert's acquaintance, Susan seized the opportunity and engaged Robert in conversation. By doing so, she made sure that Robert remembered her. Did she need Robert's help at that exact moment? No. But let's say that a month later, both Susan and Tom are working on projects that will require a bank loan. Susan calls Robert, who says, "Hi Susan—a pleasure to hear from you. How may I help you?" He then listens to her proposal. Meanwhile, Tom also calls Robert. When Robert's assistant takes the call, Robert replies, "Someone named Tom wants to talk to me about a loan? The name doesn't ring a bell. Tell him to contact one of our loan officers."

Is Susan *guaranteed* to get her loan? No. Is Tom destined to be refused? Maybe not. But it is undeniable that Susan has bent the odds in her favor. A proposal looked upon favorably by the president of the bank has a much better chance of receiving prompt approval than one submitted to a loan officer.

In all areas of life, much of your success will depend on your mental and spiritual attitude. As Zig Ziglar said, "You were born to win, but to be a winner you must plan to win, prepare to win, and expect to win."[8]

STRENGTHEN YOUR WORK ETHIC

If you arrived in a strange city with no money and no connections, you'd quickly realize that by working and making a contribution to the welfare of the city and its citizens, your own life would improve.

---

8   https://www.goalcast.com/2018/01/16/most-inspiring-zig-ziglar-quotes/

Your *work ethic* would be very important. A work ethic is more than a willingness to complete a job on time and get paid for it. That's important, but it goes beyond that to embrace a belief that hard work and diligence have a moral benefit and an inherent ability, virtue, or value to strengthen character and individual abilities. In other words, having a good work ethic helps shape you as a human being and informs how you interact with others and how they view you.

The best way to strengthen your work ethic is (obviously) to work at a productive activity and free yourself from unproductive time-wasters such as watching television. Think about it: If you feel you need to watch your favorite NFL team play a game, what are you really doing? You're watching other people work and make fat salaries while you earn *zero*. Why not use that same three hours to learn something new, exercise, or otherwise improve yourself?

The work you do must be enjoyable and give you a sense of satisfaction. Find a vocation that you love to do and would want to do anyway, even if you were not getting paid. If you truly love your work, then it will seem like fun and not a burden. Of course, every job has its boring aspects, but if you feel as though you're just working for the paycheck, you should think about what you really want to do, even if initially it means less money.

Take inspiration from this story.

In 1989, Brian Scudamore was a nineteen-year-old high school dropout. But the Vancouver, B.C. native wanted to earn a college degree (it's a long story—he basically hustled his way into Concordia University in Montreal) and was looking for a side hustle that could finance his education. One day, while waiting in the drive-through lane of a Vancouver McDonald's, he saw an old, beat-up pickup truck with a sign advertising Mark's Hauling, a trash removal company.

"I can do that," Scudamore thought, as he told CNBC's *Make It*.

With his entire life savings of $1,000, Scudamore bought an old Ford F-100 and some fliers and business cards. Even though the business was a one-man operation, he initially called it The Rubbish Boys because he wanted it to sound bigger. His father, a liver transplant surgeon, was disappointed when Scudamore dropped out of university in 1993 to focus on his junk-hauling business full-time.

In his first year in business, Scudamore made a profit of about $1,700, which he put towards his education.

Fast forward to today, and Scudamore's business, now called 1-800-GOT-JUNK?, is a $300-million business operating junk-removal franchises in 160 locations in the US, Canada, and Australia. It's the largest component of a family of O2E Brands launched by Scudamore that now includes 1-888-WOW1DAY! Painting and Shack Shine.

But is he influential? You bet! He writes a column for *Forbes* magazine. Among other awards, in 2004, he was inducted into the Young Presidents' Organization (YPO) and served as a board member for the Young Entrepreneurs' Organization (YEO). Three years later, the International Franchise Association named him "Entrepreneur of the Year." In 2012, he became a CEO Hall of Fame Lifetime Achievement Inductee with the Collegiate Entrepreneurs' Organization. He's become a leading expert on how to become an entrepreneur, and in 2018 published his first book, *WTF?! (Willing to Fail): How Failure Can Be Your Key to Success.*

As Leigh Buchanan, editor-at-large at *Inc. Magazine,* wrote, "Brian Scudamore's enthralling tale of the launch and longevity of 1-800-GOT-JUNK? is everything you want from a business yarn. This book will make you want to run—arms flung wide—toward entrepreneurship."

The story of Brian Scudamore reminds us that one way to climb the ladder of success and influence is to joyfully *do the job that no one else wants to do.*

And don't just theorize about it or talk about it. *Take action!* As Olympic gold medal wrestler Dan Gable said, "There's always ways of motivating yourself to higher levels. Write about it, dream about it. But after that, turn it into action. Don't just dream."[9]

> *"The secret of success of every man who has ever been successful lies in the fact that he formed the habit of doing things that failures don't like to do."*
> —*Albert E.N. Gray*

ALWAYS IMPROVE YOUR SKILL SET

People pay money for skills, and the better yours are, the more money you'll be paid and the more influence you will have. Always be learning and improving. If your current job is mundane, then switch jobs, take adult education classes, or work on earning a higher degree. Be forever inquisitive and look for ways to turn your knowledge into service to others.

It is almost a cliché, but it's true: If you want to make money and be influential, then you need to provide an outstanding skill or service to people who have the means to pay. If you're a lawyer, then specialize in services that rich people need, such as estate planning or divorce. If you're a housepainter, then

---

9   https://quotes.thefamouspeople.com/dan-gable-1126.php

specialize in high-end craftsmanship that the wealthy demand. If you're a chef, don't work at Applebee's. Get the skills you need to work at a five-star restaurant.

Skills are like latent wealth. You may have a skill that's not worth much on the market today, but it could be tomorrow, especially if you keep honing it. For example, see Brian Scudamore's story above. Or consider the tale of Joe Ades. In 1993, at the age of fifty-nine, he stepped off the boat from Ireland onto the pier in New York City. He had two marketable skills: He could sell, and he could entertain. Equipped with a box of vegetables and a supply of new $5 potato peelers, Joe Ades hit the streets of Manhattan. From dawn till dusk, he'd sit on a street corner or in a park and demonstrate his $5 peeler to anyone who passed by.

His engaging sales patter, $1,000 Chester Barrie suits, and stylish shirts from Turnbull & Asser eventually brought him attention and notoriety. In 2006 he was the subject of an article in *Vanity Fair*. He sold enough peelers to enjoy café society at the Pierre Hotel, on the Upper East Side, while he lived with his fourth wife, Estelle Pascoe, in her apartment on Park Avenue. On February 1, 2009, at age seventy-four, he died—only one day after being informed that he had been granted American citizenship.

He said something memorable: "Never underestimate a small amount of money gathered by hand for sixty years." How true!

LOOK FOR THE GOOD IN PEOPLE

You never want to be naïve and fail to see another person's bad intentions, but a key part of self-responsibility is the willingness and ability to objectively see the good in other people with whom you may disagree. Set aside your own preconceptions, and look for their intentions as well as their actions. So often when we understand someone else's point of view, we let go of judgment, and as a result, we become stronger and more influential.

Think back to idea #2, which says that we should be able to observe our thoughts and feelings. In the same vein, we should be able to objectively assess our position and the position of the other guy. Empathy makes this possible, and through empathy, we can try to understand why someone would want what they want.

If you've been having a conflict with someone, take a few minutes to set aside your own point of view and understand how the other person might have experienced the conflict. Do you think you'd be perceived as being inflexible and dogmatic, or willing to engage and find common ground?

CONSCIOUS RESPONSIBILITY, AND OVERCOMING REGRET AND REVENGE

Conscious responsibility for your life means living intentionally and deliberately making choices to move ahead toward manifesting your vision. When you take responsibility for your life and experience, you enter into a place of confidence. Even when you make a mistake—we all do!—you'll see the big picture, fix the error, and move ahead.

When you take conscious responsibility for the sum total of both your own actions and the external actions that have affected you, you get rid of the twin cancers of regret and revenge.

Regret comes from dwelling too much on the past and what you thought you should have done. How many times have you heard someone say, "I really regret not having taken the job that was offered to me," or, "I regret not getting my master's degree"? Does feeling regretful help you solve your problems *today?* I don't think so. And likewise, does seeking revenge for some past injustice help you improve your life right now? It's hard to let go of injuries, and we all know someone who is so obsessed with going back and re-litigating the past that their vision of the future is cloudy.

As I'll reveal in the next chapter, taking responsibility for yourself and your actions is the necessary precursor to the next step, which is becoming self-reliant.

SUCCESS ACTION ITEMS – ACCEPT PERSONAL RESPONSIBILITY

- Build your local influence among the people you meet. Take clear and decisive action to make connections.
- Envision success and then take action to achieve it.
- Look at each new problem with a fresh eye, and don't be afraid to take responsibility for finding a new solution.
- Be adaptable. Today's problems require today's solutions, not yesterdays. Flexibility is how you solve problems and is an asset.
- Recognize what you can and cannot control. If you cannot change something, put a smile on your face and keep moving forward.
- Accept the premise: I am perfect the way I am now; I must become better. Accept that the past is gone and focus on making life better.
- Choose to become self-reliant. The stronger and more self-reliant you are, the more you'll be able to help other people.
- Observe and take responsibility for your thoughts and feelings because these are the roots of all human experience.
- Be fully present in each of your one-on-one conversations. This will help you expedite trust and build stronger relationships.
- Don't victimize and quit the blame game. When you stop blaming and accept responsibility, you shift from victim to victor.
- Don't complain. Instead of complaining about a situation, ask yourself, "What is the opportunity here?
- Be happy. Being happy and taking responsibility for your life goes hand in hand with longevity.
- Create a life vision statement that will provide a roadmap for your decisions and align your choices with your best interests.
- Strengthen your work ethic by working at a productive activity and free yourself from unproductive time-wasters. Hard work and diligence have a moral benefit.
- Always be learning and improving. People pay money for skills, and the better yours are, the more money you'll be paid and the more influence you will have.
- Look for the good in people. A key part of self-responsibility is the willingness and ability to objectively see the best in other people.
- Take conscious responsibility for both your own actions and the external actions that affect you, and you get rid of the twin cancers of regret and revenge.

SOMDUTTA SINGH
CEO ASSIDUUS GLOBAL

*"The Foundation of Influence
is Survival Instinct"*

MY SUCCESS JOURNEY

BOTH OF MY PARENTS ARE doctors. For many years, my dad was the physician to Mother Teresa, until she passed away. Because of that relationship, I grew up very close to her ideology, her thought process, and her selflessness.

At a very early age, my dad introduced me to books. I read a lot about economics, from Adam Smith to Greg Connor, and the subject excited me. My mom's parents were also close to Dr. Amartya Sen, who was a Nobel laureate in economics so I became very excited about learning more about the subject. The foundation of every country is based on economics. Any businessperson doing anything is using the fundamentals of economics.

I'm an only child, and my parents wanted me to be a doctor. Unfortunately, I was terrible at dissection. I fainted when I had to cut open a frog. So when I told my parents I didn't want to be a doctor, my dad actually told me to get out of the house. I didn't take it seriously because I was fifteen years old and a rebel. I was a very intelligent girl and at the top of my class, my school, and my state. I was a trained classical music connoisseur. I could play four instruments. I wrote poetry and won a lot of awards. So I said, "I'm smart, I'll figure it out."

When I left Calcutta, where I was born, and went to Bangalore, I saw that life was not going to be easy. I went from living with all the luxuries in the world to starting my life from scratch, living in a dormitory, and having to make my own bed and clean my own toilet. At home we had four housemaids who did everything. And suddenly I had nothing. I ran away from home with less than 2,000 rupees in my pocket, which was not even thirty dollars. I used to sit at a salon. I learned how to stitch clothing. I would make chocolate in my dormitory. I learned it from a girl I met, and I sold it at my college. In my first

66

TED Talk, I talked about how my friends had the luxury of having boyfriends, while I was leveraging their luxury to earn my living. They would bring their boyfriends, and I would sell chocolates to them!

That's how my journey started. I realized I was on my own, but by the end of the first year of college, I was making enough money to not only survive but to thrive.

My dad didn't speak to me for three years until I graduated, top of the class at the university. I was a topper in college and state. The governor gave me a gold medal, and there was my dad, in the first row, standing and clapping for me. I realized then why he asked me to leave home. It was because there are many kids who say they are rebels, but they're rebels without a cause. Because *saying* something versus *doing* something are very different things. My dad taught me how to live and made me a survivor, which I think is so important for entrepreneurship.

The foundation of influence is survival instinct. You put me anywhere, and I can learn how to live.

There was no looking back. I went on to earn my PhD at the MIT Sloan School of Management, and started my first company. It was acquired by Sequel, which is a Cisco company. I built my second company, a crowdsourced fashion label. I sold that one as well. I failed at my third, because I started dating. I didn't date until I was in my mid-twenties. Because I was very focused, I felt that doing anything else beyond my career was a waste of time. I thought I didn't have time for that, even when I was in college in the United States. I was just doing my research and focusing on how I could have a great network, which I could grow from, learn from, and leverage tomorrow.

Rather than just pursue random dating, I wanted to meet someone who inspired me. It happened at one of the conferences. I traveled to Istanbul, where I met a wonderful guy. He chased me across the world, and it was euphoric. I was in my late twenties. It was so much fun. I always had men attracted to me, but it never excited me; but here was a man chasing me across the world, an entrepreneur. I wanted to make this work so much that I stopped focusing on my business. That's when reality set in. The relationship didn't work out, but it taught me balance. I rediscovered myself.

In life we often are doing one thing at a time, and we don't know how to balance the other. Balancing your personal and professional life is so important. I've always been a hardcore professional, and every time I had leisure time I would focus on more self-development. I was participating in different competitions and speaking at different conferences. Building my personal profile was so important, and I had great parents, so I never focused on my personal needs for love, affection, and relationships; so when it happened, I couldn't handle both the relationship and my business. That taught me how important it is to balance your personal and professional life.

My fourth business is going to be a unicorn. We already have a $200 million valuation. Indeed, one of the biggest beneficiaries of the pandemic was my company Assiduus Global. We're an integrated platform for brands to sell across e-commerce platforms globally. When a brand comes on board with us—let's say a Marc Jacobs or an H&M—we take them to different marketplaces, whether it's Amazon, Walmart, FC, or, in India, Flipkart, Mintra, Nika, in UAE Noon. They partner with us and we become their global distributor across these platforms. We're not just doing basic distribution, we also have technology. So we have API integration with these platforms that gives us intelligence as to which categories are going to do well, how they're going to perform, what kind of competition exists, and what the pricing should be. So we even give brands intelligence to launch new products, which is a digital first.

We have a portfolio of over fifty clients, all very marquee, Fortune 500 clients. We also have our own private label business. We have health supplements, we have beauty, we have maternity lingerie. Our health supplements line is completely vegan organic. We also have a beauty line, The Real Boss Lady, which is cruelty free, vegan, and made for aspirational women. We have our private label business, and then we have the partnership with the brands globally. During the COVID-19 pandemic, we grew business by 300 percent. I was working every single day. Every adverse situation is an opportunity.

I've had my own personal challenges. When I was born, and handed to my mom, the doctor told her that there was a problem. I had a tumor in my cerebral cortex, and even if they removed it, chances were that I wouldn't be able to speak, and my movements would be very limited. But my parents wanted to take a chance and go ahead with it. When I was six months old, they did the surgery. For four years I could walk and talk like any other child; but after that, not only could I talk, I could *sing*. I'm a phenomenal dancer and I'm trained in salsa and pragmatium. I can move. I'm not comparing myself to Michael Jackson, but I'm so flexible. I can move every bone in my body. I would go into dance competitions and the boys would be scared because if Som was coming to dance, then chances were good that she was going to win. I'm learning how to play the piano now.

But that's not where life ended. I had three other surgeries, because I started developing other kinds of issues. I had my gallbladder and a fibroid removed.

Fast forward to age twenty-eight. I was diagnosed with an aneurysm. In

2013, I had my aneurysm surgery. Today they know how to put in a stent, and I know how lucky I am. My dad is a neurosurgeon., so how much more lucky could I get? I'm a miracle child. God may have put me through a lot, but every time he put me into something better. It makes me realize my purpose in life. He made me better with every adversity. But I still have an IQ of 144. And I have an eidetic, or photographic, memory. If I read something, I remember it.

Anything that happens to you is with a purpose. It tries to teach you something.

I never take anything in my life for granted, and I share everything I do. All my employees have a stake in the company because I want them to believe that this is not just my dream, it's theirs too.

I know true success lies not only in my vision but in the execution, and I know I need amazing people to execute my vision. I always hire people who are better than I am, and give them a stake in the company so they can stay committed, even if I'm gone. I'm not building a company which is dependent on Som, I'm building a company that can run without Som, and I think that's how I want to be remembered.

I've written two books, one of which is a bestseller. I sit on the advisory board of the government of India. I was the youngest adviser to be elected to the Planning Commission, which is the EPI of the government of India. I helped the government create the first women's entrepreneurship platform. I am part of the India Israel Innovation Corridor. I went to Tel Aviv every year to talk about innovation and find ways to collaborate between India and Israel.

I am part of the global entrepreneurship network. I sit as one of their academic chairs. I'm also on the board of Dr. Philip Kotler's, Kotler Impact—the only woman of Indian origin who was not even thirty-five years old. Everybody on the board is at least forty-five, and I'm the youngest board member to support him in education for all. My first book, *Decoding Digital*, includes a foreword by Dr. Kotler.

I was in Forbes "30 under 30," and am now part of the Forbes Business Council.

I have a very empowered team that can function without much interference from my side, while I keep on innovating and thinking of new ways to cater to the consumer base that is growing and interacting with the internet so rapidly.

ENTERING A STRANGE CITY

One of the things I'm really good at is selling. I love people and I have a personality that attracts people. I can also pick up the history of a place very quickly. On landing in a strange city, I would do jobs that are more in the background while

I picked up other skills, and then keep adding value to it. I do know how to sing. I am a very good singer! I'd use that skill to attract people in order to make a little bit of money to survive. I could find menial jobs at a restaurant because I'm good with people, or at a bookstore because I read a lot. I'd get adjusted to the culture and then go from there—and then start a business of my own.

INFLUENCE

Influence means networking, and how quickly I can build a network through which I can survive. I do not believe that money equals the ability to survive. People with a lot of money are often very lonely. I'm a person who believes in friendship in the network, so for me influence is your network, that is, who can support me and allow me to grow even if I don't have money.

STRATEGIC INFLUENCE

The lifespan of an influencer is limited unless they are strategic. My social videos are not about fashion or clothing, not about success, but mostly about failure in life. I've battled depression and talked about it in a video. People who view it go back and watch it again and again, and have said it has changed their lives.

STRATEGIC RELATIONSHIP INFLUENCE

Relationships are everything to me. I harness them. I harbor them. They are the very epicenter of my life. Everything revolves around relationships.

There are three points to a relationship for me. One, relationships don't always have to convert into business. When I approach people, to me it's not just business. It's also my personal growth and my learning. It may not culminate into business. I believe you meet people for a purpose. A person may be able to guide me to become a better version of me, which can add value to my business. That is very important to me, and I don't need people with a transactional mindset. That's the reason my relationships stay active. In my company in the last few years, I have not had a single employee leave. How many people can bet their life on that? Not many. You can talk to all my employees, and they'd say they wouldn't go, even if they got better pay somewhere. They'd say they don't have this kind of culture where they're so empowered.

We don't have titles in my company. We don't have business cards with titles. It's about roles. It's what you do. You are leading operations, so you're leading operations, but you don't have a title for that, okay? You are leading design, you don't have a title for that. Tomorrow if you want to move from design to development, great, you are now part of the development team. You are part of the organization that is fluid. The moment you give a title you create a hierarchy with insecurity and incompetence. I don't want that.

I don't say I'm the CEO. I put Serial Entrepreneur in my signature because that is my identity. That tells you what I do. And it's a conversation opener. I want people to stay interested in me long-term. That's why I don't approach a relationship with a transactional mindset.

I'm personally there for my clients. I have had occasions when a client has called me and talked about something that happened in their life and said, "Hey Som, could you connect me to your dad," or, "You know I am going through this," and they have confided in me because I never betray a confidence. I keep things to myself, and I value the honesty and the trust that is there in the relationship. Because of that, I have always had people by my side.

When I go to a restaurant, I have a relationship with all the servers. When I go back the next time, not only do I get additional attention, I get free food. When somebody tells you they know Som, then they get more attention. I want my legacy to be that people know me for the human being I am, not for what I have built or for my success.

CENTER OF INFLUENCE

The center of influence is when a person is emotionally able to evoke a reaction from the audience. If I'm standing on the stage, during my first few seconds I'll be glancing through the audience to see the people. It's about interaction. It's about bringing the truth to light, and not just the superficial aspect. People don't relate to transient fiction, but to facts. When you tell them the truth, they can relate to it.

For me, emotions are the epicenter for any center of influence, because it's the only thing that can invoke attention and be long-term. Otherwise, they will get bored during your presentation, and they'll play on their phones. So, when I'm onstage, it's very important to create the emotional connection.

BEING A CENTER OF INFLUENCE

I am a center of influence. For example, to me, a stage is not always a podium. To me, a stage is an opportunity. In any medium I use, I talk about things that are relatable. I'm not scripted. It just flows. I love people, and there I'm at my best. I'm very happy when I speak.

DEEP DOWN HABITS

I'm not the same person I was when I was sixteen. Over time, I've evolved. I'm aware of my shortcomings, and not shy about them. That's why I talk about my failures, because I feel your failures are foundational to your success, and most importantly, nobody learned how to walk on day one.

Because of this awareness, to build my network and my circle of influence, I'm constantly looking for people who are complementary to me. If I'm in the center, my circle has to be in my periphery. It's very important to build that.

For the last ten years, I've never missed my time to meditate, except for when I was in the hospital. Meditation to me is not a breathing exercise. It's about setting intentions. It doesn't matter which part of the world I'm in. Even if I'm on a flight, if I'm awake, I take that ten minutes to meditate and set my intentions. I set my intentions for my day because I know there's a chance I may not see tomorrow, and it's got nothing to do with my health, it's about the reality of life.

I do not take anything or anyone for granted. I have never done that, and I never will, because each one of us are unique. The day you take a person for granted, you've lost that person in your life. So I don't take anything for granted, and that for me has been a mantra for my success. It's very important.

I try to create a sense of equity. A lot of people debate the concept of equality. I don't believe in that. Whether it's gender-wise or people-wise, perfect *equality* is not possible, because all of us have different levels of experience, biological conditions, physiological conditions, and socio-economic conditions. But *equity* is possible. One thing that has worked very well for me is to create a sense of equity, being fair, being impartial. Even when my listeners are attentive, I want to hold them accountable. If you're not listening, you're not learning. This is very important. That's pretty much how I live my life every day. I don't care about the past. They are the lessons I learned from, but then I move on. I enjoy every day and I try to ensure that people around me feel the same way.

STARTING OVER

If I had to start all over again, I would change nothing at all. Doctor Brian L. Weiss, in his book *Many Lives, Many Masters*, says, "The journey cannot be altered, but the evolution through that journey is your biggest secret."

I would change nothing. I'm so lucky. Every single day I thank God for everything I have. I don't want more, I just want to continue this life, be honest, keep doing what I'm good at with the opportunity to ask God to give me the perseverance and the guidance so I don't do anything to hurt someone intentionally.

A DEFINING MOMENT

After the aneurysm, my parents said that for three months I had complete memory loss. I couldn't even recognize them. Then one day I recognized my mom as she was holding my hand, and I remembered when I was a child, I used to sleep on her lap. I get emotional when I say it, but my mom and I both cried. It was the most amazing feeling to be able to remember those things in life. I hope I never forget my parents because they've done everything for me, from the day I was born till today. They've never given up on me, no matter what, and forgetting them and remembering them again was a rebirth for me, and that changed me as a human being. I don't take anything for granted. As parents, to see that your child does not remember you, can be heartbreaking. I don't ever want that to happen to anyone.

THE GREATEST INFLUENCER

My daughter, has been the greatest influence on me. She has taught me compassion. She taught me selflessness. She's made me smart and she's super smart. I don't care about money, and when she goes shopping with me and I ignore the price tag on something, she'll say, "Mom, hold on. You cannot waste money on that. Stop it!"

She brought me realism, she brought me adherence, she brought me commitment.

Dr. Somdutta Singh is a serial entrepreneur, angel investor and bestselling author currently operating her third venture, Assiduus Global, that enables and scales brands across global e-commerce marketplaces. Her previous ventures, Unspun Group and IRA - House of Designers have been successfully acquired.

In 2020, Dr. Som was designated as one of Fortune India's *50 Most Powerful Women and became a member of the coveted invitation-only Forbes Business Council. She is also the owner of three proprietary brands - Biotevia, Irotica and The Real BossLady Beauty, currently available in the US and was recently featured in* Femina.

Dr Somdutta Singh has served as the youngest and only woman Vice-Chairperson of NASSCOM Product Council and has been the first woman of Indian origin on the Board of Kotler Impact. She has facilitated the government of India to form the visionary Women Entrepreneurship Platform (WEP) by NITI Aayog that has helped lakhs of enterprising women across India on their entrepreneurial journeys.

Website: www.assiduusglobal.com

SUCCESS FACTOR 2: BE SELF-RELIANT

"The only person you are destined to become
is the person you decide to be."
—Ralph Waldo Emerson

T HIS BOOK IS ALL ABOUT how to build, use, and share influence. By definition, "influence" means your relationships with other people. These other
people may number in the dozens, the hundreds, the thousands, or the
millions. The implication is that we are inter-reliant, and that our survival and
success—my success and yours—can happen only through mutual cooperation
and the positive use of influence.

Look at it this way: If you were the lone survivor of a shipwreck on a desert
island, without any other people with whom you could interact, then you would
have no use for this book. You could use it as a doorstop in the hut you built
with your own hands.

The entire premise of this book is that no one lives on a desert island, and no
one is entirely self-reliant. We depend on each other, and you can learn how to
use that system to get ahead in the world. By helping others, you help yourself.

Ideally, it's a win-win situation.

If you are successful, you'll move from having zero influence (when you first
landed) to developing a small sphere of *local influence* comprising people who
know you.

Which brings me to the subject of this chapter: self-reliance.

Is this a contradiction? Why is there a chapter devoted to self-reliance? How
can our intrepid castaway in the strange city hope to survive and thrive without
building a network of interdependency? He or she needs other people to grow
food, make clothing, build houses, generate electricity, and provide medical care.
No one can do all of these things alone. Isn't that the whole point?

Yes, that is the point. But the truth is, to effectively interact with other
people and to build your network of influence, you need to start from a solid

personal foundation. You need to know yourself and your capabilities. You need to be able to take care of yourself when necessary and not be so desperate that you forge alliances with the wrong people. Recall in Part I of the book where we discussed the importance of being selective in the connections we make. A person who is weak and lacking in confidence will fall prey to grifters and charlatans and be worse off than if they had lived alone on a desert island. In contrast, a person who is confident and capable of being self-reliant will make the right choices and will be better positioned to make a contribution to their community. And as we know, there is no better way to build influence among your peers than by making a contribution and helping others to improve their lives.

Look at it this way. Let's say a big storm is coming to your town, and people need to take shelter. But many people don't have homes, so they need to find refuge with neighbors. Who would you rather be: the homeless person who must accept charity from others and stay as a guest in their house, or the owner of a fine mansion who has rooms to spare for those in need? When you first arrived as a stranger in town, you might have been one of those who needed assistance. But hopefully, your situation will improve. Most people would rather be in a position of strength and able to help others than be in a position of weakness, dependent upon their benevolence.

SELF-REALIZATION

The first step towards self-reliance is self-realization.

What does this mean?

It means that you need to have a clear idea of who you are and your strengths and weaknesses. This can be difficult because many people have a skewed idea of their capabilities.

On one extreme, we have the narcissist. This person sees themselves as someone who is grandiose, destined for greatness, admired by all, and owed every favor. They are blind to their own shortcomings (we all have them!) and assume that everything will work out in their favor. Narcissists are either overcompensating for a crushing lack of confidence, or they truly believe they're exalted. The feeling of entitlement is often instilled in childhood by parents who spoil the child, potentially resulting in the child feeling their mere existence entitles them to anything and everything they desire.

When the narcissist steps off the ship and into the strange city, he or she will expect to be greeted with open arms. Such a person is easy prey for con artists who quickly sniff a "mark" they can manipulate with flattery. Because of their inaccurate assessment of their own capabilities, narcissists often find themselves in over their heads and need to be rescued by people who are subject matter experts.

At the other extreme are those unfortunate people who have an artificially low opinion of themselves. They believe they are "screw-ups" who will never succeed.

The sad thing about these two types—both extremes—is that they are often unaware of how others see them. When things don't go their way, they think something is wrong with the world, when in fact, the world is just working the way it always has,

Most people fall somewhere in the middle of these two extremes. But to build influence, you need to interact with other people in a way that's transparent and reality-based, and doing this can be made more difficult if the image you have of yourself is even slightly skewed.

The challenge is increased by the fact that, with few exceptions, your peers—coworkers and friends—are not going to tell you that you have an irritating habit or trait. It's not considered "nice," and after all, who is good enough to judge someone else? So they tolerate the fact that you're argumentative, or always late, or indulge in gossip

Who can give you honest, useful feedback? Your parents might be able to. If you read the biographies of successful people, more often than not, you'll learn they had tough but loving parents who set high standards for their kids and taught them to be self-reliant. (I'm not talking about those overbearing "tiger moms" or "helicopter parents" who themselves suffer from a form of narcissism. I mean people like the parents of Jeff Bezos, who, despite not knowing what the internet was, invested in his fledgling book-selling business.)

A professional coach or mentor can help you develop your self-realization. When you're being coached, it's not personal. You're more like an actor being trained for an important role. If the goal of your work with a coach is to enhance your career prospects, then the advice given to help you reach that goal isn't "personal." You can step outside yourself and see yourself as others do. You can say to yourself, "Wearing certain clothes will enhance my chances for success," or, "If I speak more slowly and with better diction, I'll sound more authoritative and more like a leader."

Humans are capable of two amazing things: we can objectively assess ourselves and say, "This is me." And we can also say, "This is who I want to become."

It's like saying, "I am perfect the way I am now. I must become better."

There is a certain advantage to knowing yourself and accepting yourself. You are an individual, and there's nobody else like you. As Oscar Wilde reputedly said, "Be yourself, everyone else is taken."

ENVISION SUCCESS AND PLAN YOUR FUTURE

As I've mentioned in this book, of all the species, human beings have the unique ability to envision a *future state* for themselves.

This goes far beyond the ability of many other species to set a short-term goal and achieve it. For example, octopuses have a remarkable ability to think ahead as they pursue their prey and are adept at constructing little fortresses out of shells and other debris. On land, members of the corvid family (songbirds including ravens, crows, jays, and magpies, to name a few) are among the most intelligent birds and have been observed using tools. But none of these highly intelligent species—not even great apes or elephants—have changed their behavior over thousands of years. As far as we know, their short-term feats have never translated into long-term progress.

Humans can think much further ahead. We can envision life tomorrow, next week, or next month. We can make plans that stretch over years, decades, and even centuries. For example, on March 19, 1882, construction of the Sagrada Família basilica in Barcelona, Spain, began under the direction of architect Francisco de Paula del Villar. The next year, Antoni Gaudí took over as chief architect. He devoted the remainder of his life to the project, and at the time of his death in 1926, less than a quarter of the massive edifice was complete. Others continued the work, and in 2010 the basilica was sufficiently complete to be consecrated by Pope Benedict XVI. It's expected to be fully complete by the year 2026—the centenary of the death of Gaudí and 144 years after the cornerstone was laid.

Individuals can envision and plan their own futures. Anyone who wants to become a medical specialist, like a neurologist, must plan far ahead. You know the path ahead of you: four years of college, then four years of medical school, followed by three to seven years of internship and residency programs. It's a journey of up to fifteen years, and even then, the learning never stops. Becoming a neurologist is a very positive goal because you know you'll be helping people live longer and healthier lives, you'll be well paid, and you'll be a highly respected member of your community.

Almost anyone who embarks on a career can envision their path forward. The bank teller may see herself as one day being the bank president. The guy on the loading dock may see himself as one day being the CEO of the company. It can happen! In 1984, a high school student named Doug McMillon took a job loading trucks at a Walmart distribution center so that he could earn money for college. At the time, he earned $6.50 an hour. He liked working at the company, and over the years, he rose through the ranks, taking on titles including assistant store manager, buyer in merchandising, and CEO of Sam's Club. In 2014, he was named CEO of Walmart, with its 2.2 million employees and $523 billion in sales.

Remember to set small, achievable goals. Then, as motivational speaker Les Brown so aptly said, "As you reach your goals set new ones. That is how you grow and become a more powerful person."[10]

Set a goal and then reach it. Repeat. Then repeat again, and again—and soon you will have reached a goal you once thought was far beyond your grasp.

WE CAN CHOOSE SUCCESS OR FAILURE

To every power granted to human beings, we know there are always two opposing sides. We can be generous or selfish, respectful or rude, thoughtful or thoughtless—often in quick succession! This duality is yet another quality that separates us from the other species, who, while they may exhibit flashes of such behavior, aren't capable of planning their lives around it.

The typical discussions of our ability to envision the future assume that to a person, humans will always choose to envision a future that is positive—a better job, higher income, a bigger house, more community stature, and influence. It just seems more optimistic to think that way, and if you look at the overall arc of human development over the past several thousand years, it's pretty accurate. In general, since the days we lived in caves and carried clubs, we've envisioned and created better lives for ourselves.

But we know from experience that many people have difficulty envisioning success. Instead, they envision failure. They see the world as bleak and cheerless and themselves as undeserving of its goodness. Or they see the world as being full of cheats and thieves, and therefore they resolve to "play the game" and grab as much as they can for themselves before the next guy gets it.

These unfortunate people have often grown up under discouraging circumstances and have learned from parents or other caregivers that life is cruel and they should expect nothing from it. Very often, they are the victims of adverse childhood experiences and cannot cope with success. A sad example is musician Kurt Cobain. While his career was incredibly successful and his music hugely influential, he himself was plagued with depression and thoughts of suicide. In-

---

10   https://www.mulliganbrother.com/single-post/2019/03/31/
      top-15-les-brown-quotes-for-2019

deed, suicidal tendencies in the Cobain family date back to July of 1979, when Kurt's uncle, Burle Cobain, shot himself in the abdomen. A second of Cobain's uncles took his life five years later by a gunshot to his head. (Statistics show that if a family member commits suicide, the odds of another family member doing the same thing increase.) At age eight, Cobain's outgoing personality was darkened by his parent's ugly divorce. He spent most of his days shuffling between homes, spending a number of nights underneath a bridge. He was plagued by illness and drug abuse. There is no doubt that despite his music industry success, Kurt Cobain saw his future as something he didn't want to experience.

That's an extreme example, but the point is that no human is immune from feelings of depression and anxiety (things may possibly be bad in the future). Going back to the law of attraction, generally, your future level of success and influence will be in alignment with your power to envision them. If you envision failure for yourself, it shall be granted to you. If you envision success, you'll have a shot at it. Upon landing as a stranger in Metropolis, if you say to yourself, "This is terrible. I'm doomed,' then doomed you shall be. But if you say, "I have been given a tremendous opportunity to make a new life for myself! The future will be very bright!" then you'll *create success* for yourself.

FACE YOUR FEARS

To have certain fears can be logical and even lifesaving. Thousands of years ago, our primitive ancestors developed a set of fears that served them well. Snakes and spiders were venomous and should be avoided. The nighttime was the domain of nocturnal predators such as the wolf and the tiger. Brackish water would make you sick.

Today, we have largely tamed those fears, but we've replaced them with new ones. In our culture of material wealth, most of our fears are psychological. Few of us are bitten by snakes or attacked by wolves at night, but we have other fears that can inhibit our freedom to excel.

We're afraid of meeting new people—especially powerful people—because we may not know what to say to them. At a business meeting, we're afraid to speak up with a new idea because others might ridicule us. We're afraid to leave our dead-end job and become an entrepreneur because of the risk. We're afraid to ask for the promotion we deserve because we don't want to risk the disappointment if it's not granted. Or the flip side—we're afraid we'll get the promotion and stumble under the weight of new responsibilities.

The first step to being self-reliant is to objectively identify and face your fears. What exactly is it that you're afraid of? As business people climb the corporate leadership ladder, common fears include:

- Fear of not being good enough for the task.
- Fear of being overwhelmed by responsibility.
- Fear of being ridiculed or shamed if you fail.
- Fear of being confined to a desk all day.
- Fear that you don't deserve your success.

The truth is, you're never going to be totally ready. As Zig Ziglar said, "If you wait until all the lights are green before you leave home, you'll never get started on your trip to the top."

Along the way, you'll experience some failures. You'll learn from those failures. It's difficult to find a successful person who has not experienced failures—often repeatedly. But they set aside their fears and learned from their mistakes:

"Failure," said Henry Ford, "is only the opportunity more intelligently to begin again." Have you ever wondered why the Model T, which revolutionized personal transportation, was designated "T"? Between 1903 and 1908, Ford produced the Models A, B, C, F, K, N, R, and S, which sold modestly. The "T" was simply the next iteration, representing years of refinement.

"You may encounter many defeats," said Maya Angelou, "but you must not be defeated. In fact, it may be necessary to encounter the defeats, so you can know who you are, what you can rise from, how you can still come out of it." In other words, we learn little from victories. We learn much more from defeats, and if we have the fortitude and courage to try again, we'll start from a stronger position.

"I have not failed," said Thomas Edison. "I have found 10,000 ways that don't work." He was referring to his quest to find the elusive substance that would serve as a long-lasting filament for his light bulb. The eventual winner was a strand of carbonized cotton, which on its first try lasted a full fifteen hours before burning out.

Speaking of Edison, he also said this: "My mother was the making of me. She understood me; she let me follow my bent." Behind every successful person is a strong parent, supportive partner, or mentor!

EDUCATION AND FAMILIARITY

Fears can be powerful things. How do you confront them and then overcome them?

There are two ways.

The first is education.

Imagine you're on a ship, and you're bound for a strange new city. If you knew nothing about Metropolis, you'd probably have significant fear about being dropped off there with no friends and no job lined up. This is because people tend to be afraid of the unknown, and they imagine the unknown holds danger. Entering a strange city, you'll worry about how you'll stay safe, where you'll sleep at night, and how you'll support yourself.

Then imagine that while you were paralyzed by fear of the unknown, one of the crew told you that the ship's library contained books about Metropolis, and you could even go online and find out more information. "Knowledge is power!" you'd say to yourself as you dashed down to the library. The sailor was right, and you dive into your research. You learn all about the city, its inhabitants, its industry and culture, its crime rate, its financial institutions, and—of the most immediate concern—the location of the youth hostel, where you can find cheap lodgings while you look for work. You learn a few words of the local language and how the monetary system works.

Armed with some basic knowledge of your destination, your fear eases, and when you step off the ship onto the streets of Metropolis, you already have a plan. You might think, "My first stop should be the youth hostel. I know it's on Main Street, which should be two blocks straight ahead," and so forth. You take it one step at a time.

The other way to confront and diffuse fear is by engaging in the very activity that makes you nervous. Clearly, you have to do this intelligently. If swimming with sharks makes you afraid, and you want to overcome your fear by actually swimming with them, then you'd better get a sturdy shark cage! But in business, while many executives seem like sharks who can instill terror in the hearts of subordinates, one of the most common fears is something far less dangerous: public speaking. This includes not only giving speeches in front of hundreds of people at a convention but speaking to your boss and others at staff meetings. While you can read books and watch videos about public speaking, the only meaningful way to overcome your fear is to get up and do it. Don't worry. No harm can come to you!

In public speaking courses, they talk a lot about tricks you can use to get more confidence. They say you can imagine your audience sitting there naked, which is both silly and demeaning to your listeners. It's also something you cannot do while at the same time delivering your speech. This is the best trick of all: When you speak to people, *provide them with the information they need*. If you see yourself as the postal worker who is delivering an important letter to someone, then it's no longer about *you*. You could be the most awkward, self-conscious speaker in the world, but if you tell people something useful, and that will help them do their job better, then they will listen with rapt attention.

If you see yourself as the messenger with important information, then that takes off the table another silly device that experts say you need to do, which is to begin your speech with a joke. If there's any way to make a nervous speaker *more* terrified, it's telling them they need to tell a joke and make the audience laugh to "loosen them up." Joke-telling is a specific skill that needs to be learned, and there's no reason to add that to your list of things to do. Your job is not to entertain your listeners but to help them do their jobs better.

SKILL SET MASTERING

While on the subject of joke-telling as an acquired skill, let's dive into the broader subject of your overall skill set. As I have throughout this book, I'm going to present two seemingly contradictory axioms that, when fused together, provide valuable guidance.

The first axiom is that you must have a rare skill with high value that people will pay for.

The second axiom. You must have diverse knowledge and skills.

Why both?

In the first instance, the idea that you must have a specialized skill that people will pay for is rooted in the fact that there are seven billion people on this earth, and most of them are trying to do exactly what you're trying to do, which is make a living. If you have a *commodity skill* shared by a billion other people, like the ability to drive a cab, then the market value of your skill will be low. If you raise your fare price, then potential customers will simply choose another, cheaper driver, and you will get nothing. On the other hand, if you have a *rare skill with high value*, like being a brain surgeon, then you will be able to command a high price for your services.

In the second instance, if you also have diverse knowledge and skills, then you can leverage your rare skill in new contexts and have more impact. A simple example is lawyers and book authors. Lawyers have a rare skill with high value, and so do successful book authors. But what if you were both?

Consider John Grisham. A 1981 graduate of the University of Mississippi School of Law, he practiced criminal law for about a decade and served in the Mississippi House of Representatives from January 1984 to September 1990. Not a bad career! But Grisham also happens to be a highly skilled author. He published his first novel, *A Time to Kill,* in June 1989. Leveraging his knowledge of the law with small-town politics, it became a bestseller. Grisham kept writing novels, and to date, he has written twenty-eight consecutive number one bestsellers, and his books have sold 300 million copies.

In addition, while knowledge is good, the next step up is *wisdom*. This is the ability to see the big picture and the many parts that make up the whole. When building your influence, you'll be interacting with many diverse people from different backgrounds and cultures, and the more easily you can relate to them, the better.

In our global economy, there are more and more opportunities for people who have both highly specific and diverse skill sets. For example, in 2020, the United States imported over $500 billion in goods from the European Union. Our biggest Eurozone trading partner is Germany, and the number one German import product category is machinery and tools. Also at the top are motor vehicles—Mercedes-Benz, BMW, Volkswagen.

Let's say you are an American business person and you speak fluent German. Perhaps your parents were in the military and were stationed there, so you lived there as a kid. You are comfortable in American and German business cultures. You may also have a mechanical engineering degree. With these diverse skills, you can succeed as an American helping a German car company sell in America, or vice versa—helping an American company sell cars in Germany.

Understanding other cultures is not a trivial issue. Everyone in the auto industry remembers the disastrous merger between Mercedes-Benz and Chrysler. In this highly touted "Merger of Equals" or "Marriage Made in Heaven," in 1998, Daimler-Benz AG and the Chrysler Corporation merged in an exchange of shares. The new transatlantic company was called DaimlerChrysler AG. Valued at $38 billion, it was the world's largest-ever cross-border deal.

It wasn't long before the "Marriage Made in Heaven" was headed for divorce court. The two companies had conflicting internal cultures. Managers discovered huge differences in work habits and in the way executives planned and conducted meetings, exchanged information, and made decisions. Germans were appalled by the Americans' loose, unstructured methods, while Americans thought the Germans were hopelessly rigid and formal.

In May 2007, the ill-fated union was annulled, and Daimler sold Chrysler to Cerberus Capital Management for $6 billion. Fortunately, Chrysler survived and entered into what has turned out to be a very happy marriage with Italy's big automaker, Fiat. But just imagine what the DaimlerChrysler company could have been if more of the executives on both sides had personal experience in dealing with the other company's culture.

Remember, building your influence is *always* about being able to make a contribution and help other people succeed. Thinking only of yourself will get you nowhere. If you help others succeed, you will be handsomely rewarded.

ESTABLISH YOUR REPUTATION

This last element—your reputation—is perhaps the most important part of becoming self-reliant. It's the subjective, qualitative belief people have about you and the product or service you provide.

What elements comprise your reputation?

In a phrase, *everything you say and do.*

Obviously, we don't have space in one book to talk about everything you say and do. So we'll boil it down to the essentials.

The foundation of a good reputation is integrity, and you build your integrity by having a history of making good on positive intentions.

Let's look at that definition more closely.

Working backward, begin with *positive intentions*. When you land in Metropolis and start meeting people, project an optimistic outlook and an interest in helping people to lead better lives. Perhaps you can offer a service they need or a useful product. Or maybe what you have to offer is expertise in a subject matter or a solution to a social problem. If you have something of value, then people will welcome you.

What they're *not* interested in is negativity, your tale of woe, complaining, or your dubious schemes to get rich quick. Well, to be honest, *some* people might be attracted to those things. But these are not the people you want to associate with. A key part of a person's reputation is the other people with whom they are identified. You see it all the time with politicians; for example, the newscaster will say, "Congressman So-and-So was seen with Jimmy Gangster, who has reputed ties to organized crime." Then everyone starts talking about how Congressman So-and-So is wrapped up with criminals and must be investigated, and he's got to work overtime to burnish his image.

Positive intentions are where you start. Then you need to *make good* on those promises. Words alone are nice, but they're meaningless unless backed up by action. If you say you're going to deliver something, then do it, and do it on time. If you offer to help someone, then show up and help. If you promote a product for sale, ensure that it lives up to your marketing pitch.

Sooner or later, you may face a serious reputational problem, and you'll need to respond promptly and honestly. In the annals of corporate reputation crisis management, the textbook case is the Tylenol poison scare of 1982. In the Chicago metropolitan area, someone—the case is still unsolved—laced commercial Tylenol capsules with potassium cyanide. Over a period of a few days, a total of seven people died in the original poisonings, with several more deaths in subsequent copycat crimes. Warnings were hastily issued via the media and patrols using loudspeakers, urging residents throughout the Chicago metropolitan area to throw away all their Tylenol products.

The crime caused national headlines, and instantly the name "Tylenol" became synonymous with "deadly poison." The billion-dollar brand could have been driven from the market.

Johnson & Johnson, the parent company, moved swiftly. The company halted Tylenol production and advertising, and distributed warnings to hospitals and distributors. It issued a nationwide recall of all thirty-one million bottles of Tylenol products then on the shelves. The company asked individuals not to consume any of its products that contained acetaminophen, and when it was found that the criminal had targeted only acetaminophen capsules, offered to exchange all Tylenol capsules already purchased by the public for solid tablets.

At the time of the crisis, Tylenol's market share of pain relief medication collapsed from thirty-five percent to just eight percent. Thanks to the company's prompt and aggressive reaction, it rebounded in less than a year. Within several years, with new tamper-proof packaging, Tylenol owned the highest market share for over-the-counter analgesics in the United States.

Let's hope that you never face a crisis like that. But if you do, take a page out of the Tylenol playbook. Respond swiftly and transparently.

Finally, to establish a reputation of integrity, you need to have a *history* of making good on positive intentions. This means that you have to make good on your promises over and over again. Consistent performance will show people that they can depend on you to do the right thing, and they can turn to you in a time of need. If you're like the family doctor who will answer the phone at any time of day or night and always provide good service, people will begin to trust your judgment, and your influence will strengthen.

Your reputation is forward-looking in the sense that people will consider your reputation *in advance* of deciding how they feel about you and if they want to do business with you. Whether you're selling pizza or running for high political office, your reputation precedes you.

It is a malleable thing, both by you and by others. In fact, your reputation is constantly being constructed for you, whether you want it to be or not. If you're not in control of it, your reputation will build itself or be built by others for you. As Warren Buffet said, "It takes twenty years to build a reputation and five minutes to ruin it."

HOW MARY BARRA POSITIONED HERSELF FOR SUCCESS

Here's a clear example of someone who seized her opportunities and, over time, became one of the most influential people in America.

In 1980, at the age of eighteen, a young woman took a co-op student job at General Motors in Detroit. Her assignment was to check fender panels and hoods. After earning her bachelor of science degree in electrical engineering from the General Motors Institute (now Kettering University) in 1985, she held a series of engineering and administrative positions at GM and eventually worked her way up to become manager of the Detroit/Hamtramck Assembly plant. In February 2008, she was promoted to the position of vice president of Global Manufacturing Engineering. At this time, GM employed over 800,000 people worldwide. They were mostly men, and the executive ranks were a bastion of the "old boys" network. Top executives entered GM's Detroit headquarters through a private basement garage, worked on the fourteenth floor behind protective double electronic doors, and took their three-martini gourmet meals in private dining rooms.

Another female executive, Nancy Rottering, quit in frustration in 1987, saying the attitude at headquarters was, "We're GM. We know everything. We don't need to change."

Suddenly, the venerable company came crashing down. On June 1, 2009, General Motors filed for bankruptcy in New York, with $82 billion in assets and $173 billion in liabilities. It was the largest industrial bankruptcy in history.

In July 2009, in the middle of the massive restructuring, our heroine was made vice president of Global Human Resources. Normally this might be seen as a dead-end job, but in February 2011, she was named executive vice president of Global Product Development. In August 2013, her responsibilities were expanded to include Global Purchasing and Supply Chain.

In January 2014, at the age of fifty-three, Mary Barra reached the top of the mountain and was named the first female CEO of a major automobile manufacturer. She had come a long way from checking fender panels as a freshman in college!

Her global influence was considerable. In 2013 Barra was listed as thirty-fifth on Forbes Most Powerful Women list, and in 2014, she was named second most powerful.

In 2015, Barra was ranked number one on Fortune's Most Powerful Women list, up from number two the previous year.

In 2019, she remained in the top ten of both lists.

Clearly, Mary Barra is an example of a person who saw her life unfolding in positive terms, took responsibility, and focused not on obstacles but on opportunities.

SUCCESS ACTION ITEMS – BE SELF-RELIANT

- Be self-reliant. To effectively interact with other people and build your network of influence, start from a solid personal foundation, including knowing yourself and your capabilities.
- Have a clear idea of who you are, your capabilities, your strengths, and your weaknesses.
- Practice self-realization. This will allow you to build influence as you interact with people in a transparent manner, which will then create trust and reveal that you have nothing to hide.
- Enlist a parent, a professional coach, or mentor who can help you develop your self-realization by giving you honest and useful feedback about how others see you.
- Envision and plan a positive future by setting achievable goals. Set a goal, reach it, then repeat. Then repeat again. Soon you will have reached a goal you once thought was far beyond your grasp.
- Face your fears. Another step to being self-reliant is to objectively identify and face your fears. Learn from your failures, then have the courage to try again. You will then start from a stronger position.
- Overcome your fears by becoming educated about what you fear. People tend to be afraid of the unknown, therefore learn all you can about the things you fear.
- Jump in with both feet. Confront and diffuse fear by engaging in the very activity that makes you nervous. Learn from your failures, gain experience and confidence to move forward.
- Make skill set mastering a priority to ensure self-reliance. Develop skills of high value combined with knowledge and experience to give you the edge to differentiate yourself from the herd.
- Establish your reputation to become self-reliant. The foundation of a good reputation is integrity, and you build your integrity by having a history of making good on positive intentions.
- Make consistent performance your objective. This will show people that they can depend on you to do the right thing, and they can turn to you in time of need.
- Follow Mary Barra's example, the first female CEO of a major auto manufacturer. She saw her life unfolding in positive terms, took responsibility, and focused not on obstacles but on opportunities.

KIMBERLY CARNEY
CEO FASHWIRE INC.

"Taking Charge in Challenging Circumstances"

MY SUCCESS JOURNEY

GREW UP IN KENMORE, WASHINGTON, north of Seattle, in a *Leave it to Beaver* family. Dad was the breadwinner and a self-made man, so I think I got my entrepreneurial spirit from him.

When I was younger my family did not have a lot of money. When we moved to Kenmore, it was the first time we had a house where we could each have our own rooms, and that was a big deal.

When my dad met my mom, she was the daughter of the top police officer in Seattle, and he was painting houses for a living and sleeping in his car on Queen Anne Avenue. He then got a janitor job with ABM Industries, and put himself through college, and eventually joined management. He ended up being a senior VP and a respected businessman in Seattle. My dad was very humble. Whenever we went somewhere, like going on vacation, people would ask my dad what he did for a living, and he would say, "I'm a janitor." Even though he was a successful executive, he loved the reaction. He was a hard-working man who focused on providing for the family.

My entrepreneurial spirit came from dad, and him putting me in basketball and softball. When you grow up playing sports, you know how to work with a team. I have found in business that people who haven't played on a sports team work differently than people who have.

I went to college and worked for ABM Industries. Nobody wanted Jack Smith's daughter working for them because I was a spoiled little princess. But then one of his executives said, "I think your daughter has a knack for marketing. I'd like her to work for me."

My dad replied, "Okay—Nobody else wants her, so she's yours."

This man sat me down and he said, "You're not your dad's daughter in my office; here are the rules, here's how you're going to do it. Here's Photoshop and CorelDraw, now learn them." There was no internet back then. We had those big PC monitors. So, I taught myself. He was hard on me and made me accountable. His leadership style was really good for me because it taught me to be a self-starter.

When I graduated from college, I decided that I didn't want to work for my dad's company. I wanted to make it on my own. I got a job with AT&T Wireless working with the UWCC. We were working with all the carriers and vendors around the world on cell phone technology. I was the assistant to the head of marketing and conference of events. She ended up leaving the company. I came in one day and was told, "Your boss is no longer your boss. You need a passport. You're going to Malaysia in a few months and you are going to take over her role."

I traveled all over the world in developing countries, working with the delegates in government. I set up the conferences from start to finish, from the booths to the speakers. Two years and forty-plus countries later, which included Africa where I had the opportunity to meet Nelson Mandela. He was my keynote speaker at the conference.

The executive men who gave me the opportunity were fantastic. For a girl in her twenties and learning the ropes of this big world, I could not have had better male influencers. I was so fortunate to have met them. To this day, I'm still in contact with them.

I went from there to Discover Music. I became their head of marketing. We could have been iTunes, but we got sued by the labels. If you go back to the early days of Amazon music technology, that was our technology. We then got bought by Loudeye, a provider of digital media distribution. I was in my ninth month of pregnancy with my daughter. I took five years off to be a stay-at-home mom. I loved it, but I missed my career.

When I had baby number two, I started doing marketing consulting. A boutique then hired me to do her fashion boutique opening, and I went on a buying trip and loved it. A girlfriend of mine wanted to open a boutique, so we did it together. In 2008 I bought her out. I started over on my own. I had a successful store until the pandemic hit.

In 2009, I was at dinner with Colin Dyne, who was the head of William Rast, and Michael Barber, who had just done the Hautelook acquisition for Nordstrom. At dinner, I told Michael, "I have this idea. I think consumers and designers can be on one platform, and we can direct them to all these brands."

They said, "Kimberly, you're five or six years away from that."

Five years later, I started facilitating the FashWire idea because I saw tech becoming a key factor in driving buying decisions. We had gone from writing on paper to orders going digital. I hired my first developer, who was expensive. I'm pretty sure I paid for the engagement ring he gave to his fiancé.

In 2015, I hired a new developer, and he built a prototype that made it possible for us to go to the trade shows. Being an owner of a boutique gained us entry and allowed me to get feedback on the beta test version to get designers signed up. It was back before swipe technology, so the original idea was to choose "yes" or "no" for the brand's products. After a year of shows, we got designer feedback and I realized that consumers were not going to adapt to our app. The developer tried to improve it. We ended the relationship and determined it was best to check the code, and the code wasn't usable, so I had to start over. It was painful.

Shortly afterwards, we exhibited at TechCrunch in New York. I needed to show the app to key investors, but my previous developer had expired it, so I couldn't even show the beta version. I didn't know what I was going to do. There was a booth across from me featuring a dog app. A man from the dog booth came over and said, "You look a little stressed, can I help you?"

"We're having tech issues," I replied.

"Maybe I can help."

"We are actually a tech company, this is not an animal app. I don't think you can do anything, but it was super kind of you to offer."

I then started talking to the guy next to me, who had an amazing app. I asked, "Who built your app?"

"The guy you sent to the doghouse," he laughed. "But he's cool, he'll come back."

The Dog App guy came back over. I apologized and he said, "No worries, obviously you're stressed."

Within an hour he had us up. He saved us.

The new developer and I agreed to meet. I wanted to see his offices. So, I walked in with my NDA and said, "Will you please sign this?"

"On one condition," he replied. "You let me bid on the project. You don't have to pick me, but let me bid."

"I'm really close to signing a contract with one of two other developers," I said, "and I've got these investors who want me to pick one of them."

Again, he said, "Let me send you a proposal."

I said okay, and he signed my NDA. He was neither the most expensive nor the least expensive and I ended up going with him.

One of the big entrepreneur mistakes I made was in my choice of words when writing to my investors. Instead of saying, "I'm going to trust my instincts," I said, "I have a great feeling about him."

A couple of my investor advisers responded, "You have a 'good feeling' about him? Okay, explain this. You just met him."

I had him fly to Seattle. We met with investors from my neighborhood at a corner restaurant, and I just threw him to the wolves.

The developer pulled me aside and said, "This is an interview, isn't it?" "Pretty much," I replied.

The next day we sat with my whole advisory board and they got it. Hooman is my development partner today. He's like family to me.

I hired him in 2017, and the next year we launched with a Google partnership. He and I got to spend the day together with the Google team. We had thirty brands then. We hired somebody I was already working with out of the fashion industry to help us go after brands. I tried to go with bigger affiliates, but they said I would never get brands, and so I said, "Watch me." We hit the shows and we cold-walked instead of cold-called. We grew from thirty brands to nearly 400 today, and that's in three years. Capitalizing on the success of Fash-Wire, we recently launched GlossWire, a separate app and web-based platform with the same compelling experience for the beauty industry.

FashWire, on the B2B side, is designed to drive and navigate consumer demand, improve margins, and increase profitability for the brands. For GlossWire, it's designed to navigate consumer demand but help improve and streamline their brand strategies. It's a data play for both of the platforms, giving brands real-time actionable insights on consumer shopping behaviors. For the consumer on both platforms, they get to have that fun immersive swipe voting and social integration that lets them have an influence on the brand's decision-making in their product offerings.

Both mobile apps have a small one-time fee of $2.99. $1.00 of that is donated to a philanthropic cause. Every month we support a different charity. We had been free, but changing to a paid app, we got fewer downloads but more shopping. The philanthropic causes have really helped us increase our downloads to a broader scope of consumers because people get behind their charity.

Coming in the future, we are planning FashLuxe, which will be for the luxury consumer, and then FashPlus for the plus-size market.

The biggest thing I think I've learned is you have to have a great development partner. A lot of people have asked me why I don't bring development in-house. I say, why would I? Not only do we have a true development partner, but Hooman and his team believe in it as much as we do. Each month they go above and beyond to drive our technology forward and keep us relevant in our perspective industries. To have a partner that you trust instinctively is a good feeling.

My vision for the future is to be business intelligence for prospective industries. I believe our data-driven platform will change the face of fashion by keeping the consumer at the heart of decisions. Right now, you've got shifting consumer behavior that is unpredictable. People are starting to shop again, so we're moving out of sweatpants and back into luxury. We have a pulse on real-time insights with our contemporary market, and soon we'll have the same data on the luxury market.

LANDING IN A STRANGE CITY

If I were dropped off in a strange city, the first thing I'd do is get a job. I would probably go where I could make the quickest money. I would try to get a job at a restaurant, to be in a place where I could communicate with people because that's the way I'm wired.

As I am working my job, I would start to develop a plan of what I could do that could help the community. I would talk to people about the cleanest and safest place I could live for the least amount of money. I'd rebuild myself, just like I've rebuilt myself in the past. You have to have money to survive, so get a job first and take it from there.

As soon as I could, I would get myself a tech job. I would go directly to the top and try to get myself into a tech company where I could show my value. And then on the side, I would try to come up with something I could create on my own, probably in fashion.

INFLUENCE

For me, influence is being able to have an impact on someone who can learn from you. For example, I'm part of the New York Fashion Tech Lab, and I am a mentor to startups. I'm an influencer in the tech industry, not because of social connections, but because of my background and what I've accomplished. An influencer is somebody who is driven, well networked, and has developed good relationships.

INFLUENCER

I'm an influencer because I can make an impact on our brands by giving them the opportunity to grow their businesses with our platform and pitch competitions. We hosted a pitch competition for our fashion brands in December 2020 after winning First Place in the Startup Grind Global Pitch Battle in September 2020. That was the first-time fashion had won in tech. That was a big win. I was able to take the pitch, which is on YouTube, and give it to the fashion brands. They said it was super helpful to see my pitch. Additionally, we did a pitch competition for our beauty brands in March 2021. What FashWire accomplished in the pandemic was impactful to the fashion industry because everything was shut down and we were able to give the brands a reliable platform to showcase their brands and interact digitally with a global consumer base. As I became an industry expert, the Council of Fashion Designers of America (CFDA) recognized me for an opinion piece and the New York Fashion Tech Lab placed me in their Expert Network. We had powerful press with Oprah and Marie Claire and grew our portfolio of brands from 225 to 400 because of my drive and passion with FashWire and my incredible team. We kept moving forward, which was super important and contributed to our success.

STRATEGIC INFLUENCE

Strategic means that you're able to adapt and plan how to move forward, whatever you're coming up against. It's that ability to navigate your path forward with your influence to where you need it to be, whether it's marketing or technology, or strategy in itself.

It's interesting being a CEO and having had different teams over the years. When hiring somebody to be an executive, they have to be strategic and be able to work with this team of strong females. I need people who can be adaptive to a startup life because it's very different from corporate life. When I'm hiring, my strategy is to make sure they can collaborate and work well with the team. When interviewing, I always ask if they've been on a sports team. I don't require a college education if the candidate is outstanding, but I always go back to the team sports thing. There is something to that edge, that street learning that you get from being on a sports team. They have to be a team player and they have to be able to wear different hats.

I'm very strategic in the way I go about my relationships. On my Advisory Board, I've been very strategic with whom I've brought in. They have all invested. The strategy was having stronger, better expertise in their respective fields than I have. When I am not the smartest person in the room, I'm challenged and I have the opportunity to educate myself. I love to learn from people, and I know my lane. I know where my value lies. I love my Advisory Board. I choose not to have a board of directors because my advisory board acts like one. They all have different areas of expertise and that has been such great help to me. As I push forward as CEO, they guide me. The longevity of authentic relationships is super important.

CENTER OF INFLUENCE

I think a center of influence would be the person who can influence one person who then goes and influences a third person. I have a lot of those people in my life, and I think I'm also one of those people. If one of my advisory board members connects me to an investor or company for potential partnership, then they're at the center of that; and then if I can connect that next person, then that full circle comes around. You're able to make an impact not only with connection A but with connections B, C, and D, and then they can go make an impact.

I believe I'm a center of influence in my industry. The New York Fashion Tech Lab named me on their industry expert network list and connected me with the brand Reflekt Me. Being a mentor is part of how I'm a center of influence. CFDA put an opinion piece about me on their site about how I see digitization, which gave me further validation as a center of influence.

I never thought I was a center of influence until Fashion Group International asked me to be on their beauty panel. I said, "You guys realize we just launched beauty and we're just learning the industry."

They replied, "We're going off your fashion background." It was because of the technology that we won FGI's Rising Star Award. All of a sudden, I started getting invited to participate on podcasts, panels and then people wanted to do pieces on me, and I realized, oh my gosh, this is getting real.

DEEP DOWN HABITS

It's my ability to self-start, to stay focused and my tenacity and passion for what I believe in. All of those things have helped me to be an entrepreneur and to push forward, even when I didn't want to.

I think being driven is staying focused on your brand narrative and keeping people accountable for their roles so that you can do your job. Sometimes as a startup CEO you find yourself doing the work that your team should be doing which makes it challenging to move forward. Being driven means you hold your team accountable, and you make yourself accountable right there with them. Being driven means that you can't just sit back and hope it's all going to work out. If you don't push forward and get the work done, it's just not going to happen.

Pre-COVID, the team was able to meet up at the different industry trade shows around the world. Once a month we would see each other in different countries or some other spot in the US and we were able to connect and talk to each other. We would spend our days working the trade shows and I would host team dinners in the evenings so we could discuss the shows and bond together as a team. Then when the pandemic hit, I started these weekly Zoom calls, and that really helped the team to re-connect. We go around the zoom room and each person gives an update on their deliverables. The team then will ask questions, offer advice. We all work together to try and help. Even now it's collaborative with the team. Everyone has that same entrepreneurial spirit, but they're all very driven and passionate about the company.

KEEPING ON TRACK

I have a treadmill that I use every night. Some people drink wine, but my night-time routine is to get on my treadmill, put on my music, pretend I am a rock star, and just go for four or five miles.

That helps me, and so does time with my kids. Spending time with them, where I can just shut it off and focus on how their day was and what they are doing, really helps me.

ONE DEFINING MOMENT

When I worked for my dad and Chris Arlen, who was my boss, I led a privileged life. I had great parents. I never wanted for anything. I am not going to lie. I was self-absorbed and a spoiled brat. I was very much my dad's daughter with my drive to want a career. My dad hired me during college to give me work experience, but I behaved like a princess, so nobody wanted "Jack Smith's" daughter working for them. But then Chris Arlen saw something in me that nobody else did. He said to me, "You have a creative mind, you think out of the box, and I think you could be really great at marketing." He was the first person to ever say that to me. It made me want to learn everything. I got out of my head, I changed my "spoiled brat" attitude and started to focus. I knew the career I wanted, and that moment launched my marketing career, which led me here.

MY GREATEST INFLUENCER

My dad is my greatest influencer.

What changed the course of FashWire and made us successful today was a conversation I had with Daymond John, from FUBU and *Shark Tank*. He was a big influence on how I moved FashWire to the next level. I was in the middle of looking for a developer, and Daymond took time with me and gave me some really critical advice. I was not 100 percent ready to hear it, but I listened. He went through our old app and he gave me the best advice on how to move forward. I took his feedback to heart, and he was right. I saw him after we launched with Google. I told him, "I just want to say thank you for taking that meeting with me. Your advice that day guided me to move in a new direction and because of that, we were able to partner with Google for a successful launch." I will always be grateful for that meeting. It was a big deal for me to receive his advice. I believe people come into your life for a reason.

Kimberly Carney is Founder and CEO of FashWire *and GlossWire, two high-growth global app and web-based platforms. Kimberly combined her previous 20+ years of experience in tech with her 15+ years of working in the fashion industry to develop a two-sided global marketplace where fashion brands could leverage data-driven insights in an innovative, low-cost scalable way to bridge the connection between designers and consumers. Conversely, consumers can use swipe and social technologies to directly interact with designers. Since FashWire's launch in 2018, and finding success in a global pandemic, FashWire has grown to 400+ designers from 40+ countries. In addition to disrupting the fashion space, Kimberly recently launched into the beauty industry with GlossWire. She has been recognized in the* CEO Publication *as one of the Top CEO's of 2020,* New York Fashion Tech Lab *as an Industry Expert and by* Authority Magazine *as a disruptor in the digital space.*

Website: www.fashwire.com
Instagram: www.instagram.com/fashwire/

Website: www.glosswire.com
Instagram: www.instagram.com/glosswireofficial/

SPHERE OF RELATIONSHIPS

SUCCESS FACTOR 3:
DEVELOP A NETWORK OF INFLUENTIAL CONNECTIONS

"The business of business is relationships;
the business of life is human connection."
—*Robin Sharma*

Y OUR JOURNEY TO THE NEW city has so far been rewarding. Since landing in Metropolis with no friends and no connections, you've managed to
establish your first two spheres.

In the Sphere of Accountability, you accepted personal responsibility for
who you were and your situation at that moment. You knew that what happened
yesterday was in the past, and what would happen tomorrow was unknown. Did
this mean, for example, that if you had been sent to Metropolis by no choice
of your own, which was offensive to you, that you needed to re-write or ignore
historical reality? Of course not. Facts are always facts, and reality is reality. But
it did mean that as far as your *mental attitude* was concerned, you looked at the
world around you with objectivity. You didn't play the blame game, and you had
a proactive mindset. Regardless of what had happened to you in the past, you
had work to do: you needed to meet people, secure gainful employment, and
provide for your basic necessities. With a strong work ethic and marketable skill
set, you bent the odds in your favor and adapted well to your environment. Your
sphere of influence was small and very local, but growing.

From there, you progressed to the Sphere of Accountability, where you
became increasingly self-reliant. You faced your fears—we all have them—and
used the power of self-realization to become both self-sufficient and a contributor to society with a growing reputation.

And now, still focused on your local environment and having local influence, you're ready to develop your Sphere of Relationships and a network of
influential connections.

Why do we use the word "relationships?"

Because developing relationships with people represents the next step towards meaningful influence. When you meet someone and get to know them, your association with that person goes through a series of phases or steps. In marketing, they're called "touchpoints," a term that works pretty well here, also. Here's the progression of relationship touchpoints.

RELATIONSHIP TOUCH POINTS

1. NO CONTACT

You are a stranger. You don't know the other person, and they don't know you. There has been no interaction, and you have no knowledge of the other person, nor they of you.

2. REPUTATION CONTACT

Here, one person learns about the other person through a third-party source—a conversation, a news article, or on social media. On this basis, an opinion may be formed. People and brands go to great lengths to manage their reputations and maintain a favorable image in the minds of consumers and possible partners. And, as we've seen in so many cases, a person's reputation can be "trashed" by unfavorable rumors or reports.

Your reputation often precedes you and can be important when people who can open doors for you consider you. For example, let's say that you've met quite a few people in Metropolis, and you're ready to join the exclusive golf club. You apply. The membership director receives your application, but he doesn't personally know you. He will ask the membership committee, "Who knows Jane Smith? She has applied for membership." Hopefully, several people will raise their hands, and each will say, "I know Jane Smith, and she's a terrific person and will be an asset to the club." They convey your good reputation to the membership director, who nods approvingly as he accepts your application.

This "reputation" step is optional. Sometimes you go directly from step 1 to step 3, "first personal contact," by meeting people and getting to know them.

3. FIRST PERSONAL CONTACT

Let's say you've landed in Metropolis and you go to a grocery store. You know nothing about the store; it's just the first one you found. You buy a loaf of bread from the clerk. You notice her nametag: Jenny. She seems nice, and she treats you fairly. You will remember her, and she might remember you too.

First personal contact often happens at social or business gatherings, where you meet someone for the first time, like when Susan met Robert, the president of the First National Bank. Of course, Susan knew that the bank had a president—all banks do—but she had never met Robert and, until that moment, had no information about him.

Especially in business, while it's nice to think that a person's "inner soul" is what really matters, first impressions are important. Imagine that when Susan had met Robert at the business event, she had been visibly tipsy from too much white wine. It could have been a one-time slip-up and uncharacteristic of her, but the first impression that Robert received would have been unfavorable. (This is the reason why many business people never drink alcohol at such events—it's just better to be absolutely safe!) In contrast, if Susan had presented herself in a professional manner and had come across as a good team player, Robert's first impression would have been positive.

4. INTERACTIONS

In this step—which you've been doing in the Sphere of Accountability—you interact with other people, perhaps more than once. At the grocery store, you buy things from Jenny on regular occasions. You can count her among the group of people you can say you "know" in Metropolis. You're not yet friends, nor do you have a relationship outside of being a customer at her store.

You might open an account at the First National Bank and become a known customer. In this phase, monetary transactions are simple and low-risk. The requirement for trust is very low. But with repeated interactions, familiarity is developed, and *consistency of behavior* is noted. If Robert, the bank president, has a series of low-stakes interactions with Susan, and she's consistently pleasant and professional, he'll be pleased that his initial positive impression of her has been validated.

5. RELATIONSHIPS

Here, your interactions are of sufficient value that a higher level of trust is required. Your interactions with Jenny at the grocery store may never rise to this level—you could shop there every day and never have a business relationship. But if you get a loan from the First National Bank, you're going to have a relationship with your loan officer (assuming it's a small local bank). You might join a nonprofit board where Robert, the bank president, also serves. You might work on a project together and form a relationship in which the elements of *trust* and *dependency* are introduced, in which something of value is exchanged. For example, let's say you serve on a nonprofit board committee with Robert, and the committee must oversee the annual fundraising event. You take on the job of lining up sponsors, and over a period of a few weeks, you do it well, thereby fulfilling your promise to the committee. Robert will note that you're trustworthy and capable of delivering something of value that helps the committee reach its goal.

Another ubiquitous way to form business relationships is on the golf course. People who don't play golf might scratch their heads at the idea, but through repeated low-risk interactions, even while playing eighteen holes, a trusting relationship can develop, and deals can be made.

6. PARTNERSHIPS

These are much deeper and more productive relationships, which we'll discuss in the next chapter, Sphere of Influence. Generally, partnerships are long-term, have substantial value at stake, and there may be legally binding contracts involved.

This chapter is about building your sphere of relationships.

PERSONAL RELATIONSHIPS DON'T SCALE

These examples, and countless more, show that social media and internet influence can be scaled. But this book is about deeper personal and professional relationships. Earlier in the book, I mentioned the Jenner-Kardashian family and their hugely successful reality TV show *Keeping Up with the Kardashians*. When thinking about influence, the story you should know is how the program first got on the air. The *original* influencer—the person with Hollywood clout—was Ryan Seacrest. In 2006, Kris Jenner, who knew him, told him about their idea for the show. One Sunday afternoon, Seacrest sent a camera crew to film the Kardashian family as they were having a barbeque. (They used a video camera Seacrest bought at Best Buy.) Seacrest liked what he saw and sent the seven-minute tape to some friends who were executives at the E! network. But the executives told him they couldn't buy a show based on only seven minutes of video. This was perhaps the expected default response from mid-level managers who were afraid to make a mistake. For most "suits," saying "no" is much safer than saying "yes"!

Here's where Seacrest's industry influence came into play. Undeterred, he picked up the phone and made another call directly to the man who was the head of E! at the time. Seacrest talked him into green-lighting the show.

In August 2007, E! announced that the Kardashian and Jenner families would star in a yet-to-be-titled reality show described as a "new non-scripted family sitcom." Ryan Seacrest was a co-producer, along with Bunim/Murray Productions, which had previously produced Paris Hilton's *The Simple Life*.

The twentieth—and supposedly final—season of *Keeping Up with the Kardashians* was slated to premiere in March 2021. All told, it's estimated the family earned $2 billion from the show. As for co-producer Ryan Seacrest, he earns an estimated $75 million a year from a wide variety of entertainment business ventures, including *Keeping Up with the Kardashians, American Idol,* and his syndicated radio show. In Hollywood, Ryan Seacrest has real influence—the kind that can get a television show on the air.

Let's get back to scaling. Personal relationships, of the kind that allowed Ryan Seacrest to pick up his phone and call the head of the E! network and pitch the show to him, are *not scalable.* They are nurtured slowly, over months, years, and sometimes lifetimes. They depend on a high level of personal trust. They cannot be contrived or fabricated, and they are created one person at a time.

It's important to note that a relationship of any kind can continue indefinitely—for months, years, even a lifetime—without becoming a partnership. A relationship is transactional, meaning you buy something from me. It can be low-value, meaning we're engaged in a project of mutual interest, but the stakes are low. Or it's potentially valuable, just not yet.

For example, you can have a checking account at your local bank for your entire life. It's a pleasant relationship, but not a partnership.

You can have a friendly relationship with your neighbor, and wave hello to each other each morning, and borrow his lawn mower once in a while, but even if the good feelings last for decades, it's not a partnership.

Ask any parent whose adult child has been in a romantic "relationship" for years. After a while, the typical parent will say in exasperation, "Enough with the 'relationship!' When are you two getting *married?*" In this case, the potential for a partnership is there, but it's not happening yet.

DEVELOP YOUR NETWORK

Networking is a business I know well since I built a national business networking concept named Trustegrity. Networking is the act of creating a set of personal connections who will provide support, resources, business referrals, feedback, insight, and information. At its most basic level, it means meeting people and forming personal or professional relationships with them. You may recall the old expression: "It's not *what* you know, it's *who* you know." The implication is that no matter how smart and skilled you may be, you will not have the same competitive edge as someone who is well connected. There's a lot of truth in that expression.

Networking means you have to get out and personally interact with strangers. You cannot achieve the same results by becoming successful on the internet or social media. During the COVID-19 pandemic, our nation's self-imposed social isolation was crippling and had an adverse economic effect on huge sectors of the economy. Large business meetings, business networking gatherings, conventions, and symposiums were all canceled, making it much more difficult for people like Susan to meet and interact with people like Robert, the bank president. Relationships that existed were frozen in place, while new relationships were much more difficult to form. One potential benefit that came about purely out of desperation during the pandemic is virtual meetings. Virtual meetings can also be referred to as cyber meetings or online meetings, defined simply as meetings that happen online rather than physically. These types of virtual meetings are projected to become much more commonplace than they were prior to the pandemic because of their ease of use, no requirement to travel, and cost savings.

Because of its one-on-one nature, networking is simultaneously one of the most obviously useful and one of the most dreaded developmental activities that some aspiring leaders must face.

Regardless of how you feel about it, if you want to build and use influence, networking is a requirement. It's the quality of the relationships in your personal network that ultimately determines your success in business.

People who grasp this fact tend to fall into one of two groups. Those who are socially adept embrace it and love it. They see it as an opportunity to become part of something bigger than themselves. To them, it's the fun part of their professional life. And let's face it—networking events often involve food and drink and the chance to unwind.

Those who are less socially confident resist and resent networking. They think, isn't it enough that I do a good job? Do I have to go out and constantly sell myself? They have the misconception that networking is something you do in order to *get something*. That attitude usually does not produce good results. Those who think that networking is somehow phony don't understand what it's really about. It should never be forced or laborious. You should never feel like you're selling yourself. At its best, it's an enjoyable diversion from the everyday routine of the job while helping someone else solve a problem.

In fact, the golden rule in networking, which makes it a positive experience, is this: *Give more than you get.*

You don't sell, you contribute. A skilled networker gives to her network by sharing information, lending a hand to a project, and introducing people to each other. You can simply invite someone to lunch (and pay for it), and have a nice time. The conversation will gravitate towards areas of common interest, which may be business, or it could be something else. If you network by joining a committee or project, either at work or in your community, then the shared goal provides a framework for conversation.

Figure 5.1 illustrates the three basic types of networking.

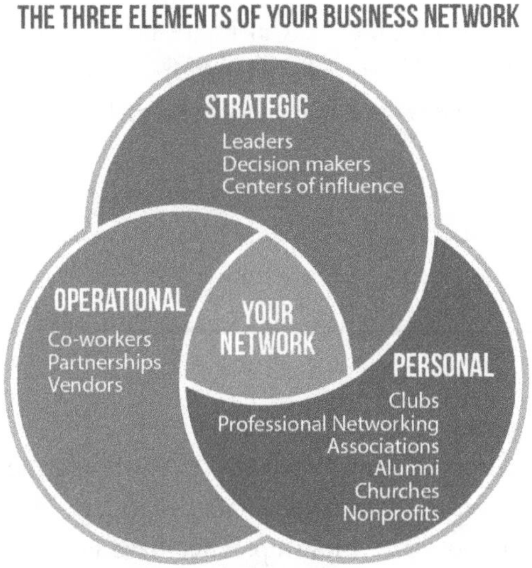

THE THREE ELEMENTS OF YOUR BUSINESS NETWORK

Figure 5.1

THREE ELEMENTS OF NETWORKING

PERSONAL

These opportunities are not directly related to your nine-to-five job. They are largely external, composed of discretionary links to people with whom you have something in common. They include professional associations, alumni groups, clubs, churches, nonprofits, and personal interest communities.

What makes a personal network powerful is its referral potential. Personal network connections are valuable to the extent that they can help you reach, in just a few connections or "degrees of separation," the person in your orbit who has the information you need. With these interactions, you can gain new perspectives that allow you to advance in your career. The contacts you develop can provide important referrals, access to new untapped industries, information you may be seeking, and even developmental support such as coaching and mentoring

OPERATIONAL

Here, you collaborate with others on a project that has a goal. This could happen at work, where you join a team that includes people you may not know very well, such as from another department or even a vendor or partner from another company or government agency. For example, real estate developers who build houses, apartment buildings, and commercial spaces must collaborate with a wide variety of other people, including bankers, lawyers, contractors, government zoning and licensing officials, real estate brokers, appraisers, and many more. Over time, they build trusted relationships so that when a new building project is launched, the developer only needs to make a few phone calls to assemble his or her team.

On operational teams, you quickly discover which team members are reliable, active partners, and which are deadwood, or even worse, counterproductive. And it's here where you learn how much influence you have over others—or, to be more precise, how much influence they will accept from you.

STRATEGIC

Strategic networking happens in two arenas.

The first arena is networking with the goal of a future relationship. For example, when Susan meets Robert, the bank president, she may have no immediate reason to propose a relationship. They have no interests or projects in common. But she knows that months or even years from now, there could be a basis for a relationship, and so she makes it a point to meet and greet Robert whenever the opportunity arises.

The second arena is when you and others are engaged in high-level planning of projects and initiatives that have long-term ramifications for many people.

In business, this type of high-level strategic networking can happen in the C-suite and the boardroom, where long-term strategies are proposed and formulated. A corporate board of directors is responsible for helping the organization set broad goals, supporting executive duties, and ensuring the company has adequate, well-managed resources at its disposal. They are responsible for articulating the mission of the company and assuring that all decisions are related to and support that mission. The board can change the mission, but only after careful deliberation.

To strengthen important relationships, directors are often linked to major vendors. For example, given their mutually beneficial relationship, you'd expect to see a top executive of The Coca-Cola Company sitting on the board of directors at McDonald's Corporation, or vice versa.

Often, deals are made because of the influence one executive has with a potential partner.

Let's say a maker of frozen pizzas is rolling out a new line of organic pizzas. They are to be sold in supermarkets, where shelf space in the freezer aisle is highly coveted. If the company cannot get advantageous positioning in the freezer—the choice spot being at the end of the aisle at eye level, not down by the floor—the product may not grab the attention of the consumer. Fortunately, you worked in sales for many years, and you happen to have a relationship with Joe, the vice president of frozen foods at Walmart, which is ramping up its grocery division. You volunteer to contact him at the Walmart headquarters in Bentonville, Arkansas. The CEO gives you the green light, and you call Joe and send your proposal. Because Joe knows you and trusts you, and he knows that your company has the capacity to deliver, he feels comfortable placing a purchase order for 100,000 frozen organic pizzas, which he promises to display at eye level near the end of the aisle. Your influence has made the difference.

Now that you have progressed in your journey to the Sphere of Relationships, *Figure 5.2.* illustrates the types of connections that will give you the greatest opportunity in your developing business network. Quadrant 1 offers little opportunity since these connections have low levels of influence and offers little motivation in developing a relationship. Quadrant 2 includes potential team members or employees, if the relationship is built on trust, but no real business networking value given that these connections have low influence capacity. Quadrant 3 is your target group where you should be focusing your attention. These business people have high influence and are the business contacts with whom, once a trusted relationship is developed, can offer the greatest strategic opportunity. A word of warning, highly influential targets offer limited value if their profiles don't align with your industry, values, markets and targeted client base. Quadrant 4 is the highly valued subset of business connections that you

Figure 5.2

have worked hard to develop trust and strategic relationships with. Each of these connections should be regarded as a highly valuable asset and be treated as such.

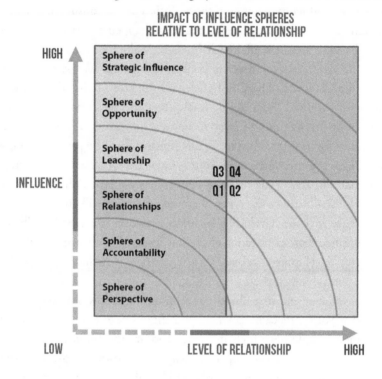

Figure 5.3

Figure 5.3 represents an expanded model of the previous figure. The purpose of this diagram is to illustrate that the sphere of strategic influence you achieve makes a tremendous difference in your ability to warrant an introduction to high profile connections. As your level of skill set, reputation, expertise and influence expands, your network will naturally grow attracting more and more influential business people to your personal sphere of influence. Likewise, individuals of higher influence will also take note of your developing reputation and will be open and perhaps even interested in becoming connected. Some may even proactively contact you. Notice in the diagram that the spheres of influence you achieve expand outward, eventually arriving in that coveted quadrant where high-level strategic influencers are present. This quadrant is where centers of influence are located. It could take an entire career to arrive there, but the aim of this book is to teach you not only how to develop influence, but how to cultivate relationships with high-level, strategic influencers called, Centers of Influence. Your opportunity lies ahead.

PROFESSIONAL NETWORKING AND AFFINITY GROUPS

In addition to networking within the upper echelons of a corporation or at the board level, you can meet people very effectively by joining a structured business networking or community service group. Historically, networking began with "old boys" and women's clubs. In the United States, the Schuylkill Fishing Company in Andalusia, Pennsylvania, was the first private social club. Founded in 1732 and devoted to angling, it was and remains the oldest continuously active social club in North America.

For women, social clubs emerged in the mid-nineteenth century to provide them with a non-denominational, independent avenue for education and active community service. For example, the American Association of University Women began in January 1882 when Marion Talbot and Ellen Swallow Richards invited a group of alumnae from eight colleges to a meeting in Boston, Massachusetts. They founded the Association of Collegiate Alumnae, AAUW's predecessor organization, to create an organization of women college graduates that could help them develop opportunities to use their education, as well as promote and assist other women in attending college. The association also sought to improve standards of education for women so that men's and women's higher education was more equal in scope and difficulty.

For exclusivity, few organizations can rival the Union Club on Park Avenue in Manhattan. Its doors first opened in 1836, and over the years, its highly influential members have included Presidents Ulysses S. Grant and Dwight Eisenhower, publisher William Randolph Hearst, banker J.P. Morgan, diplomat W. Averell Harriman, and many others.

Along with private clubs came service groups like the Rotary Club, which was started by Chicago attorney Paul Harris in 1905 so business people could exchange ideas and form meaningful, lifelong friendships. The Chamber of Commerce dates back to 1599 in France and since 1912, the U.S. Chamber of Commerce has promoted pro-business issues via lobbying efforts at the national level.

Kiwanis International was founded in 1915 by a group of businessmen in Detroit, Michigan. The organization was originally called the Supreme Lodge Benevolent Order of Brothers but soon changed its name to Kiwanis. The name was coined from an American Indian expression, *"Nunc Kee-wanis,"* which means, "We trade."

There are many more—Greek fraternities and sororities, the Elks Club, the Loyal Order of Moose, the Freemasons, the Junior League, the Professionals of Color Social Club. They are all loosely defined as affinity groups or clubs, formed around a shared interest or common goal, to which individuals formally or informally belong.

Business-oriented networking groups are flourishing, including Business Network International (BNI), the largest referral networking organization with members and chapters in seventy countries. LeTip, founded in 1978, offers members the opportunity to meet weekly to exchange qualified leads, build solid business relationships, develop strong presentation skills, and become proficient networkers.

As mentioned earlier, in 2013, I launched a national business networking concept named Trustegrity, dedicated to being a better and more efficient way to connect, confide, and collaborate with businesspeople. We believed that when experienced business people received the right connections and the right strategic advice, that anything was possible.

In 2013 we had just two small groups, and over the next seven years, we expanded into a national, coast-to-coast organization. I sold it at the end of 2019, just prior to the COVID-19 outbreak.

The difference between Trustegrity and other business referral groups at the time was a deep focus on relationships built on trust with integrity, along with a mastermind knowledge-sharing component. Business referrals were a natural byproduct of the relationships and knowledge-sharing experiences.

This book, *The Power of Strategic Influence!*, introduces a new, next-generation approach to strategic business networking. It builds upon the central theme of *Positive Influence* combined with *Strategic Relationship Building*. In referring to Relationship-Centered Influence, this book teaches you how to get access to it, how to develop it, how to utilize it, how to expand it, and later how to be generous with it to help others.

LEARN TO BE INTER-RELIANT

For influence to exist, there must be more than one entity in a system. Recall the example of the desert island: If you were wholly independent and did not need the opportunity for interaction with other people, then the concept of personal influence would not be needed and would not exist. Influence presupposes a universe of multiple participants seeking to change the behavior or thinking of others by means of persuasion, setting an example, or some other means.

Influence is not a one-way street. It's based on a foundation of reciprocity, where value is exchanged equally. This exchange is not always literally equal, but according to each one's ability to pay. No one expects a successful retired CEO to act as a mentor to a younger executive and be compensated for every scrap of information; he or she is paid with the satisfaction they have helped another person lead a better life and have enhanced everyone's overall standard of living.

For you to increase your personal influence and build relationships, you must begin by contributing and helping others succeed. Expect nothing in return. Over time, your colleagues and partners will see you as increasingly indispensable. You'll be the person who "gets things done," the "go-to" person, who can be turned to for expert advice, knowledge and who is consistently dependable.

Will some people take advantage of you and accept your help while giving nothing in return?

Yes. This is a fact of life, and you will never change it. Do not become angry or bitter at such people as it is a poor use of your valuable time. The "taker" mentality is deeply ingrained, and in a workplace setting, you're not going to change them. What you can and should do is detach yourself from such people as much as you can. Know in advance their contribution will be minimal or nothing and plan accordingly. If you are an employee of an organization, it's likely that you will have little control over who your colleagues are and how your superiors want you to work together. You just have to make the best of it, and if the situation becomes intolerable, move on to greener pastures.

THE THREE TYPES OF OPERATIONAL INTER-RELIANCE

In practical terms, in a workplace setting, inter-reliance takes three forms.

SEQUENTIAL

This type is linear, like an assembly line. You receive a work product from the person preceding you. You perform your task, and then you pass the product along to the next person. Each person adds value to the product so that when it's complete, it's ready for the end user. If you're a diligent worker, you'll become frustrated when someone or something ahead of you in the process causes the product flow to stop or slow down. Conversely, you'll feel pressure when you don't have enough time or resources to complete your part of the job, and you're the one perceived to be the bottleneck.

You'll find this form of inter-reliance in office settings when, for example, you need to write a report based on data sent to you. If you don't get the data in time, or it's incomplete, you can't do your job. It's also common on construction projects; for example, if you are the contractor responsible for installing the interior wallboard in each room, you can't do your job until the electrician has done the wiring and the plumber has installed the pipes in the rough framing. In building construction, a key task is the coordination of the various subcontractors; you want them coming in and out of the project with no overlap and as little downtime as possible.

As an individual contributor to a sequential project, you have very little influence over its overall success. The failure of one person or team could derail the effort.

POOLED

This type resembles the hub and spokes of a wheel. You're responsible for your part of the project, and then you submit your work to the person or team at the center, who coordinates and assembles the end result. It's like a product launch, and you're the advertising director, and your job is to shoot the TV ads and deliver them. Once you've done your job and delivered the ads, it's up to the product launch manager to put the pieces together. If another team fails to complete their part of the project, the entire enterprise could suffer, and unfortunately, you may have very little influence over it.

COLLABORATIVE

Here, the dynamic is very fluid, and team members work together in cross-functional roles to achieve a goal. It's akin to a military campaign, where many equally skilled actors are deployed to accomplish various tasks. If one team falls short, another team can be sent to assist. Resources can be sent where they are needed, and as the project or battle progresses, assets can be re-assigned.

In an office setting, influence over a project is determined not just by rank (CEO, director, manager, employee) but by the dedication and skill of each participant. If you are involved in a collaborative team, you have the opportunity to increase and leverage your influence. This is because if you are more highly qualified or more dedicated to success than your teammates, you can assume more responsibility and push the project ahead more aggressively.

Business communities and networking groups can also be highly collaborative by partnering in such a way that provides more value to each other's clients. Examples of collaborative partnering can include bundling of products or services, developing joint marketing campaigns, facilitating cross-training for sales and support people, and so on.

FOCUS ON SYNERGY

It is in such a collaborative setting where, regardless of your job title or position in the pecking order, you can personally develop your influence over the group and the project. In the process, you must be careful not to simply take over and try to do it all yourself—if you do, you'll burn out, and the others will take the credit anyway. You need to focus on developing synergy, which occurs when two or more people work together to make a greater impact than they would separately. By uniting collective talents and strengths, the combined result for the organization is greater than the sum of its individual parts. It is not a "touchy-feely" idea, but a practical approach to getting results—and when you know how, it's not all that difficult to create.

Synergy does not always happen naturally. You need to cultivate it. Lack of team synergy is caused by normal human characteristics such as differences in individual priorities, ego, habits, talents, and interests, as well as poor management and coordination, individuals not playing as team players, ineffective communication, poor leadership and followership, or people simply not adding their own contribution.

How can you develop and assert your influence? Primarily by setting a good example, being indispensable, and not alienating your colleagues. You gain influence by helping others to reach their goals and keeping a positive attitude. Will some people abuse your collaborative approach? Yes, but that's just how some people are, and you cannot change them.

TRUST-CENTERED RELATIONSHIPS

At the end of the day, influence is based on trust. In any relationship, the influence you are granted by your colleagues will depend upon how much they trust you and feel as though they can depend on you to do the right thing.

If you're like most people in business or in life, you aspire to a position of leadership, whether that's in your organization, your industry, or your community. Leadership is something that must be given to you by other people. The CEO of a public company is hired by the board of directors. If you are an entrepreneur and you own your company, your degree of leadership—the growth and size of your company—is determined by your customers (or lack thereof) and investors. It is they who have the final say over your level of success and the influence you have over the marketplace.

Through bad or misguided behavior, trust can be eroded, relationships dissolved, and influence negated. While CEO resignations or firings can be the result of business downturns for which the CEO must be held responsible, many others are caused by unethical behavior.

In February 2020, Tidjane Thiam, CEO of Credit Suisse, resigned after it was revealed he had a private investigator spy on a former executive who had joined another bank. In an episode that seems almost silly, the problem stemmed from the fact that Thiam and Iqbal Khan owned adjacent properties on Lake

Zurich, and they disagreed on some trees growing on Thiam's property. (We should all have such problems.) This disagreement was eventually followed by Khan's departure for the rival bank, UBS. Credit Suisse then began surveillance of Khan to see if he was trying to poach employees or clients.

While an internal investigation cleared Thiam of misconduct, the scandal had damaged the credibility of his leadership, and his influence evaporated.

In September 2020, Trevor Milton, founder and CEO of Nikola, a manufacturer of electric trucks, announced his resignation following scathing accusations by Hindenburg Research that he had lied about the company's proprietary battery technology. At the time, he was under investigation by the US Justice Department for misleading investors. In a tweet, Milton said, "I intend to defend myself against false allegations leveled against me by outside detractors." But investor trust had been shattered, and the once-influential entrepreneur found himself on the outside, looking in.

Whether in business or private life, trust is the foundation of all successful relationships, and when trust is lost, so is influence.

SUCCESS ACTION ITEMS –
DEVELOP A NETWORK OF INFLUENTIAL CONNECTIONS

- Develop your network. Networking is the act of creating a set of personal connections who will provide support, resources, business referrals, feedback, insight, and information.
- Establish high-quality relationships. It's the quality of the relationships in your personal network that ultimately determines your success in business.
- Give more than you get. You don't sell, you contribute. A skilled networker gives to his or her network by sharing information, lending a hand to a project, and introducing people to each other.
- Be aware that there are three basic types of networking.
  - Personal, composed of people whom you have something in common such as professional associations, alumni groups, clubs, etc.
  - Operational, originating from work contacts or subcontractors you use to complete a project.
  - Strategic networking is when you and others are engaged in high-level planning of projects and initiatives that have long-term ramifications
- Join a professional networking group. Meet quality people by joining a structured business networking group.
- Learn to be inter-reliant. Influence is not a one-way street. It's based on a foundation of reciprocity, where value is exchanged equally.
- Become the "go-to" person. Increase personal influence and build relationships by contributing and helping others to succeed.
- Prioritize collaborative environments to gain influence. Business communities and networking groups can be highly collaborative by partnering that provides more value to each other's clients.
- Focus on synergy. This occurs when two or more people work together to make a greater impact than they would individually. By uniting collective talents and strengths, the combined result is greater than the sum of its individual parts.
- Develop and assert your influence. Do this by setting a good example, being indispensable, and not alienating your colleagues. You gain influence by helping others to reach their goals.
- Cultivate trust in your relationships. Influence is based on trust. In any relationship, the influence you are granted by your colleagues will depend upon how much they trust you and feel as though they can depend on you to do the right thing.

DANIELA CIOCAN
CEO ACCESS BEAUTY INSIDERS

"Relationships are My Specialty"

IMMIGRATING TO THE US.

WAS BORN AND RAISED IN Transylvania, in communist Romania. The president, Nicolae Ceauşescu, was a dictator. He had this idea we'd be the only nation in the world that didn't owe money to anyone. Anything produced in the country was exported, and nothing was imported. Everything was rationed, from flour, to butter, to sugar. It was very challenging to have a good lifestyle, but we were all very educated because the Communist Party provided education. I was very much looking forward to being educated and going to the university.

In 1985, my father decided to come to the United States to visit his sister. He called my mom and told her that he was not coming back. All the phones in Romania were tapped by the secret police. The next day, my mom was called into the president's office, and there were two men present from the secret police. They told my mom, "We know your husband is not coming back. This is not going to look good for you. You need to make him come back. If he does not return, then we will make sure that you don't get a visa to emigrate. We will fire you, and your daughter will not be able to go to school anymore."

My mom didn't convince my dad, so we decided to come to the United States. They kicked me out of school, which was very traumatic because I had just turned thirteen. It was nearly two years while we waited for a visa.

I had a private tutor. I learned English and math at home. I would go and wait for my friends as they would come out of school so I could hang out with them. But that put me in a different category. I was no longer part of the group.

In communist Romania, you were taught from a young age to be very careful about what you said. You could never voice opinions against the government or the president. You could never share conversations that happened at home.

It was a culture where everyone told on the other person, so you didn't know whom to trust. That all stayed with me, as I am very reserved.

We came to the States, where my dad lived in New York City. He didn't live in a very good area. I went to one of the worst public schools, Newtown High School, located in East Elmhurst, in Queens.

I had an accent. I understood and I could speak, but I didn't want to speak because I sounded different, so I was very quiet. Also, things were very different since I came from a culture where everyone looked like me, and suddenly I was at a school where there were Latinos, blacks, Indians, people from all over the world, and there were kids outside smoking weed and drinking. There were no uniforms. At the school in Queens, girls were wearing miniskirts and they had red lips. I saw some girls my age, sixteen at that time, who were pregnant. It was such a shock for me. I did not fit in.

Nevertheless, I was a very good student. I didn't know what I wanted to be, so my parents consulted with other Romanian families, and decided that a good career for me would be an accountant, a CPA. I had no idea what that was. I enrolled at a private university. After the first semester, I thought, if I have to do this for the rest of my life, I'm going to kill myself.

I switched to business administration and I didn't like that, and I finally dropped out of school because I didn't feel I connected with any of the programs. I got into modeling and partying a lot, and my dad was very strict. My dad finally said, "Listen, young lady, either you get a job, or you move out, but you cannot continue partying like this."

And I replied, "A job? I've never had a job!"

So what could I do? One of my friends said, "I bet you could get a job in a store." I ended up walking into a J.C. Penney's. At the time they were selling high-end cosmetics. The store manager gave me a job selling beauty products behind the counter, and I loved it. There was an older lady working there. Every time I would go to work, she told me, "Daniela, you cannot sell beauty products behind the counter for the rest of your life. You're too young and you're too bright. You need to go to school." To prove her wrong, I decided to search for a university where I could get a degree and work in the beauty industry, which I was sure didn't exist.

Well, I was wrong. There was a New York state university that had a program, which to this day is supported by the cosmetics industry.

So, I enrolled and I went full-time. I was so excited.

I graduated in three years. I graduated *magna cum laude,* and I loved the industry. I ended up doing my internship for Estée Lauder Companies corporate.

Around 1997, the fall of communism was happening, and all of Eastern Europe was opening up. Estée Lauder Companies, which is a massive multibillion-dollar company, wanted to open up a new office in Romania. I was working under the vice president of Origins. She called me in and said to me, "Daniela, I have this awesome opportunity. We want to make you country manager and send you to Romania, and you will build the business there."

This would have been an awesome opportunity. But my parents reacted, "Are you kidding us? We sacrificed ourselves to *leave* the country and now you are going *back?*"

I went back and forth on this. I am Romanian, but I had left the country so long ago and I didn't know the landscape there anymore. I was more American in many ways. So I decided not to take the opportunity.

The executive who had vouched for me seemed to be very disappointed with my decision. Since I'm in the industry and I've developed a high profile, I have bumped into her several times, and even after she retired, I don't think she ever forgave me.

I ended up working for the fourth-largest Japanese cosmetics company. They were massive in Asia and Japan, but they had no distribution and no experience in the Western market. They had signed a distribution deal with a Japanese gentleman, who hired me. He knew zero about cosmetics, but he was a great salesperson. I learned a lot about business etiquette from him.

I was the second person hired, and we started having conversations with luxury retailers who were interested in the brand. I was making $28,000 a year. I got a call from one of the luxury retailers. We were launching on Fifth Avenue. The store buyer said, "Daniela, you need to come to the store and you need to hire a counter manager."

I was so new and so green. I asked, "How much are we paying this person?"

And they said, "The range is around $55,000." So I had to hire someone who was twice my age and making twice as much!

I was not equipped, so I went to my boss and said, "I can't do this."

He said, "Yes, you can!"

I hired a woman, and I was intimidated by her since she was older, a very traditional department store woman, with full makeup face on and perfect hair. It turned out that behind my back she would tell my boss that every time I would do a store visit, she would go crying afterward because apparently, I was so hard on her.

I tried to understand why she felt that way because I'm a kind person, but very quiet. I mostly say what needs to be said, and no more. Because I was intimidated by her, I didn't try to engage her on a personal level. My style was offensive to her, but *I was scared of her* the whole time.

The brand grew and I was responsible for putting together a team. For nine years, I traveled all over the country meeting with department store managers. I was proud of the amazing people I had brought together.

I went to Japan several times, and that was interesting because Japanese culture is very different. It's very male-dominated. I would meet with the man who ran the company on behalf of a billionaire family. The Japanese market is also very distinct in the sense that it's very homogeneous, with similar skin tones and similar preferences. Here in the US, we have many skin tones, different climates, and different texture preferences. The Japanese leaders did not understand that they needed to adapt to the market. The first time I had a meeting with the president, I felt he was talking down to me. He treated me like a young girl who didn't know what she was talking about. I went there two or three times, and after that I told my boss I never wanted to go there again. I was not respected and the people sitting around the table were older men who did not understand cosmetics. The young girls who *did* understand were there to just translate or get coffee.

After nine years, we signed a huge deal. I learned that relationships are crucial. Neiman Marcus was one of our largest distributor accounts. The vice president who ran the account there moved to Bath & Body Works. I was very close to her. Before she left, she said, "Daniela, I'm going to move, and I want you and your brand to come with me." I promised her I would make it happen.

Moving to Bath & Body Works required a sudden conversion from an environment of beauty advisers consulting with customers to a self-serve environment where they looked at the shelves and chose products on their own.

The problem was that our packaging was not designed for a store like that. Japanese packaging was very clean, pretty and simple, and had no product information on the box. So I went to Japan for the last time. I told them this could be massive for the business, but the packaging needed to be adjusted. They said no problem, just sign the deal and then we'll do it.

We got a great deal, and we rolled out to four hundred stores, but then the company didn't make any changes. I told them the company would not survive and they would go under. I resigned, and less than a year later, they shut down the business in the United States.

In 2005, I moved to Las Vegas with my now ex-husband, and wasn't quite sure what I wanted to do next.

I quickly realized that there was no beauty industry in Las Vegas. Then I learned that there was an international trade show for cosmetics named Cosmo-prof. They had hosted their event in Las Vegas for years. They were looking for someone to turn around the show who had relationships with retailers, and had a European background. I was born in Europe. Romania is very close to Italian culture. They also wanted someone who understood working with international partners. They wanted me to be the bridge between the Italian partners and the American partners.

I knew nothing about exhibitions. The marketing language is different. It took me almost two years to get familiar with the language. But I was savvy enough to understand that luxury retailers wanted to have exclusive beauty brands.

The show was large, with around 700 companies, but no nice brands like I would see in a Neiman Marcus or Sephora. My job was to bring the retailers, but how could I bring them if I didn't have confidence in what was on the floor?

I asked Cosmoprof to give me a section we would call, "Discover Beauty." It would be like a show within a show. In that section, I could have a say as to who could buy space, and have integrity in inviting buyers to come, and meet up with those brands I chose. That was revolutionary for the trade show business, because no one had ever really created a show within a show. We extended those areas from Discover Beauty, to fragrances, to organic beauty and Black & Brown Beauty. Those special areas, although small spaces, made close to 15% of the revenue by the time I exited the company. We changed the trade show dynamic whereby we were not selling square feet, we were selling a package, an experience. It was the access that you got, which was why we could charge much more for premium areas.

Cosmoprof North America became one of the most awarded trade shows. I twice won the marketing genius award from *Trade Show Executive* magazine.

I was suddenly in the spotlight with all of the largest tradeshow organizers. I developed a name in the tradeshow and beauty world, which helped several companies become huge. In one of the special areas I created, IT Cosmetics had the opportunity to meet with the director from QVC. Nine years later, IT Cosmetics sold for $1.3 billion to L'Oreal. Also there, Drunk Elephant met a Sephora buyer, and a few years later sold for a little under a billion dollars to Unilever.

In 2018, after thirteen years, everyone knew me as a tradeshow expert because I put Cosmoprof on the map here in the States. I also did fun things while at Cosmoprof, like creating kind of a beauty Shark Tank with Mark Cuban and John Paul Dejoria, who owns Patron Tequila. That was a large event. We had 1,500 people sitting in the audience and Mark enjoyed it, and he actually offered mentorship to a company that he really liked from the three who were pitching him live.

After leaving Cosmoprof I decided to start my own event company. In 2019 I launched my first event, focused on beauty, in downtown Las Vegas. The event is called Unfiltered Experience. I wanted it to be my own unfiltered vision of what an event should be, and it certainly should be an experience.

What I wanted to do with Unfiltered Experience was help smaller companies in the beauty space connect with local buyers from spas, boutiques salons, and with influencers because I saw the dynamic change when going direct to consumers. I featured an up-and-coming artist because I wanted to create an experience. We won the BizBash best influencer event of the year.

I had an opportunity to work with a digital TV channel called Bespoke TV, which has a reach of about 35 million homes. They're into fashion, lifestyle, and beauty. We worked out a deal launching a pilot show called *Behind the Mirror*, with six episodes, showcasing twenty-four indie companies in the beauty space through founder interviews, talking about what their motivation was to start their business, and to allow beauty lovers to discover those brands.

I was also executive producer for *The Look: All Stars* tv program, which had two seasons that aired on Sinclair Stations and CW. The next season will be produced on Bespoke.

GOING TO A STRANGE LAND

If I were put ashore in a strange city with little money, with no connections and no knowledge of the local culture, I'd first have to get the lay of the land, to understand where I could connect with people. Whether it's business or personal, it's all about the connections. So it's understanding, "Here I am, where can I go to make human connections?" It is really trying to assimilate and absorb what the locals do, and creating some bonds and connections with locals, so they can help you navigate.

That's what we had to do when we came to this country. My parents went to ask advice from others who had kids—Where should we send our daughter? What should she do? So that would be the most important thing, trying to understand with whom I could connect. Then trying to get as much information about how to survive.

INFLUENCE

Influence is the equity that your name brings to the table. We all have equity, be it good or bad. Equity are the things you have done that people have experienced with you. It's your behavior, your accessibility, your willingness to provide input or advice or help.

I would define influence as the impact on the community on people around you, and impact is really defined through the equity of things you're known for.

STRATEGIC INFLUENCER

Strategic influence means that you are very instrumental. You're very well positioned for a specific segment. I'm a strategic influencer in the B2B beauty space. Am I a strategic influencer for consumer beauty like social media? No, I'm not. I'm not so strategic there because my brand equity doesn't parlay so well in that space.

Being a strategic influencer means you have the right qualifications to make an impact. You could know a lot of things but you're not really strategic if you come to a different industry and you're lacking some of those inner, very fine understandings of what makes things tick. In order to be strategic, you need to have a very keen sense of those smaller elements that are not so glaringly obvious. Being strategic also means being very purposeful, being very honed-in on a specific outcome or segment.

STRATEGIC RELATIONSHIP INFLUENCER

Relationships are crucial. I've been very good at building relationship networks and I was very active at it even through the pandemic. I try to remember to touch base with certain individuals. I have conversations so that I stay in the know. I find out what's happening. I ask for other connections. These things widen my network and put me in touch with other ways of thinking, where people may come from a different perspective, which is going to help me be better at what I do.

Then I have a deeper understanding and a broader perspective. One thing leads to another. I had the opportunity to work with Mark Cuban. It was always my belief that if I wanted to get to Mark, I was sure, if I thought really hard, I would have friends who will know a friend who will get me to him. That's how I have built my career. So I think that relationships are crucial to getting you ahead.

MAINTAINING CONNECTIONS

Even though I'd been home during the pandemic and had not been on a plane for a year, and there were no industry events, I have tried to maintain communications with different individuals including journalists, retailers, and people on the brand side. I want to know what's happening. Who did you see in New York? What did you see in L.A.? What are you hearing? Having constant communication and touching base is very important. I send a lot of texts, saying I'm thinking of you, and I ask for calls.

CENTER OF INFLUENCE

If you're at the center of influence, when you walk into a room, people gravitate toward you. They know that you will be able to connect them. You will be able to deliver value. To be a center of influence, you have to have authenticity and you need to be genuine. Those are the only ways you can become that. You cannot buy it. You cannot fake it, because eventually people will see through it.

Apparently, I'm a center of influence. Even without the Cosmoprof name, I'm still on several boards, and I get regular calls when new companies get created. When people want connections, I feel like I'm the 411 office because I always get hit up.

DEEP DOWN HABITS

It's wanting to do my best, which is hard because I have very high standards, and sometimes it's challenging for others to understand and keep up. In a way, that makes it harder to be part of a team because you keep driving and striving for a higher level, whereas some people are just complacent.

With the pandemic, I tried to be a bit more mindful. So I started trying to meditate more regularly because when you lack a regular routine I felt my mind was so scattered. With events not happening, it's like where am I? What am I doing right?

I try to work out regularly because I feel like it makes me feel better about myself and that helps with my outlook. I try to read something every day. I think keeping up with what's happening in the industry is important. In terms of product project management, I have these mile markers. I ask myself, where am I compared to where I need to be?

IF I COULD START ALL OVER AGAIN...

I always say that even mistakes are learning experiences, and you need those to become who you are. The person I am today is because I've had some things happen to me that I may not be proud of, but they defined me, made me kinder, and more humble. I think that my journey served me well.

ONE DEFINING MOMENT

Professionally, my defining moment was starting to work in the trade show business because it exposed me to a life of purpose and wanting to help others, and I loved it.

MY GREATEST INFLUENCER

It was my dad, who sacrificed everything to come to the States, to a country where he didn't speak the language. He had to work really hard, physical work that he never had to do in Romania and he did it for me. I was an only child and he wanted me to have a better life.

And now that's part of the reason why I'm always wanting to be better and to do better so that I can make him feel proud. I still like learning from him. He is very hard-headed and very determined. And when he sets on the path, it's like he's unleashed. I look up to that because I'm a bit softer and more accepting. I also forgive people that do me wrong. I don't hold grudges. I respect him because he's very much about, "You did that to me, so now you're in this category, out of my life." So, I want to be that way. I love that about him. He's very determined.

Daniela Ciocan is the Founder/CEO of Access Beauty Insiders, a company created as a joint venture partnership with TARSUS MEDIA GROUP UK. A two-time winner of Trade Show Executive's "Marketing Genius Award", Daniela is credited with growing the COSMOPROF NORTH AMERICA annual tradeshow from infancy to become one of the most awarded exhibitions in the country, continuously listed as one of America's "50 Fastest Growing" and "Top 100 Gold Shows" by Trade Show Executive and TSNN with over 1,400 exhibitors and 40,000+ attendees from across the globe. Actively involved in the industry, Daniela serves as a board member for CEW (Cosmetic Executive Women) and IBA (Independent Beauty Association), providing regular content to B2B magazines and thought leadership insights to national media outlets such as VICE, Forbes, Yahoo News and NewBeauty.

E-mail: Daniela@accessbeautyinsiders.com
Instagram: @danielamciocan

SUCCESS FACTOR 4:
FORM TRUSTED PARTNERSHIPS

"Trust is the glue of life. It's the most
essential ingredient in effective communication.
It's the foundational principle
that holds all relationships."
—Stephen R. Covey

W HEN YOU FIRST SET FOOT in Metropolis, you knew you faced a daunting personal journey. To succeed, you had to begin with the basics, which included accepting personal responsibility for your situation and your actions. You had to be able to say, "This is my life, and I'm in charge of it, and I'll accept whatever happens as I strive to always do better."

Having embraced personal responsibility, you developed your self-reliance. You took stock of your skills, learned how to leverage them, and through simple interactions began to establish your good reputation. Your exchanges with others became more frequent and more complex, and over time, through a series of low-stakes interactions that were a "win-win" for both parties, you developed relationships. You opened a bank account and became a trusted customer, and then you took out a loan—perhaps to buy a car or even a house—and the relationship became more formal. People with whom you dealt began to trust you, and your reputation for honesty preceded you so that even if people didn't know you personally, they could verify your reputation with others.

Now you're ready to take the next step up, from maintaining successful relationships to forming trusted partnerships. If successful, your sphere of influence will move you from local to regional reach.

WHAT MAKES A PARTNERSHIP

In business, partnering between companies begins when a business—Company A—seeks to accomplish a goal that is beyond the company's capability, and organic growth is not the answer. For example, a car manufacturer might say,

"We need to offer a GPS service that tells the driver his or her exact location at any moment, but we don't own a satellite, and we don't intend to enter the satellite industry." Or a movie studio might say, "We have a new superhero film in production, and we need a toy company to make the action figures and a national fast-food chain to give them away."

With a goal in mind, Company A looks around among the other companies that could become trusted partners. The potential partner—Company B—needs to have a good reputation and products or services that are compatible and align well with Company A's customers. (If they have the same customer base, they need to be selling products that are complementary, not directly competitive.) Talks ensue, and if common ground is reached, then a deal is made, and the companies create a new product, promote one another, bundle offerings, plan customer events—whatever the joint venture calls for.

When a good match is made, a key element in any successful partnership is the commitment and ability to "stay the course"—that is, follow a strategic plan long enough to bring it to fruition. Too often, business partnerships collapse prematurely because one of the partners doesn't have the stability or resources necessary to carry out the mission.

In its simplest form, the salient characteristics of a partnership comprise three shared concepts: common purpose, value, and reward.

COMMON PURPOSE

Every partnership needs a "why"—a reason to come together and jointly pursue a common goal. It could be developing a cross-marketing campaign with trusted business partners or even launching a company together. While they share their goal, the partners should bring different talents to the table. In business especially, there's no point in having a partnership of two people who have the exact same skill set. Generally, one person tends to be more creative while the other is more pragmatic. Such was the case with Larry Page and Sergey Brin, who met at Stanford University. Page had the idea for a World Wide Web search engine that could rank links based on how often they were being linked by other pages. Brin helped make it a reality, and in 1996 they launched PageRank, which they later renamed Google.

Another partnership example is the story about Ben Cohen and Jerry Greenfield. They were childhood friends from Merrick, New York. While Greenfield finished college, Cohen dropped out of school. Looking for something to do, in 1977, they both completed a correspondence course on ice cream making from Pennsylvania State University's creamery. This was their shared interest. But

Cohen had severe anosmia—a lack of a sense of smell or taste—and so relied on "mouthfeel" and texture to provide variety in his diet. Clearly, he wasn't going to be responsible for the *flavors* of Ben & Jerry's Ice Cream! The partnership worked, and in April 2000, they sold the global company to Unilever for $326 million.

THE VALUE EACH BRINGS TO THE PARTNERSHIP

Partners share the workload. The most well-rounded pairs recognize their individual limitations and respect what the other brings to the partnership.

Perhaps two of the most famous business partners in history are Steve Jobs and Steve Wozniak, who in 1976 founded Apple Computer. They had become friends at a summer job in 1970. Wozniak was building a computer, and Jobs saw the potential to sell it.

In a 2006 interview with *The Seattle Times*, Wozniak explained, "I was just doing something I was very good at, and the thing that I was good at turned out to be the thing that was going to change the world.... Steve was much more, further-thinking. When I designed good things, sometimes he'd say, 'We can sell this.' And we did. He was thinking about how you build a company, maybe even then he was thinking, 'How do you change the world?'"[11]

Sometimes, a partner can join the founder during the company's emergent phase and propel the effort to new heights. Such was the case when Sheryl Sandburg joined Facebook. The company had been founded in 2004 by Mark Zuckerberg and some college friends as a cool social media site, but he didn't know how to monetize it. In 2007, with Facebook growing rapidly, Zuckerberg met Sandberg at a Christmas party. While he had no formal search for a chief operating officer (COO), he thought of Sandberg as "a perfect fit" for the role. In March 2008, she left Google and joined Facebook.

In September 2009, Facebook announced it had achieved positive cash flow for the first time.

In asking Sandberg to join Facebook, Zuckerberg knew he was partnering with someone with much more business experience than he had. He was twenty-four years old, while she was thirty-nine and an industry veteran. "When I look at my friends who are running other good companies," Zuckerberg said on "Masters of Scale," the podcast hosted by LinkedIn Co-founder Reid Hoffman, "The single biggest difference that I see in whether the companies end up becoming really great and reaching their potential or just pretty good is whether

---

11 https://www.businessinsider.com/10-successful-cofounders-and-why-
their-partnerships-worked#steve-jobs-and-steve-wozniak-3

they're comfortable and really self-confident enough to have people who are stronger than them around them."[12]

REWARD

Here's where the "trust" component of a partnership is tested. A hallmark of a true partnership is the sharing of the rewards. (It also can include the sharing of risk, which I'll address in the next section.) The sharing need not be 50/50, but it needs to be clearly spelled out in advance of any rewards being available—namely, at the moment of the first investment, whether of time or money.

The primary causes of partnership disagreements are disputes about financial rights and obligations. They generally arise when the company is undergoing financial stress, and without clarity in the partnership agreement about how profits will be shared and liabilities handled, serious problems among the owners may occur.

A perceived misuse of assets for personal use is a common source of financial disputes between partners. For example, one partner may think it's fine to use company funds to pay for a home remodeling, while the other does not.

Partnerships between family relatives can work well, as shown by the relatively harmonious history of the Walton family, which controls the vast Walmart business empire. But too often, such partnerships are marred by a lack of trust and acrimonious accusations. For example, in 1935, S. Prestley Blake and his brother Curtis Blake used a $547 loan from their parents to open a small ice cream shop in their hometown of Springfield, Massachusetts. Due to their rigorous work ethic, Friendly Ice Cream was a success: One brother worked nights making ice cream, and the other ran the shop during the day. In the following years, the brothers opened more locations. Curtis focused on finding personnel and training them to be family-friendly, while Pres, as he was called, focused on finance, sales, and other hardcore business matters.

They decided who would be president of the company by flipping a coin. Curtis won.

For decades, the relationship between the Blake brothers fit their restaurant's image, which in 1989 was renamed Friendly's. But in 2007, following pressure from an activist investor, the board hired Goldman Sachs to help it explore a possible sale. Pres, who was then ninety-two years old, supported the sale, while Curtis, age eighty-nine, vehemently opposed it. In reference to his brother, Curtis told *The Boston Globe*, "I'm very disappointed. He was my best friend for

---

12   https://fairygodboss.com/articles/why-mark-zuckerberg-hired-sheryl-sandberg

eighty-five years. It would have been a nice story if we ended up best friends for our entire life."[13]

Sadly, the company struggled in the twenty-first century, and its network shrank from a total of 500 restaurants to about 150 by 2019. In November 2020, citing the impact of the COVID-19 pandemic in the United States, Friendly's announced that it would file for Chapter 11 and sell "substantially all its assets" to Amici Partners—an affiliate of Brix Holdings—for a mere $2 million.

Because this book is not about the mind-numbing intricacies of the laws governing corporate behavior, let's get back to your goal of establishing and increasing your influence among the citizens of Metropolis. As you develop relationships with influential people—business leaders, politicians, cultural icons—you'll have opportunities to enter into a partnership with one or more of them, in which you'll have a formal or legal relationship and commitment to work together in a shared interest, with shared effort, and enjoy a shared reward while shouldering shared responsibilities.

If and when you have the opportunity to forge a partnership, here's how you need to approach it.

ENTERING INTO A PARTNERSHIP: THE 10 FOUNDATIONS

Here are the ten foundations for a successful partnership of any kind. For the purposes of this discussion, I'm using "partner" in the singular form, as if the partnership consisted of you and one other person; but the same rules apply if you have three, four, or more partners.

1. SHARE THE SAME VISION

For a partnership to be successful, both parties involved must agree on the same strategic direction for the company. Each must be excited about reaching a specific goal or breaking new ground. "Making lots of money" is not a sufficient vision. You must delineate how you intend to bring *value* to your customers or marketplace.

2. SEE THE BIGGER PICTURE

When you first landed in Metropolis, seeing the big picture and planning a year or more ahead was not your priority. Your task was to get to know your immediate surroundings, survive day to day, meet people who could help you build your life, and provide the basics for yourself. Your sphere of influence was zero. Since then, you've developed a local sphere of influence. When forming

13   https://www.bostonglobe.com/business/2007/03/18/feuding-friendly/IB6A4RJwSGo5yq4xI82GCJ/story.html

a partnership—for any reason—the implication is that you have a long-term result in mind. You're seeing a path forward, beyond today. You're able to grasp how things work in your community and how they might work in the future. If you and your partner do *X,* then the future result will be *Y.*

3. DETERMINE THE PARTNERSHIP STRUCTURE

The partnership structure can be informal with both parties retaining independence, in which case no legal business structure is required. Both parties may choose to establish a formal, legal partnership. In this case the structure you choose for your business will determine how you and your partner pay taxes for the business.

If you're going to be doing business under a name other than your own, most states require you to register that name, also known as a "doing business as" name or "DBA." To register, you'll need to fill out a form and submit it, along with a filing fee, to your state agency in charge of business filings.

4. THE PARTNERSHIP AGREEMENT

It is simple to set up a general partnership because there are no legal documents to file. Because it's so easy, a partnership is often nothing more than an oral agreement between two or more parties. Even though they are legally binding, in case of disagreements, purely oral agreements can present problems. You should avoid them by drawing up a partnership agreement.

According to the Small Business Administration (SBA), your partnership agreement should include the following:

- Description of the type and nature of the business
- Amount of equity invested by each partner
- How profits and shortfalls will be shared
- Partners' pay and other compensation, such as bonuses
- Policies of decision-making
- Restrictions regarding authority and expenditures
- Parameters of a dispute settlement clause
- Exit strategy and the distribution of assets upon dissolution of the business
- Provisions for changes to the partnership or for dissolving the partnership
- Settlement of the business in case of death or incapacitation
- Expected duration of the partnership

5. CLEARLY DEFINE BUSINESS ROLES AND RESPONSIBILITIES

Because a successful business partnership leverages the strengths and skills of each partner, business roles must be apportioned according to each individual's strengths. For example, if one partner is strong in product design and marketing, and the other partner excels in sales and finance, then split those tasks accordingly.

Remember that in a general partnership, each partner has sole authority to enter into contracts on behalf of the entire partnership. For example, if your partner is responsible for distribution, he or she could enter a contract with a wholesaler without bothering to confer with you. You should define this ability with an agreement specifying that both (or two or more) partners must agree. By agreeing who can make these kinds of decisions, you mitigate the risk of conflicts down the road.

6. AVOID THE EQUAL SPLIT

With just two partners, it may seem logical and fair to equally split decision-making, input, and profit-sharing. However, this can lead to a stalemate when you can't come to a compromise. You may want to develop a mechanism to resolve differences.

If this is not possible, then consider using an outside source to analyze the situation and give their opinion for a course of action. If needed, get more than one opinion.

I'll discuss partnership financing in more detail in the pages ahead.

7. CREATE A WAY TO SETTLE DISPUTES

Not many people will agree with each other one hundred percent of the time, and there will be occasional conflicts. As onerous as it may seem—not unlike a prenuptial agreement when you get married—you should plan how you are going to handle disputes, not only with each other but with suppliers, employees, customers, or any other stakeholders. You might want to include a mandatory arbitration clause in your partnership agreement and the contracts you make with other entities.

Another option is the activation of a buy-out clause, allowing one partner to resolve the deadlock vote by purchasing another member's partnership interest.

8. HOLD PARTNER MEETINGS

A strong business partnership is built on open communication. Meet on a regular basis so you can analyze your daily operations, share constructive criticism, review roles, and discuss your strategic plan for the growth or direction of your business.

9. MANAGE GROWTH

Hopefully, as you and your partner work together, your business will grow over time. As your business grows, you may want to readdress your partnership agreement. You may need to hire employees, add more partners, and include expansion agreements.

You could include this in your initial agreement, but it might be better to wait until you are in a position to consider growth and expansion.

10. STAY THE COURSE

The success of the partnership depends upon both parties sticking with the venture until its completion. This does not mean being inflexible or rigid—quite the opposite. If you've ever sailed a boat or flown an airplane, you know that if you set out from your home base and aim for a faraway destination, you'll begin by charting a straight line. After you set off, the wind and the current—the changing conditions in your environment—will alter your course. You'll need to re-chart your course, and perhaps change direction, to get to your destination. You may have to do this several times.

Recall the ill-fated Apollo 13 mission, which was launched from Kennedy Space Center on April 11, 1970. Two days into the mission, an oxygen tank in the service module (SM) failed. Suddenly, the mission's goal was changed from landing on the Moon to one that was more urgent and fundamental: Orbit the Moon and return the three astronauts safely to Earth. The people at Mission Control, using primitive computers and slide rules, as well as imaginative problem-solving, made the adjustments, and on April 17, the craft splashed down. They truly "stayed the course" and turned a potential disaster into a success.

CULTIVATING TRUSTED PARTNERSHIPS

As you become more comfortable in Metropolis, build your reputation, and develop relationships, your sphere of vision will expand from what's immediately around you to the bigger picture. Having mastered the basics of survival, you'll see how people are interconnected and who wields influence. While you constantly make new connections (this process will never stop) and develop lasting relationships based on successful transactions or mutual interests, you'll learn there's a difference between people who are connections and those with whom you have a special relationship.

From the steady stream of new connections, over time, a handful of them will become special or strategic. They will fall into the category of *trusted partner*. These are the relationships with whom you have regular contact, and you can work with not just formally, as in a business partnership, but in an informal and committed partner-type relationship.

To become trusted partners, *Figure 6.1* identifies 6 foundational building blocks a trusted partnership must contain:

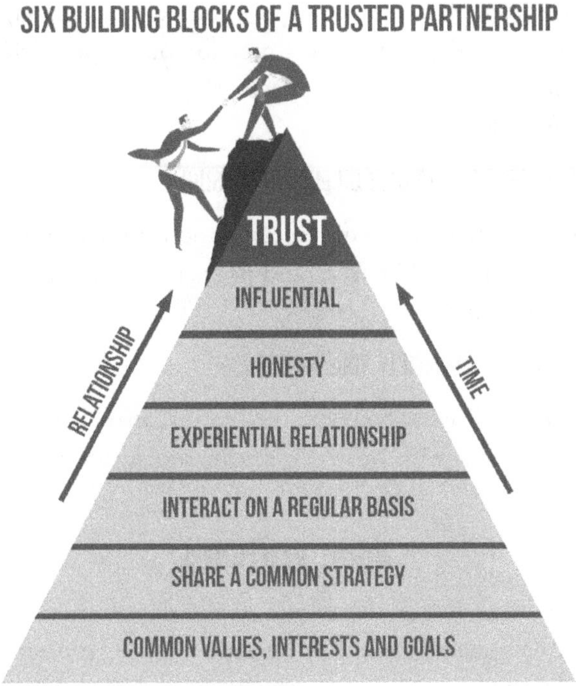

SIX BUILDING BLOCKS OF A TRUSTED PARTNERSHIP

Figure 6.1

SIX BUILDING BLOCKS OF A TRUSTED PARTNERSHIP

1. COMMON VALUES

Have common values, interests and goals. This usually occurs naturally, because people gravitate towards others who share similar interests.

2. SHARE A COMMON STRATEGY

In a partnership with a common goal, problems can arise when partners disagree on how to *reach* their goal.

3. INTERACT ON A REGULAR BASIS

While the interactions need not be high stakes, they should be of substance—that is, not just sitting at the same table at a meeting, or passing each other in the hallway. Meetings should be engaging and have a sense of purpose and value to each person.

4. HAVE A RELATIONSHIP THAT CONTAINS EXPERIENCES OVER TIME

Unless you have ironclad assurance from a mutual connection, it's unwise to make someone a trusted partner who's new to you. Experiential relationships mean two parties engage in activities, developing a higher sense of comfort regarding a working relationship.

5. EXHIBIT HONESTY AND AUTHENTICITY ON EVERY OCCASION

People who are dishonest will be dishonest for no reason, or for a trivial reason. It's just in their operating DNA. You need partners who are scrupulously honest every minute of every day.

6. INFLUENTIAL - BE ABLE TO MULTIPLY YOUR INFLUENCE

In the next chapter I'll talk about the concept of "marrying up," and why it's always better to partner with people who can add to your growing sphere of influence.

JOINT VENTURES

Joint ventures are short-term or long-term partnerships formed by two individuals, companies, or organizations. The purpose may be to create and exploit a marketing agreement to cooperate in business, bundle product offerings, or promote each other's brands.

For example, in June 2012, Microsoft Corporation and General Electric announced a 50-50 joint venture called Caradigm. The objective was to improve patient experience and the economics of health and wellness by providing the health system with advanced system wide data and intelligence. The name "Caradigm" evolved from "care" and "paradigm" because the two global giants intended a paradigm shift in the system of healthcare delivery.

The Caradigm board of directors and leadership team was composed of executives from both parent companies. "The combination of people and technology from GE Healthcare and Microsoft will allow us to drive the dramatic change that is needed in healthcare," said CEO Michael Simpson, who came from GE Healthcare. "By forming Caradigm, we can offer innovative healthcare solutions, including an open platform and tools that enable software developers around the world to address the complexities of population health today."[14]

Joint ventures are often preceded by personal networking and the nurturing of relationships that are non-competitive and where the products or services perfectly align and complement each other.

Two business owners, business professionals, solopreneurs, or entrepreneurs can have informal but strategic partnerships based upon trust and history with each other. Let's call them "trusted partners." Of all the hundreds of connections you might have, you would reserve only a handful of spots for strategic and trusted partners. These partnerships agree to endorse each other's company. They may introduce each other at customer events or even promote each other's products as part of a bundled solution. They are not necessarily based upon legal agreements but strong and tested strategic relationships.

Not every joint venture succeeds.

THE RISE AND FALL OF INTEGRION FINANCIAL NETWORK

At the dawn of the internet era, the banking industry realized that online banking was going to be the wave of the future, and they needed to get on the bandwagon. In March 1997, sixteen big banks and computer giant IBM announced the launch of Integrion Financial Network, an online banking service. At the heart of the network was the Gold Standard for Electronic Financial Services platform, as the Integrion system was called, which was designed to offer a wide variety of services over the telephone, personal computer, automatic teller machine, and the internet. Integrion had access to a powerful customer base, counting among its sixteen members half of the retail banking population in North America.

Sounds good! The problem? Too many chefs in the kitchen.

As *American Banker* reported, the consortium was unwieldy from the start. Marquee members included IBM, Visa USA, Bank of America Corp., Bank One Corp., Citibank, First Union Corp., Royal Bank of Canada, and Wells Fargo & Co. Other heavyweights included ABN AMRO Holdings NV, Comerica Inc., Fleet Financial Group Inc., Liberty Mutual, Mellon Bank Corp., Michigan National Corp., PNC Bank Corp., and US Bancorp. Each company initially contributed $4 million to the consortium's internet banking and e-bill efforts.

Analysts quickly pointed out the unlikely partnering of obvious competitors. Integrion insiders agreed, and within a month underwent restructuring.

---

14 Microsoft. https://news.microsoft.com/2012/06/06/
microsoft-and-ge-healthcare-complete-joint-venture-agreement/

Several member banks left the partnership's management and investor side, while remaining as customers.

David Fortney, chief development officer at Integrion, admitted, "It's hard to build a consensus when you're dealing with twenty companies. Winnowing down our member base left us in a much better position to react to the marketplace we compete in and make better decisions. Having lots of owners is a great idea until you try fitting them all into a boardroom."[15]

By 1999, the company was still not performing as well as hoped. Integrion was supposed to have had one million people using its services but had only about 807,000, with fully half of them coming from Visa Interactive, which Integrion had bought in 1997.

As ZDNet reported, just five banks used Integrion's services to offer online banking. Even though experts said a restructuring was likely, Integrion denied it was in trouble. "We're going to be a player going forward, and we're going to be a strong player," said Emily Mendell, a manager of planning at Integrion. But she did admit the group was considering "making some revisions."

Lots of powerful partners with competing interests made the joint venture precarious. Some Integrion members began to hedge their bets. Citibank became a part-owner of Transpoint, a Microsoft-backed bill presentment venture. Brian Maimone, a senior analyst at Furman Selz, stated, "Banks want to make sure they don't have all their investment in one model."[16] In March 2000, *Computerworld* reported that Integrion was folding "after continued turmoil in its management ranks."[17] The platform's services were handed over to the member banks.

---

15   American Banker https://www.americanbanker.com/news/high-times-for-integrion

16   ZDNet.com. https://www.zdnet.com/article/dissension-hits-net-banking-alliance/

17   Computerworld. https://www.computerworld.com/article/2592491/online-banking-group-dissolves.html

SUCCESS ACTION ITEMS – FORM TRUSTED PARTNERSHIPS

- Be agile. You must have a plan, but you must also be willing to modify it as conditions change. For this, you need a close working relationship with your trusted partner.

  Now you're ready to take the next step up, from maintaining successful relationships to forming trusted partnerships. If successful, your sphere of influence will move you from local to regional reach.

- Choose the right partnerships. The potential partner needs to have a good reputation and products or services that are compatible and align well with those of your clients. A key element in any successful partnership is the commitment and ability to "stay the course" that is, follow a strategic plan long enough to bring it to fruition.

- Have a clear and concise mission and vision statement. This is especially important with joint ventures because you may have two organizations that have their own missions and may even be in different industries, so the mutual goal must be crystal clear.

- Follow these three concepts to provide the best opportunity for a partnership to succeed.

  1. Common purpose. Every partnership needs a "why"—a reason to come together and jointly pursue a common goal.
  2. Value each brings to the partnership. The most well-rounded pairs recognize their individual limitations and respect what the other brings to the partnership.
  3. Reward. A hallmark of a true partnership is the sharing of the rewards equitably.

- Cultivate trusted partnerships. From the steady stream of new connections, over time a handful of them will become special or strategic. They will fall into the category of *trusted partner*.

- Qualify a trusted partnership by stipulating the following requirements:

  - Have common values, interests and goals,
  - Share a common strategy
  - Interaction of substance on a regular basis.
  - Have an experiential relationship over time.
  - Exhibit honesty on every occasion.

Each is capable of multiplying the other's influence through introductions into new circles of influence.

BRIAN J. ESPOSITO
CEO ESPOSITO INTELLECTUAL ENTERPRISES, LLC

*"I Succeed by Helping Others
Solve Problems."*

THE FIXER

LIKE TO BE THE PERSON we all call "the fixer." When people used to call me with a problem, I used to laugh and say, "If you're calling me, you really must have nowhere to go." But then I quickly realized it was something I was good at, so maybe in this new world, with all the experience that I have, I could be a problem-solver for them, and that could be my value. There's nothing better than word of mouth and somebody saying, "All you need to do is call Brian to get that resolved." Or, "Hey, call Brian. He'll find a solution for you." Many of the intros and momentum I've had were people having an issue and not knowing where to go, and I was the one to be able to give them a path to succeed or a path to fix that problem.

You rely on your strengths. In my case, people can come to me, and I'm willing and able to help them solve their problem.

At the beginning, I have no expectations. My nature is to help people, but also, I think because of my persona or the air I give, people are very comfortable telling me things. It used to be awkward in the past. I'd be like, "Why is this person telling me their deepest, darkest secrets or problems?"

I don't judge. I don't make fun of people. People feel safe around me. That can turn into the feeling that there's a reason I'm in this moment. This person feels obligated to tell me things, and I'm not a psychiatrist, and I'm not asking them any questions. They're just pouring it out. So as it relates to business and meeting other people, it's great to have the ability to make someone comfortable telling me a problem. They don't feel insecure about it, and they don't feel like their privacy or ego is wiped away.

They also know that with me, it stays with me. If someone asks me about somebody else, I say, "Well, ask them. That's their story to tell. I'm not writing an autobiography about them. If you want to find out what they're doing or who they are and they want to tell you, that's up to them. That's not my role."

One of my character flaws—or traits, is that I believe everybody's inherently good and that people will do the right things. So, if I'm there helping them, and I don't have expectations or ulterior motives, and they sense that I appreciate their values and morals, I believe they'll do the right thing.

HOW I'D SURVIVE IN A NEW LAND WITH LITTLE MONEY AND NO CONNECTIONS

If I were stepping off the boat into the city of Metropolis, and I knew no one, then the dollars in my pocket might be irrelevant, so I won't even bring them out until I learn the basis of the local economy and what type of commerce they find valuable. For all I know, it could be bartering.

I'd have to find out with whom I could immediately communicate. I'd find out who speaks English to help me get a good foundation as to where I can begin to work. Obviously, I'd need shelter, food, water, and some clothes, or at least a place to wash the clothes that I have. So I'd have to get the easiest, quickest job I could, just to have a place to go, and have value for myself, where I have a purpose in that new land. I wouldn't care what the job was. If it were digging holes twelve hours a day, I would do that, but until I understood what the need was on that land and how I could help, I would probably have to start at the bottom. It would be just like going into any business with no relationships, or going into any corporate job without having a lead-in or the proper degree, like starting in the mailroom somewhere. I probably would just use that as a basis as a foundation.

But knowing what I've done over the last twenty years, I would quickly adapt and grow. I'm not phony about anything. I'm going to always be me. If I have to speak a different language, then I just have to figure out how to be me.

Building a reputation is important. I always ask, how do I add value to what's already there? My goal isn't to take the resources or the opportunities given to me and put them in my pocket. My goal is to say, "I'm here to help. I want to add value."

I want to increase whatever it is—building awareness or creating new revenue. That's just how I'm wired. I want to add value. I want to create win-wins for everybody, and I would just carry that over into this new land. I think that mindset is very basic, but in today's world, it's few and far between. The majority of people are looking out for themselves, and I get that, but you can't really build long-term relationships if you're not bringing something to the table. And hopefully, in my case now, I'm bringing more than I'm getting back.

The first thing is to show up. If I say I'm going to do something, then I want to do more than I say I'm going to do. Just show up! Back my words with actions, and obviously be reliable.

INFLUENCERS

I hope that the word "influencer" will once again have a more long-term impact and meaning. It's been watered down a lot. For example, an influencer today is like a celebrity promoting a cosmetic brand on social media, and she sells fifty thousand lipsticks as an influencer, that is in the moment.

I love the word, and I like the idea that someone of substance with some kind of reach and awareness is able to make a change. And hopefully, it's something that they really believe in. For the majority of influencers, the problem lies with money. The problem lies with the manager of that celebrity or actor, entertainer, influencer. And with many people, their core value idea was to really make an impact, and then all of a sudden, it gets diluted in continuously making money because their manager or their agent has to get their ten percent. So they're forcing new things down their throats, and people/influencers lose themselves.

The idea of what is today's influencer is just a mess. One day they're promoting something here, the next day, they're promoting something there, and there's no consistency in their messaging for the most part.

I think we need a new word. The idea of someone believing in something so dearly, and they'll put all of their resources, talents, relationships, and fans or supporters behind it, and making a long-term impact or a long-term change. Not something for an immediate financial reward or result.

STRATEGIC INFLUENCERS

The way I operate, a strategic influencer is somebody who's in it for the long-term and knows it's not going to be easy. It's something not a lot of people are dedicating time or resources to because it all depends on the strategy that makes it a success. A strategic influencer is someone who will have a legacy behind them. It's something that they're putting in place that their kids and their grand-kids will continue with the drive.

I think having a strategy around it means it's worthy of your time to sit down and understand what needs to be done and how you're going to accomplish it, whether it takes a day or ten years. The idea of having a strategy means that it's something you're going to give all you got, and it's not like the quick mention or the quick press release that makes you look good for a moment. It's something that you really live and breathe.

Strategic is where the person who needs your influence, your connection, and your introduction to the right people, and where you, as the influencer, need to be a good fit. On the flip side, there's the influencer who is being asked by hundreds of people, and they've only got so much time.

Your network is your bloodline. It's about who you are and obviously about the value that you bring to the network as a whole. If you have the confidence to bring a coveted relationship into the mix, that has to make sense. You can't bring somebody into an idea that you want to get behind and make a change or an impact if their vision and what they do with either their own company or their own network or one of their holdings isn't in alignment. You can't create hypocrisy, so you've got to be very strategic as to what relationships you bring into that. Otherwise, you're obviously risking your network.

You have to believe in it so much that you're going to go out and bring in people on whom you depend, and you call friends, allies, and business partners and ask them to be part of it. Now is when you're putting yourself at risk. Because of your relationship, they're going to feel obligated that they have to, if the relationship is that important to them. You want to make sure that they're in it for the right reasons. If you bring the right people into it with the right resources, and the higher level you are in life, and you have access to certain inner circles, it's pretty amazing the awareness and the attention you can get.

INTEGRITY AND RELATIONSHIPS

You build long-term success by building a magnet for people to come to you. When you build that magnet, it needs to have a filtering process because both good and bad people will be drawn to you. So it's really important to have a good radar and life experiences to know which people you want to work with and which people you don't.

I'm thankful for being older now, not because of the experiences, but because I feel by your mid-to-late twenties, you are who you are. And maybe you can change a little bit, or maybe you can see God in your life from a life and death situation. But when I meet an adult, and they have values or morals or questionable characteristics, it's not my job to fix them. I'm not a priest. I'm not here to help them become a better person, but it is my job not to let them impact my network and my relationships.

As we get older and become more experienced in life, when you meet somebody who has questionable maneuvers, you've got to run away. There's no need to have their life impact the good that you're trying to surround yourself with. You only need one good person in your corner to really do amazing things, and if you have more than one, then you are extremely lucky. That's why I say it's all about integrity and relationships, and work on getting one good person at a time, and then you have a really powerful army behind you.

CENTER OF INFLUENCE

Being a center of influence means you're an authority in that space. People come to you for direction. They come to you for resources. They come to you obviously because they want to work with you. You become a target. You really become an exploitation target, too, for people to use you as that center of influence for their benefit.

You're a hub and spoke. It's just like a cell tower—everybody comes to you for the connectivity tissue that allows them to be in the world that you created.

You cultivate relationships with centers of influence directly to them. That's where it gets tough, where it gets stopped, because it needs to be direct to direct. If they are a celebrity or athlete, for example, it can't be through management because then it's a financial component, and it has the wrong foundation.

If you want to be connected to the center of influence, to someone you want to do good things with, and you want to work with, then you must have patience and maneuver through the handlers and all the people who have their hands out that benefit from you and that person.

That money the manager of an influencer wants to take, whether they earn that or not, is money that's taken out of the pie that could actually do good. I'd love to get statistics on how many managers, agents, representatives, accountants, and lawyers put money back into the focuses of those centers of influence. I'm sure it's not a lot. I'm sure when they get their money, they go and buy a car. They are going to offer nice dinners, but I'm sure the money's not going back, and I'm sure a majority of the money's not going back into the pie.

You don't want to have to pay to get introduced to someone. It needs to be more organic. It can be through a trusted friend—someone who trusts you and can introduce you. It's got to be direct. That's from my experience.

Another center of influence can be a direct contact who can introduce you. I used to sell nail polish, and everything in the world that I live in now it's continuing to grow my career, and your reputation is everything. I've always done what I said I was going to do, including becoming a trusted friend and partner to many incredible companies and people. So the larger your network gets, the smaller the world gets, so that's why you must have patience. Just like most great real estate deals get done principal-to-principal. They don't get done with a bunch of agents or law firms in the middle. The best deals get done with one person and the other person because they know how to create value. I've seen so many great deals dissipate because of greedy brokers, greedy go-betweens, greedy success fees, and it's appalling the mentality that there are people in this world who would rather get nothing than a little smaller percentage.

DEEP DOWN HABITS

Personally, I don't consider myself to be a center of influence. Others may disagree. But I have some deep-down habits that I've developed over the years that have helped me to become successful.

Working twenty-four hours a day and always being accessible has led to a successful business side, but also to an unsuccessful personal side. So, it's being successful when there is a problem. You know, you succeed by diving headfirst into it and fixing it, not going into the corner in a fetal position and crying like a lot of people do. I've been faced with so many problems, more than the average, it seems, for whatever reason. It's just the cards I get dealt.

One of the things that I've got to get better at—and again, that's the sacrifice on the personal side—is when I hear someone say, "I can't make that meeting. I've got to take my daughter to swim class," my head wants to explode. Hey, I think, don't say that. Take care of your family. Family's first, I get that, but when I've taken the time to set up a meeting to get fifteen people involved, a meeting that you've agreed to, and now we have to go back to everybody and reschedule it because you suddenly announce you've got to take your child to swim class—well, you're not going to succeed with that mentality. And that's fine; you may be happy with where you are in life, and you're complacent, and I may be very envious of you, but don't mess up my world or waste my time when I'm here trying to help you, and I put all these pieces together, and then I've got to hear that's your reason to cancel. The comfort some people have with the idea that it's okay in business to do that is why there is so much confusion going on. And for me, I'm glad, because the more confusion, the better opportunities are for me, because I'll go out there and pick up all the pieces that people are not properly managing or cultivating, and I say, yeah, fine, keep operating like that, because I'll just keep winning.

IF I COULD START ALL OVER AGAIN

I've learned how to monetize myself, and I'm the value; that may sound arrogant, but for fifteen years of my life, I did not monetize myself because I didn't understand how you put a price on yourself. But now, I see things differently. I know I can create opportunities in a flash that have real value and can get real traction behind them. And I've done that my whole career. But for years, I did it and let other people flourish. I did it and watched major deals get done, and I had no part of the outcome even though I was a key spoke in the wheel during that process.

If I had to start over today, I would continue to do what I've learned, to monetize myself, create value, use my network, and use my relationships. It's crazy what you can accomplish if you know A and B, and you want to make Z. It's great, but the only way you get to do that is if people subscribe to you and trust you. That's why it goes back to your character and your integrity.

ONE DEFINING MOMENT

In February 2016, I got into a bad car accident. I shouldn't have walked away from that accident. It made me realize that I was here for a reason.

I had maybe thirty percent of the companies and the holdings that I have now. But it was my world, and when I was taken out and incapacitated, I realized I had the wrong people involved and running, maintaining, and managing those situations and those companies. Everything fell apart. My whole world turned upside down, and this is where I had a choice as a human being.

One choice was to be angry and bitter and get nowhere. Or since that gets nowhere, have all the current problems, and be angry and bitter on top of it did not seem like a smart formula.

The second choice was to figure it out. Salvage what I could salvage and rebuild. But the most disheartening thing at the time in the business world was that there was nobody there to help.

And there were people whom I had helped create enormous companies. There were employees for whom I had co-signed, on homes to help them get cars, and I was overly generous to them; at that moment, I realized, well, maybe you really are in this world by yourself. In the business world, it really may be kill or be killed, but how do I do that with a smile? How do I do that and still be me? How can I do it now, without hurting anybody in the process?

THE ONE CRITICAL RELATIONSHIP

My greatest influencer was my dad.

I've met a lot of incredible people. If we're going to say money is success—and that's not how I think, but I've met a lot of billionaires, and I'm in a lot of those circles—to me, they could have one dollar in their pocket or billion. I don't care. I'm always being myself, but I love the fact that I've earned the ability to be in those rooms, and it's just the same feeling over and over again with those people. I'm honored and privileged to be in that room, so there's not one of them that I sat back and said, "Well, I'm like a sponge, and I want to soak up what they know." No, because I look at them as equals. I know I can do what they've done. I just have that feeling.

But when it comes to my pops, I've always tried to emulate the positive side of him, and what I felt I wanted to be, so I'm always trying to grab those features and characteristics, whether I naturally have them or I wanted to emulate them. And it was everybody taking his calls and everybody calling him back that I admired, as well as his ability to be the center of a room and attention. He always wanted to help people, but I'd always see people hurting him, and that's one of the reasons why I didn't want to get bitter or angry because you know, I've seen what life has done to him, and it would chip away at his soul every time he has had his hand out to help people, and it got bitten. So again, how do you be who you are and not shift into the dark side?

He's been my biggest influence. Obviously, as a son and father relationship, you want to make your father proud. That's just natural. But there's been nobody. I wish there was somebody I could have that obsession with in the business world, but I don't.

I get this question a lot. Do you read books? Do you have any mentors? No. My mentors are the streets. Anybody can give you advice. But you have to live it, experience it.

Ranked among the World's Top 10 CEOs for 2020 in The World CEO Rankings Awards by Adria Management, LLC, Brian J. Esposito is the founder and CEO of Esposito Intellectual Enterprises, LLC, (EIE). An award-winning serial entrepreneur and business leader. In December 2019, he was featured in The Corporate Investment Times, the next-gen investment magazine in the Middle East, and in 2020 was recognized as being a member of The Top 100 Magazine for the top 100 People in Real Estate. (EIE) www.eie.rocks, a holding company for over 20 years of work, business startups, and investments. Focuses range from manufacturing, distribution, retail, hospitality & hotel development, restaurants, commercial real estate, technology, crypto, blockchain, eSports, gaming, professional sports, media, energy, oil & gas, aviation, space, maritime, esports, music, TV & Film, education, beauty, medical technology, security, hemp, fashion, and much more. Wholly owned by Brian, EIE currently has over 65 entities within it and over 150 joint ventures that have been accumulated around the world.

Website: www.eie.rocks
Twitter: www.twitter.com/brianjesposito
LinkedIn: www/linkedin.com/in/brianjesposito

PART THREE:
INFLUENCE EXPANSION AND THE END GAME

SPHERE OF LEADERSHIP

SUCCESS FACTOR 5:
ASSUME THE ROLE OF INFLUENCER

"Sometimes the greatest things are right in front of
us. Look around - opportunity awaits!"
—Unknown

W HEN YOU FIRST ARRIVED IN Metropolis, you were a newcomer with
no relationships and no partnerships. You were alone, and while you had
skills to offer, your very first interactions were with people who had more
influence than you. (They had more of just about everything than you!) For
your basic necessities, you depended on them, and for the most part, none of
them had to depend on you. Sure, the grocer was happy to take your money and
sell you bread, but if you had gone somewhere else, it wouldn't have made much
difference to him. You applied for a job, but there were probably many other
candidates from which the employer could choose. In the workforce, you were
strictly paid labor; management existed at a level higher up, and leadership still
higher.

You built relationships, but they were often lopsided. When you work for
a boss, you might have a long-lasting relationship, and even a close one; but at
the end of the day, your boss could fire you and take away your paycheck, but
you could not fire your boss and take away his paycheck. The relationship was
imbalanced.

If you had influence, it was on an *ad hoc* basis. Perhaps your boss gave you
a project, and you did it well, and you came up with a new solution. Your boss
was impressed. For that brief moment, you had influence over the outcome of
the project. But then it was back to business as usual, and your relationship
continued as employer and employee.

Some relationships were equal. You made friends or worked on projects with
colleagues. Your influence was strictly local—that is, confined to the boundaries
of the relationship.

Then you developed one or more partnerships. Here, more was at stake for each side. You saw the bigger picture and contributed to a project that required a shared interest, effort, and reward. Unlike employees, partners have *equity* and a voice in the direction of the enterprise. Your influence expanded from local to regional, meaning it became oblique, with the ability to impact people who were not directly in a relationship with you.

Having risen to that level, now you're ready to take on more autonomy, and rather than be a reflection of others around you and a follower, become a source of influence to whom others look. You are prepared to enter the Sphere of Discovery. Opportunity awaits.

CAPTAIN OF YOUR OWN SHIP

One of the hallmarks of assuming the role of influencer is that you have the capability of executive leadership, whether as the head of your own enterprise or within a larger one.

The title of this section is "Captain of Your Own Ship." At first glance, the casual reader might think, "Well, if I'm the captain, then I can do whatever I want and tell my crew—my employees—to jump at my command. I'm the boss, and it's my ship."

Not exactly!

No human is ever 100 percent influential—that is, autonomous and able to act freely in society or business, without the need to persuade others to follow along. (For the one exception, see below.) Look at it this way: As we move through life and experience its varying degrees of influence, we begin as babies with zero influence and no autonomy. We're totally dependent on our parents for everything. You might say the ratio of dependence to autonomy is 0/100. In our scenario of stepping off the boat onto the dock at Metropolis, you have some adult skills, so let's adjust the dependence/autonomy ratio to 10/90—a bit better than being an infant! You're like an ordinary deckhand on a ship at sea or a private in the army. You have some rights and some limited influence, but mostly you just follow orders.

Then, as you develop relationships, your dependence/autonomy ratio shifts incrementally, perhaps to 30/70. You have more influence in your community and some ability to shape your future. You are less dependent upon the largesse of others.

When you form partnerships, the ratio might shift to 50/50, at least as it applies to your enterprise. You're on an equal footing with your partner, and you share in the responsibilities and rewards.

Now you're entering the phase of being an influencer. As you gain more influence, the thing about the dependence/autonomy ratio is that it can *approach* 100/0—total and complete autonomy—*but it can never get there*. You will never be totally autonomous. You will always be accountable to someone.

The captain of a ship is accountable to the owners of the ship. When Christopher Columbus sailed west in 1492, he reported to King Ferdinand and Queen Isabella of Spain, who had funded the voyage. He had considerable influence over the expedition—after all, it was his idea—but the Spanish court was paying the bills. They were majority partners.

When you're the captain of the ship or the CEO of your company, you have an unwritten contract with your crew or employees. Or, more broadly, a contract with your stakeholders, who include your investors, your board, your customers, your suppliers, and your community. In exchange for the influence you wield, you pledge to act in the best interests of your stakeholders, run the company efficiently and ethically, and provide a good return on investment.

In a corporation, the chief executive officer reports to the board of directors. The board is accountable to the investors or shareholders and also to government authorities. In government, elected representatives are accountable to the voters.

The only way you can be totally autonomous and accountable to no one but yourself is to take your solo boat, with only you on board, and sail out into international waters. There, your dependence/autonomy ratio will be 100/0. On the open water, with no human interaction, you may enjoy your unlimited freedom for the remainder of your short life.

INTER-RELIANCE

American cultural mythology celebrates the loner who gets the job done all by himself, like the solitary inventor who, alone in his lab and late at night, makes great discoveries. In real life and throughout history, the greatest deeds have been accomplished by people working together toward a common goal. Each person makes a contribution, and each relies upon the other to do their part. It's the leader's job to coordinate and focus the efforts of the team.

For example, in his sprawling lab complex at Menlo Park, New Jersey, the great American inventor Thomas Edison, widely mythologized as a solitary genius, oversaw a group of several dozen assistants whom he called the "muckers."

Men fresh out of college or technical training school came from all over the US and Europe to work alongside the famous inventor, who relied upon them to build and test his ideas.

In many of our most important activities and projects, we are inter-reliant on each other. This is how it should be, for healthy inter-reliance brings strength. It's like the old-fashioned custom of barn-raising. When America was being settled, and people were establishing farms, a necessary part of every farm was a barn. Now a barn is a large structure, and you can't build one yourself. So the settler would lay out the framing for the walls, flat on the ground. Then a barn-raising would be announced, and everyone from miles around would converge on the farm and literally raise the walls into position. A good time was had by all, and at sunset, they'd head home. Then, if you got the call to a barn-raising for your neighbor, you'd reciprocate, take an afternoon off from work, and help with the project, just as you had been helped.

If you tried to build your barn alone, it would take you months to succeed, if you could do it at all. As Charles Darwin wrote, "It is the long history of humankind (and animal kind, too) that those who learned to collaborate and improvise most effectively have prevailed."

Instead of going it alone, you need to reach for more potent *synergistic* opportunities. While we all want to see ourselves as being independent, there is only so much one person can achieve. In order to soar and reach the highest levels of success and influence, you need to align yourself with other high achievers who have complementary skills and circles of influence who can help you expand your reach, your influence, and your successes. This is the essence of inter-reliance. Once you have counted the costs, put in the time, made the sacrifices, and built a powerful reputation of influence, the real opportunities reveal themselves through the positive and constructive leverage called inter-reliance. This is where exponential growth and success can happen!

UNCHARTED WATERS

As a new arrival in Metropolis, your primary task is to learn and master the existing system. You are not there to "rock the boat." You need to establish relationships within existing social and industry structures. You'll open an account at an established bank. You'll apply for a job that has familiar requirements in a company that has a track record of solvency. You'll join the ubiquitous chamber of commerce and Rotary Club. In short, you'll walk down a familiar and well-trodden path towards acceptance and increased autonomy.

When you step up to the role of influencer, you're ready to leave your apprenticeship behind and begin to affect change in the world around you. The essence of life is innovation, and in business, the rate of change is accelerating. What worked yesterday will probably not work today. Merely mastering the existing system may have been sufficient years ago, when the rate of change was much slower, but it's no longer sufficient today.

This concept can be seen in stark reality in Moore's Law. In 1965, Gordon Moore, the co-founder of Fairchild Semiconductor and CEO and co-founder of Intel, saw that digital technology and manufacturing capabilities were accelerating. He posited that the number of components per integrated circuit would double every year and projected this rate of growth would continue for at least another decade. Remember, if you double a number every year, growth is not arithmetic but exponential—2, 4, 8, 16, 32, and so on. In 1975, looking forward to the next decade, he revised the forecast to doubling every two years. Generally speaking, what has become known as Moore's Law has been accurate. It has been used successfully in the semiconductor industry to guide long-term planning and to set targets for research and development. These accelerating changes in digital electronics have been a driving force of technological and social change, productivity, and economic growth.

Every leader is in uncharted waters. While certain truisms will always hold, such as "people need food and water" and "people need to see a brighter future," the various mechanisms by which these truisms are translated into real life are constantly changing. For example, back in 1980, you would have been smart to invest in VHS home video technology. The Sony platform was ascendant, and the video rental market was exploding. Soon every town had a Videosmith or other VHS cassette rental store, where you could rent Hollywood movies and view them on your own TV set at home, whenever you wanted. It was truly an amazing new world of entertainment!

The VHS boom lasted until the digital DVD was introduced in 1997. Almost overnight, and only seventeen years after they had been introduced, clunky VHS cassettes were obsolete. The DVD was the new amazing world of entertainment!

That is, until the rise of cable streaming services. 2005 was the peak year for DVD sales, after which the decline began, spurred by platforms including Netflix, Hulu, and HBO. Today, DVDs are quaint antiques, like landline telephones and cars with manual transmissions.

Some companies, like Blockbuster Video, enter uncharted waters, eventually strike a rock, and sink. Others, like Sony and Apple, successfully navigate those same waters, and by being inter-reliant and innovative, thrive decade after decade.

ESTABLISH YOUR PERSONAL BRAND

Everyone knows about the concept of brands as it relates to products. When attached to a product or service, a brand conveys two things.

1. A GENERAL SENSE OF VALUE, QUALITY, AND INTEGRITY

We talk about some brands as being good and full of value, while about others, we say, "I wouldn't buy that product—it's cheap and shabby." A product's reputation must be built slowly, over time, as consumers learn to trust it. A brand can be easily tarnished if that trust is broken. For example, consider the Deepwater Horizon oil spill, an industrial disaster that began on April 20, 2010, in the Gulf of Mexico on the BP-operated Macondo Prospect. Considered the largest marine oil spill in the history of the petroleum industry and one of the largest environmental disasters in American history, the event was a public relations nightmare, made worse by the seemingly casual response by BP CEO Tony Hayward, who said, "I'm sorry. We're sorry for the massive disruption it's caused in their lives. There's no one who wants this over more than I do." Then he added this tone-deaf comment: "I'd like my life back." Since then, BP has spent years repairing its brand image and now positions itself as super-friendly to the environment. They've made sustainability a key part of their brand, and the effort seems sincere.

2. A BRAND POSSESSES SPECIFIC FEATURES AND DELIVERS CERTAIN BENEFITS THAT DIFFERENTIATE IT IN THE MARKETPLACE

For example, on paper, Coke and Pepsi are nearly identical. They're made of carbonated water, caramel color, sugar, and flavorings. They're sold in much the same way. But there are subtle brand differences in flavor, to which consumers are highly sensitive. Pepsi is sweeter, which is why it fares well in blind taste tests where the participant is sampling only a small amount, not the whole bottle. In the 1980s, in response to a series of such taste tests, and in an effort to lure Pepsi's younger demographic, Coca-Cola adjusted its secret recipe. On April 23, 1985, at a big press conference, Coke introduced "New Coke," designed to appeal to the Pepsi crowd. It got mixed reviews, which became worse over time. The company's network of bottlers—very important stakeholders!—saw great difficulty in trying to promote and sell a drink that had long been marketed as "The Real Thing," as reliable as night and day, and which now had been changed.

On the afternoon of July 11, 1985, just seventy-nine days after the introduction of New Coke, Coca-Cola executives announced the return of the original formula.

Your personal brand is no different. It will project your basic values and character traits—honesty, a good work ethic, ability to influence others—as well as your personal skills, such as being good at marketing or having experience in finance. Like a product brand, your personal brand can take years to establish and minutes to destroy. As Benjamin Franklin said, "It takes many good deeds to build a good reputation, and only one bad one to lose it." Two hundred years later, Warren Buffett echoed the same thought: "It takes twenty years to build a reputation and five minutes to ruin it. If you think about that, you'll do things differently."

MARRY UP

Let's return to your efforts to establish yourself in Metropolis. Forming strategic joint ventures with other people or organizations—whether established or up-and-coming—is a time-tested way to create synergy, with the result that 2 + 2 = 5. Obviously, you do not want to enter into a joint venture with someone whom you'll have to "babysit" or who cannot make a strong contribution. Ideally, you'll want to "marry up" and partner with a company with greater reach and resources than your own. But you don't want to marry up too far because you want the joint venture to be a partnership in which both parties make a strong contribution.

For a joint venture to work, Partner A needs to contribute something of value to Partner B, which Partner B doesn't have, and vice versa. A typical joint venture might involve an entrepreneur who has an idea and an angel investor with cash. Each has what the other wants, and hopefully, the "marriage" is made in heaven.

Some joint ventures are "no brainers." For example, IHS Holding Limited Group, based in the Republic of Mauritius (an island off the east coast of Africa), is a major provider of cell phone towers in Africa. (Cell phones are exploding in Africa, in numbers far outstripping traditional landlines.) The company currently has 27,000 towers in the emerging markets mobile market. In 2014, IHS announced a joint venture with MTN Group Limited, formerly M-Cell, a multinational mobile telecommunications company based in Johannesburg, South Africa, which operates in many African, European, and Asian countries. The deal gave the smaller company, IHS, full operational control of MTN's

9,151 mobile network towers in Nigeria and was expected to reduce MTN's operational cost, boost network efficiency, and expand its voice and data capacity.

Issam Darwish, CEO of IHS, said, "This is a significant and transformational agreement for IHS that doubles the size of our business and confirms our position as the leading mobile infrastructure company in Africa."[18]

By outsourcing the management of its physical cell towers to IHS, MTN was able to focus its resources on its core business, which is not tower maintenance but digital phone and data service.

An important part of this or any other joint venture is *trust*. Clearly, the leadership of MTN and IHS trusted each other to act in good faith and support the joint partnership.

This is in stark contrast to the relationship between Chrysler and Daimler, which I talked about in Chapter 2. It was pitched as a "marriage of equals," but the German executives at Daimler never believed this. They saw Chrysler as the partner who was marrying up. When the divorce was announced in 2007, as Mat Moore wrote for the Associated Press, "Through it all, there was the simmering resentment of German shareholders, who felt that something pedestrian, unimpressive—indeed, American—had dulled the lustrous sheen of one of their country's greatest carmakers."[19]

The moral of the story? Marry up—but not *too far* up. If you're the junior partner, you need to ensure that you can provide more than your share of value and, as they say in the boxing business, "punch above your weight class."

CULTIVATE RELATIONSHIPS WITH CENTERS OF INFLUENCE

At this stage in your climb up the ladder of influence, having built solid relationships and entered into one or more productive partnerships, you should be well positioned to both have access to people who are *Centers of Influence* and form relationships with them. This is how influence is multiplied. For example, let's say you have an interest in the fine arts. Once you're established in Metropolis, you seek out the most prestigious art museum. You want to join and eventually contribute. As a real-life example, take the Metropolitan Museum of Art in New York. You can volunteer there and work your way up the ladder of citizen supporters. You will need to provide cash donations, too. In time, you'll be eligible to join one of the various "Friends Groups." These volunteer groups are involved with The Met's libraries, conservation, and curatorial departments. As

---

18 Telecoms.com. https://telecoms.com/281201/
 ihs-to-take-over-mtn-nigerias-towers-through-joint-venture/

19 *San Diego Union-Tribune.* https://www.sandiegouniontribune.com/sdut-
 billed-as-a-marriage-made-in-heaven-daimler-and-2007may14-story.html

The Met says on its website, "Through special programming and events, Friends build relationships with museum curators and like-minded patrons in intimate, behind-the-scenes settings."

You'll need money: "The Met's Friends Groups dues provide an important source of support for the museum and departments. Annual dues range from $2,500 to $15,000, and benefits include those of a Patron Circles' Membership and recognition in the museum's Annual Report, among other privileges."

Can anyone join a Met Friends Group? No. Membership in a Met's Friends Group is by invitation only.[20]

Having become comfortable as a Met's Friend, you might then be ready to join the museum's board of trustees. There are only about fifty seats available, and the price of admission hovers around $10 million. Even at that price, many aspire, and few are invited. As *The New York Times* noted, "A spot on a cultural board is among the most coveted prizes in a city of strivers and mega-achievers. And spots are limited: the New York City Ballet, for example, has forty voting members; the Museum of Natural History has fifty-six. The rewards of service are many: social status, the personal satisfaction of doing good, the chance to rub shoulders with Rockefellers and Lauders, and a say in setting the intellectual course of the nation, if not the world, through a leading museum or performing arts institution."[21]

If you can bring some other form of value to the board of The Met, then being able to write a personal check for $10 million is not an ironclad requirement. Nonprofit boards look for "time, talent, and treasure," so if your treasure is on the skimpy side, your time and talent can compensate. Even so, most boards like The Met have an ironclad rule: "Give, get, or get off." If you can't give $10 million, then use your connections and your influence to find donors who can. If your influence is so weak that you can't even do that... then goodbye. Go back to being a Friend.

5 STEPS FOR CULTIVATING RELATIONSHIPS WITH CENTERS OF INFLUENCE

There's the hard way and the easy way to expand your circle of influence.

The hard way is to go it alone. You can spend your entire life working, building a personal reputation, gaining expertise, and establishing yourself as a credible contributor in your operational circle of influence; but unless you gain access to people with higher influence, your ability to succeed will be greatly

---

20   The Met. https://www.metmuseum.org/join-and-give/
      support/curatorial-friends-groups
21   *NYT*. https://nyti.ms/3wuomFI

limited. This is not to say that passion, hard work, skill sets, expertise and competencies are not important—they are, as will be explained in Success Factor chapters 7 and 8. That said, since this book is about the Power of Strategic Influence, combining your purpose, passions, and expertise with strategic access to people of higher influence will increase your chances for much greater multiples of success.

Figure 7.1 reveals the Five Steps for Cultivating Relationships with Centers of Influence. Let's dive in.

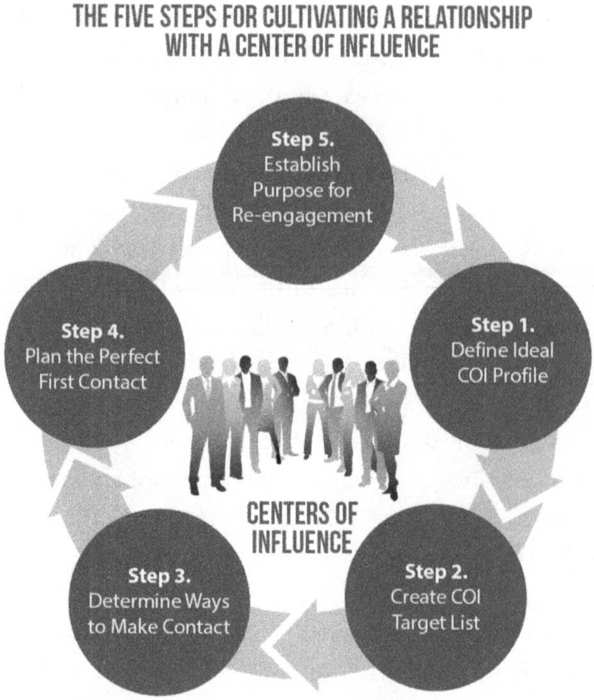

THE FIVE STEPS FOR CULTIVATING A RELATIONSHIP WITH A CENTER OF INFLUENCE

Step 5. Establish Purpose for Re-engagement

Step 4. Plan the Perfect First Contact

Step 1. Define Ideal COI Profile

CENTERS OF INFLUENCE

Step 3. Determine Ways to Make Contact

Step 2. Create COI Target List

Figure 7.1

STEP 1. DEFINE AND IDENTIFY THE IDEAL CENTER OF INFLUENCE PROFILE

One would think that any influence is good influence, but that is not always the case.

Before rushing to connect with just any business influencer, we need to establish some ground rules for cultivating centers of influence as represented in Figure 7.1.

A business influencer with expansive influence is called a *center of influence*

(COI). A COI can be a deeply embedded businessperson in a community, state, or multi-state region, or a nationally known or even a global business leader.

Step 1 requires taking time to define and identify the ideal center of influence profile. What does that mean? It simply indicates the need to list the relevant matchup criteria we'll use to define the ideal COI for our particular business. Example criteria can include a COI's geographical reach, experience in your industry, reputation in your industry, technical expertise related to your products and services, and—perhaps most critical—high-level connections to potential clients or other industry influencers.

STEP 2. CREATE A CENTER OF INFLUENCE TARGET LIST

Now that we have established the criteria for the profile of the perfect COI for your business, next you should create a list of target COIs.

Start by listing the reputable and well-connected business people in your industry. Think of leaders or experts who are mentioned in trade magazines or are speakers at industry events and tradeshows.

Next, ask your trusted partners including business associates, employees, investors in your business, customers, and family members with whom you have strong relationships, as well as advisers and board members whom they know. If you attended business school, contact business leaders in your academic circles, and even professors who may have relationships with business influencers.

Finally, you can search LinkedIn or even Google to identify names for your target list.

This should be a very select list of COIs numbering 10, 20, or if you are lucky, 50 individuals. Though there is some truth to a numbers game, the strategy you should be focusing on is building a list with quality, not just quantity; a strategic fit, not merely influence; and possible access. Though there are some celebrity business influencers, the chances of making contact are very slim unless you or one of your trusted contacts has a personal relationship.

STEP 3. DETERMINE WAYS TO MAKE CONTACT

It does you no good to create a COI target list without an introduction vehicle to connect with potential COIs. The first move should be to prioritize the list by its "low hanging fruit," or influential people whom you know or who have knowledge of you or your company in some way.

Next, prioritize the list by trusted relationships who can introduce you to people on your list. These include those trusted partners identified above in business circles, associations you belong to, academic circles, investors and consultants involved in your business, as well as trusted customers and family members who want to see you succeed.

Immediately after prioritizing who you will contact, establish a schedule for making contact with those you personally know and with your trusted partners. Set a goal to contact two to four contacts on your list every week.

When contacting trusted relationships, and once you have identified potential and matching COI influencers, then ask your contacts for the best way to get or facilitate an introduction.

STEP 4. CREATE A SUCCESS PLAN FOR MAKING THE FIRST CONTACT

As Will Rogers once said, "You never get a second chance to make a first impression." So true! This is especially applicable to highly influential businesspeople. In fact, if you get the chance for an introduction to a highly influential business leader or COI, if it doesn't go well, it will be a one-time experience. To succeed in making the first contact, you must prepare, plan, rehearse, and perhaps even pray that your time with this person will be productive.

How do we go about that? As mentioned above, there are three tasks that can increase your chances of making a positive connection with a COI, and this is after you have completed Steps 1 through 3 in getting to this point.

TASK 1: RESEARCH THE INFLUENTIAL PERSON.

Start by looking up his or her social profiles. Next, do searches on their name to become familiar with their past accomplishments. Read up on what they are currently involved in their business and other newsworthy activities. If they have posted videos, podcasts, or interviews online, take time to view or listen to them. Take specific notes about their interests, their accomplishments, and their goals. You need to be able to relate to them and identify areas that you have in common, or needs they have that you may be able to help them solve, including making introductions for them to other COIs with whom you have a relationship.

TASK 2: MAKE A PLAN.

This means writing down what you are going to say. Since most often these introductions are just a few minutes in duration, create a short pitch and introduction that will hit all the hot points about your value proposition. Mention something of value you can offer them such as an introduction or involvement in a project that fits their passions and goals. Bring them a sample product if you feel they will like it as a gift. If you are an expert yourself and have written a book, bring them a signed copy. Make this experience one they will not forget.

TASK 3: REHEARSE.

I highly recommend you find someone with whom you can role play and who will give you honest feedback. Rehearse your approach, introduction, and pitch with them. After the feedback, adjust and improve your approach, and rehearse it again. Preparation, researching, planning, and rehearsing will give you the best chances of succeeding.

STEP 5. ESTABLISH A PURPOSE FOR RE-ENGAGEMENT

Congratulations are in order if you have made it to this step. It means that your hard work paid off. You successfully created a fitted COI profile, developed a well-matched target list, determined the best introduction methods, and finally did an outstanding job preparing, researching, creating a customized pitch, rehearsing and delivering a message that was well received. As the title of the comedy by William Shakespeare, *All's Well That Ends Well,* suggests, your effort and sacrifice to get this point is well worth it if you get a positive result. Even if the introduction did not result in a successful relationship, the practice and experience will provide you with the experience to do better the next time. If your efforts are 1 out of 2, or even 3 out of 10, the opportunity to align yourself with a highly influential strategic contact will pay itself back many times.

Before we conclude this exercise, it would be a wasted effort if you got this far and then didn't take the opportunity to establish a reason to *re-engage* with this new COI. Before you conclude the meeting, come prepared to offer a good reason to connect soon after the introduction if possible. Possible ways to do that are:

- Offer to facilitate an introduction of interest to your new COI.
- Confirm that you will send a follow-up email with information from your company that your COI showed interest in.
- Offer to send a VIP ticket to an event you are promoting.
- Show interest and commitment in getting involved in some initiative that is important to them. The key to re-engagement is to offer something of value that the COI has interest in and cares about. It might just be the opportunity of a lifetime, so do it right the first time!

TAKE CALCULATED RISKS

It's an ironclad rule of business—or in life, actually—that without risk, there's no reward.

When Christopher Columbus sailed west in 1492, he was taking a big risk. Not that the earth was flat and he'd fall off the edge; navigators had known since the days of the ancient Greek geographer Eratosthenes that the earth was round. Columbus knew he'd eventually reach Asia by sailing west. The question was, how far would he have to go?

In 200 BCE, Eratosthenes had correctly calculated the circumference of the earth to within one percent of its actual girth. But in making his own calculations, Columbus made two mistakes: He followed the reasoning of the medieval Persian geographer, Abu al Abbas Ahmad ibn Muhammad ibn Kathir al-Farghani (a.k.a. Alfraganus), and he also misinterpreted the distance of an Arabic mile. Columbus thought the circumference of the earth was 16,305 nautical miles. In reality—and according to Eratosthenes—it's about 21,600 miles. So if Columbus could sail in a straight line westward from Spain to Japan, he and his crew would have starved to death long before they made the journey of 15,000 miles. By a lucky chance, there was an unknown landmass blocking his path: the continent of North America, which made his voyage a tolerable 4,000 miles.

In business and investing, the higher the risk, the greater the reward. The lower the risk, the lesser the reward. As you gain influence and the experience of relationships and partnerships, you'll become better positioned to use your executive authority to commit resources to projects that involve risk.

For example, Elon Musk has taken one risk after another and come out on top every time. Two days after beginning undergraduate classes at Stanford University, he dropped out to form his first company, Zip2 Corporation, with Kimbal Musk (his brother) and Greg Kouri. The company provided and licensed online city guide software to newspapers. They sold it to Compaq for $307 million. Using his seven percent share from the sale, Musk co-founded X.com, a first-of-its-kind online payment company. Just a year later, X.com merged with PayPal, and Musk became a part-owner of the new company. Then eBay bought PayPal for $1.5 billion. Musk took the $180 million he made from the sale of PayPal and threw it into three projects: SpaceX ($100 million), Tesla ($70 million), and SolarCity ($10 million).

All three were huge risks, particularly SpaceX. Musk had no illusions about his chances for success. During a press conference with NASA in March 2019 at the Kennedy Space Center in Florida, Musk said of founding SpaceX, "I always thought we would fail… I thought maybe we had a ten percent chance of reaching orbit starting out." The people around Musk were skeptical too. Musk added, "When we started SpaceX, they said, 'Oh, you are going to fail.' And I said, 'Well, I agree. I think we probably will fail.' They said I would lose all the money from PayPal. I was, like, 'Well, you are probably right.'

"I had so many people try to talk me out of starting a rocket company. It was crazy," Musk told Scott Pelley on CBS's *60 Minutes* in 2014. "One good friend of mine collected a whole series of videos of rockets blowing up and made me watch those. He just didn't want me to lose all my money."

Sure enough, the first three SpaceX rocket launches failed. Musk knew he had one more try. "A fourth failure would have been absolutely game over," Musk said at the International Astronautical Congress conference in 2017. "But fate liked us that day. So, the fourth launch worked."[22]

Influencers are drawn to calculated risks because they know they produce the biggest rewards. As Jeff Bezos said about walking away from a successful career on Wall Street to start Amazon.com in his garage, "I knew that if I failed, I wouldn't regret that, but I knew the one thing I might regret is not trying."

Pharmaceutical companies are accustomed to taking big risks on new medications that may not work. They've learned how to manage risk at every step and be comfortable with the possibility of failure. As Ina Kamenz, former CIO of Eli Lilly and Company, said, "By establishing milestones, gates, and questions along the way, you're ensuring that you're being smart about the risks you're taking. And as hard as it is, you've got to be ready to say, 'We are stopping.'"

The greater your influence, the more you're able to persuade others to take a calculated risk. Be sure to do your homework, know the odds of failure, and be honest about them to your stakeholders. If you then experience a failure, you'll be able to turn it into a new opportunity for success.

---

22 CNBC.com. https://www.cnbc.com/2019/03/06/elon-musk-on-spacex-i-always-thought-we-would-fail.html

SUCCESS ACTION ITEMS – ASSUME THE ROLE OF INFLUENCER

- Assume the Role of Influencer. You're ready to take on more autonomy, and rather than be a reflection of others around you and a follower, become a source of influence to whom others look.
- Embrace inter-reliance. Do not try to go it alone. The greatest deeds are accomplished by people working together toward a common goal. This is where exponential growth and success can happen!
- Align yourself with other influencers. In order to soar and reach the highest levels of success and influence, you need to align yourself with other high achievers who have complementary skills and circles of influence who can help you expand your reach, your influence, and your successes.
- Prepare yourself for new opportunities. When you step up to the role of influencer, you're ready to leave your apprenticeship behind and begin to affect change in the world around you.
- Navigate new opportunities by being inter-reliant and innovative.
- Establish and expand your personal brand and reputation by creating value, quality, and integrity.
- Marry up! Partner with leaders and companies with greater reach and resources than your own.
- Joint ventures require that each partner contribute value to the other. Marry up—but not *too far* up. If you're the junior partner, ensure that you can provide more than your share of value.
- Multiply your influence by cultivating Relationships with Centers of Influence. You are well positioned to both have access to people who are *Centers of Influence* (COI) and form relationships with them. The five steps for cultivating relationships with COIs are; 1) Define the ideal COI profile, 2) Create a COI target list, 3) Determine ways to make contact with COIs, 4) Plan for the perfect first contact, and 5) Establish purpose for re-engagement.
- Take Calculated Risks. It's an ironclad rule of business—or in life, actually—that without risk, there's no reward. As you gain influence and the experience of relationships and partnerships, you'll become better positioned to use your executive authority to commit resources to projects that involve risk.
- Leverage your influence with integrity. The greater your influence, the more you're able to persuade others to take a calculated risk.
- Do your homework, know the odds of failure, and be honest about them to your stakeholders. If you then experience a failure, you'll be able to work together to turn challenges into new successes.

TOM ZIGLAR
CEO ZIGLAR INC.

"Leadership is Humility and Confidence"

GROWING UP AS THE SON OF ZIG ZIGLAR

A s THE SON OF ZIG Ziglar, I had a front-row seat to the incredible impact and inspiration he provided that influenced more than 250 million people worldwide. As I grew into adulthood, here's what my father told me: "Son, whatever you want to do, just do it two ways: With 100 percent integrity, and with 100 percent effort." I've spent my life following that advice, developing the unique gifts and voice God has given me to enable Ziglar, Inc., to carry on the messages of motivation, inspiration and belief that my father first began sharing more than sixty years ago.

RELATIONSHIPS

In 1938, the Harvard Grant study began when researchers enlisted the sophomore class at Harvard, all of them young men, and they also took about an equal number of young men from the Boston tenement housing projects and followed them for seventy-five years.

Profiles, careers, lifestyles, relationships—all these through four generations of research. In the seventy-fifth year, there were only ten percent of the people still alive because they were all in their nineties.

They asked them a question: "Are you happy and satisfied with your life?" And for the ones that said, "yes," they went back in the data and discovered that when they were in their 50's, their number one focus wasn't money or travel or retirement or starting a new business. Or a hobby. Their number one focus was *relationships.*

If you want to be in your nineties and happy and satisfied, we know what the secret is: it's relationships.

HOW I WOULD SURVIVE IN A NEW LAND

If I were to arrive in a strange city, being an optimist, I would be very confident that I would survive and thrive.

My first take would be that I would be absolutely excited for the opportunity. Maybe a little nervous at first, just as you get your feet underneath you. But I've learned that if you help enough other people get what *they* want, then you can have everything in life that *you* want.

I would look around. I would walk the streets and take a look at what people are doing. I would try to pick up a local newspaper.

I'm very focused on solving problems, and I would know that I had a problem, and that problem is I need to earn my keep. I would look for problems I could solve for other people. I would look for what is holding people back by checking in with some local businesses.

I would probably seek out somebody in the direct sales area, retail sales, anybody with a sales personality, and I would explain my situation and ask them whom they might know. I would do that because if they're a true professional, they'll know a lot of people, and they might have some ideas or some leads. And then I would ask if there's anything I can do for them. If my short order of survival is to get through the next few days, then I would be very bold and ask, "Is there something I can do here, or something for the day?"

There's a quote that I love from Rabbi Daniel Lapin, who's a good friend of mine and a mentor, and he says this: "Opportunity seeks out the generous." So, my mindset, my mode, is always to try to be generous. And this is especially important when you don't have much to be generous with!

Somebody once asked me if my dad, Zig Ziglar, had a number one secret. They wanted me to boil it down to one. There are hundreds! But I replied that every day, he spent the first three hours reading, researching, studying God's word, knowledge, information, wisdom, self-development, all these different things; but his reason for doing it was to internalize it, simplify it, so that he could then share it with someone else, for their benefit.

That's the key and the reason: the motive behind it is for someone else's benefit.

INFLUENCER

An influencer has the ability to motivate and inspire and get others to take action, think things, do good things. I look at the combination primarily on the action—what actions have they taken, what's the behavior that I can see, and then see if that matches the words they say.

We pay far too much attention to people's words without taking the context of what their actions are, so influencers must have a track record of consistency. They need to be congruent in their beliefs, their actions, and their words.

Influencers come on all levels. I had breakfast with Dr. Ken Blanchard, and he gave me a great quote. He said, "Hey, do you know what the two most important leadership qualities are?"

"What?"

"Humility and confidence."

I would say these could also be influencer qualities.

Dr. Blanchard looked at me and smiled, and he said, "They seem like the opposite, don't they? Think about it this way. It's having the humility to know that without Christ, you can do nothing, and the confidence to know that with Christ, there's nothing you can't do. When I look at an influencer today, I'm looking for somebody who's humbly confident."

What seems to happen in leadership is we get an extreme. We get somebody who's so confident they go into arrogance. And then we lose trust. One of my sayings is, "Trust is the byproduct of integrity." So when we look at that, then the other side is you've got other leaders who are so helpful.

Influencers and leaders must really master that combination of being humble enough to say, "I don't really know it all, tell me more, what can I learn," and always seeking to discover what's true; but the confidence to let people know, "Hey, this is what I believe, here is where we're going, this is how it's going to happen."

Influencers have the ability to transfer their own confidence to other people, and that confidence has to be rooted in a foundation of integrity.

I BELIEVE I'M AN INFLUENCER

One of the ways people know if you are a leader is whether you have followers. So influencers would have people who are following through on whatever is that they're recommending. At the end of 2019, I re-looked at our mission statement as a company. As the CEO for twenty-six years, it was a personality-driven company. Zig Ziglar—what better way to launch a company! Dad passed away eight years ago, and it's gone through a major transition. Not in the content or the primary things that we do, but in how we get the message out.

Dad's reach was to the individual, the salesperson, the small business owner, and always from the bottom up. Our mission is to encourage, transform, equip, and support.

There are four areas in which we work—people who are building an intentional legacy, coaches, trainers, and speakers. My primary objective is to encourage, equip, and support those who are taking our message out to the world. I have a great responsibility to influence them. The communication channels are wide open all the time. It's a living, breathing relationship.

Without influence, our business wouldn't exist. We couldn't get partners to come in and carry that message forth.

STRATEGIC INFLUENCER

Strategic to me is all about legacy and helping those you love grow through life's most difficult challenges. Strategic to me simply says that we can't avoid the trials and tribulations of the world. Something's going to happen. We don't know what it is. It could be an illness; it could be a relationship breakdown. We've got to prepare in advance for that. Dad had a great quote—he said, "Expect the best, prepare for the worst, maximize what comes." Strategic to me is always being solution focused. We're always thinking that today is a day of gratitude, and we're going to make a difference. It's our job and our responsibility.

My mission statement is very simple: It's to create the atmosphere that allows you to become the person that God created you to become. To me, being strategic starts from the inside out. It's how I'm creating the atmosphere, how I'm creating the space and the ability for other people to flourish in the way that God created them.

Then there's the long-term view of strategic, which asks, where are we going to end up? What is it that's going to be different? How do I become the person who produces those results?

One of my sayings is, "A tree's fruitfulness depends on its rootfulness." It's probably quoted through the generations, and I'm sure some preacher sometime, somewhere, said that.

We talk about seven roots: The mental, the spiritual, the physical, the family, the financial, the personal, and the career. Strategically, I've got to nourish each one of those seven roots. And I like to take purpose out of the theoretical and put it into the practical, so if I have a clear design or purpose in my life, and things that I want to accomplish strategically, and I write those down, and I define what my PPAs are. A PPA is simply a "purpose-producing activity."

So strategically, I know this is where I want to end up. In fact, I have defined certain activities that I can do on a regular basis that will automatically produce that fruit. A good habit is simply a purpose-producing activity done every day.

CENTER OF INFLUENCE

All of us have three relationships in our life. We have a relationship with ourselves. We have a relationship with others. And I believe we have a relationship with God. And until we get the one with ourselves and God right, the relationship with others is always going to struggle.

When I think of center of influence, we do a lot of work with business owners. And if the business owner is right—meaning personally—then their business has a great chance of success. If they're not, it's going to be a struggle. They can put all the systems in, they can bring the consultants in, they can have the big idea, but if they're struggling in those areas—the mental, spiritual, physical, family—their relationships are going to struggle.

The first center of influence in that perspective is the individual. And then we've each got to have a standard that is higher than ourselves. Something to aspire to. If *we* get to make up the rules, then people with the power or the wealth are going to make the rules, and morality has no factor in it.

One of the questions I heard recently is, "Can you love someone else more than you love yourself? Can you respect someone else more than you respect yourself?" Because ultimately, you can't give something you don't have.

DEEP DOWN HABITS

The number one habit is choosing my input—what I read, listen to, with whom I associate. I believe that everything starts with thought. I believe we create the future we see. And what is the future that we see, and what influences that? It's what we read, what we listen to, where we spend our time. So, the first habit is putting in the right information.

The second is one that I've created, and I wrote about it in my book, *Choose to Win.* I call it the "perfect start." Every day I try to start the same way. I get up early—five-thirty—and have quiet time. Bob Beaudine wrote a book called *Two Chairs.* And the idea is that for five minutes first thing in the morning, you set up two chairs—one for you and one for God. And you ask God three questions: "God, do you know what's going on? God, are you big enough to handle it? God, what's the plan?" And so for four and a half minutes, you just listen.

You just *listen.* Because in my belief, it is a relationship. So the relationship is what we're going for. Then after that, it's scripture reading, or devotional, and then I plan my day. I've got my performance planner, which is built around goals and what we are going to do today. Then I do a mental model of any appointments, meetings, or speaking engagements. It's sixty seconds of picturing in my mind exactly what's going to happen, how it's going to go, what questions they will have, what obstacles they face, so that I could be prepared.

I'm kind of a brain nerd, so all the neuroscience says that even if you prepare and the meeting ends up being completely different, you're still better off having gone through that kind of mental model than if you didn't.

The last practice is the time capsule, the forty-five minutes to ninety minutes of the number one priority: What are we going to get done today?

Those are my two main habits. The perfect start has about five or six habits in it, but one of my thoughts is that there are people to whom life happens, and there are people who happen to life. And if we can happen to life in the first part of the day, then everything else goes from there.

HOW DO YOU KNOW YOU HAVE A BAD HABIT?

I was once asked a great question by a young man named Caleb Miller. Dan Miller is his grandfather and Kevin Miller is his father and the host of the Ziglar Show podcast. Dan wrote *48 Days to the Work You Love*. He's just dynamite. Caleb asked me, "How do you know if you have a bad habit?"

It seems like an easy question to answer. But it's actually a fantastic question because you don't know if you have a bad habit if you don't have any goals. If your goal is to get lung cancer, then smoking is a good habit. So we criticize people for having bad habits, for not being strategic, when the reality is that they don't have a purpose of why, a dream, a goal, an aspiration laid out and defined.

MY GREATEST INFLUENCER

My greatest influencer would be my dad, Zig Ziglar.

Somebody once asked me, "What was your dad's greatest spiritual quality?" I actually did a study on, from God's perspective, what we should develop in ourselves. If you study the Old Testament, you might come up with obedience. In the New Testament, it's going to be love and humility. I found this word, "brokenness." It doesn't mean that you're broken and no good. It means that you have this understanding there's nothing of eternal significance that you can do without God's help.

One of the character qualities of someone who is broken is they never worry. I heard Dad say a thousand times, "I never worry." And, of course, I'm not there yet.

Another hallmark of a broken person is they realize they only have two responsibilities.

The first one is to have a vibrant relationship with God.

The second is to speak God's truth and love. When Dad went on stage, he had that confidence and that boldness. He went out there knowing that he wasn't there to please the audience, he wasn't there to please the guy paying the bill, and he wasn't there to get laughs.

He was there to please God.

The second one is the big one, truth and love. Today there is a lot of truth spoken, but it's not in love. There is a lot of love spoken, but it's not based on truth. When you speak the truth in love, you have no responsibility for how it's received. When Dad would get offstage, and he would have all these rounds of applause and standing ovations, I would say, "Dad, how did you do?" He never judged his performance by the reaction of the audience. He judged it by asking himself, "Did I speak God's truth and love, and did I prepare as much as possible?" That was it. And then he was very careful to say, "Look, you can't always prepare as much as you like because circumstances change, but, did you do the best you can with what you have?"

That was how he did it. Seeing that balance of setting the highest standard and yet offering the deepest grace was the way Dad lived, and he never backed down on the standard. If he ever failed to lead with grace, he'd come and apologize.

He apologized to me for things I didn't think he had done. So that's an influence.

THE NUMBER ONE DO-OVER THAT I WOULD DO

When I look at my career, and I started working at the company, and dad was speaking and traveling, every year he had at least fifteen to twenty corporate engagements, where it was their big convention, it was their big deal. And all the executives, all the leadership, all the people from that company would be there and there might be from 250 to 25,000 people at these events. And I was back at home, working in the business, working my way up, doing sales, doing different things. If I could change anything, I would give myself the assignment of traveling with him on every one of those events. And my only responsibility would be to take care of him, anything he needed and to meet and develop relationships with all of those influencers and leaders that he met on these trips. So, we get our priorities wrong. We think it's about climbing the ladder when it's really about forging relationships. That's what I would change.

DEFINING MOMENTS

The story of when Dad passed away was just filled with—there's no other way to put it—miracles.

There's a scripture, 1 Thessalonians 4:13-18. Once, when my sister Julie left Mom and Dad's house and was driving back to her home, she saw in the clouds a perfect "Z." So she grabbed her camera on her phone to take a picture of it.

When my dad went into the hospital two weeks later, and he was going to die, and they've given him just hours, and it's in the middle of the night, Julie said, "Hey, you need to see this picture. It's a Z-cloud, and our last name is Ziglar, so I noticed this. I've never seen a Z-cloud."

I said, "I want to get a screenshot of that." We got the screenshot, and that's what we put on the announcement when Dad passed away.

On Thursday, we went to the pastor to plan the funeral. And Dad had already written out all the instructions, so then we left. As we were walking out, I said, "Wait a second, we're having two services. We're having the big one at the church and also a graveside service, and all we did was plan the church. I told the pastor we hadn't planned the graveside service.

"What do you want to do?" he asked.

"Short and simple, because it's just for the family and a few close friends."

He said, "Okay. I got it."

Friday night was visitation, and before we went to visitation, Julie said, "Look at this, it's actually the Z-cloud, but it's not a picture. It's a video." She had been driving down the road at sixty miles an hour, and she pulled out her iPhone to take a picture, and she must have swiped across to video. She played the video, and it lasted four seconds. The radio was playing in the background, and there was a pastor preaching on 1 Thessalonians 4:13 through 18. We looked at each other, and we said, "I wonder what that verse says?" We looked up the verse, and it said, "But we do not want you to be uninformed brothers about those who are asleep, that you may not grieve as others do, who have no hope."

The verse said, "Don't grieve." This was good. So, it was like God saying, "Okay, here's the 'Z' so you'll pay attention, and then here's the verse." It's about our hope in Christ, and the last verse says to therefore encourage one another with these words.

Dad's Sunday school class was called the Encouragers Class. On Saturday morning at the graveside, the pastor came out, and he said, "I want to share a verse. And the first thing he did was recite the passage from Thessalonians.

It's like God said, "Okay, I'm going to give you a cloud, then I'm going to give you a picture, then I'm going to give you an audio and a video, and then if you still don't believe it, I'm going to have the pastor back it up."

I went to the pastor, Jack Graham, right after that, and I asked, "Did you hear about the video of the Z-cloud?"

He said, no, he hadn't seen it.

In the book, *Choose to Win*, we have a link to that video so people can go and watch it. To me, that was a turning point. That was like God reaching down and saying, "Look, you know."

If you go to Ziglar.com/Zcloud, you can see the whole story.

Tom Ziglar has had the rare privilege of spending his entire life surrounded by world-class leaders, innovators, and motivators. Family dinner included the presence of the world's TOP motivator, his father, Zig Ziglar. As a result, Tom's arsenal of experience and information is absolutely unparalleled.

As CEO of Ziglar Inc, Tom Ziglar carries on the Zig Ziglar philosophy: "You can have everything in life you want if you will just help enough other people get what they want." Tom has written two books: Choose to Win *released in March of 2019 and* 10 Leadership Virtues For Disruptive Times *to be released in the fall of 2021. As a speaker and writer Tom is dedicated to equipping Business Leaders, Coaches, Speakers, and Trainers to achieve their dreams and goals.*

Website: www.ziglar.com
Facebook: www.facebook.com/ZigZiglar

SUCCESS FACTOR 6: PREPARE AND PLAN FOR THE ULTIMATE JOURNEY

"No matter how many goals you have achieved, you must set your sights on a higher one."
—Jessica Savitch

THE PURPOSE OF THIS CHAPTER is to *prepare you* for the next section of two success factors which comprises the Sphere of Opportunity.

What does this mean?

Ever since you landed in Metropolis, you've been presented with opportunities—to get a job, to establish your brand, to form relationships, and then partnerships. And judging by your progress, you've recognized and seized these opportunities. That's how you got to where you are today. But those opportunities were largely the product of you responding to your environment and what it had to offer. You needed a job, so you looked on job boards to see what was available. You needed relationships and partnerships, so you made yourself available. You made the best of the situation you were in.

It's as if you were the captain of an old-fashioned sailing ship powered by the wind. In those days, the mightiest clipper ships and men o' war could travel great distances, but they depended on the wind. If there was no wind, then they drifted, becalmed. They could be in the middle of the ocean, making good time, and suddenly the wind might die, and there they would sit, sometimes for days. Opportunities would pass them by. They were at a standstill until the wind picked up.

Now imagine you installed a powerful engine in your ship. Suddenly, you'd be capable of purely autonomous movement! If the wind died down or came from the wrong direction, it wouldn't matter. You could take your ship in any direction, any time of the day or night. You could *make your own opportunities.*

That's what the upcoming section is about. Having taken responsibility for yourself, becoming self-reliant, and having formed relationships and partnerships with the opportunities available to you, you're now preparing to begin the ultimate journey as the Captain of your own ship. As a leader and influencer, you will be able to plan your destiny, be proactive, and create opportunities, even in situations where none are apparent. Alas, before we venture off to this new land, and before we can create new opportunities, we must first prepare for the journey.

GAIN PERSPECTIVE

Given this newfound potential for creating your own opportunities, what's the first thing you should do?

To go back to the example of the old-fashioned ship, the very first thing you'd do is send a sailor high into the crow's nest to search the horizon. Today, you'd look at the radar screen and gather satellite information. You need to know what's out there. Are there threats, like submerged rocks or dangerous currents? Are there opportunities, like new places to trade? Now that you can go in any direction you want, which direction do you favor?

Sailing aimlessly from here to there without being mindful of the passage of time is not a winning strategy. To build influence for power and profit cannot be done overnight. At the very least, it takes years; and at the most, it can take a lifetime. There is no time to waste.

Consider the president of the United States. Getting yourself elected president is perhaps the most powerful achievement of influence we have today. A few people have made it happen at a relatively young age. The youngest to be elected president was John F. Kennedy, who was forty-three years old at his inauguration. Other young presidents have included Theodore Roosevelt, Bill Clinton, Ulysses S. Grant, and Barack Obama. Most of these men, while relatively young, ran for office after having already built up their influence within their parties; and Theodore Roosevelt, John F. Kennedy, and U.S. Grant were boosted by their impressive military records.

But to attain the position of president of the United States, youth is the exception. The median age of ascendency to the office of president is currently fifty-five years and 354 days—therefore, nearly fifty-six years. For most people, this is more than thirty years after first entering professional or public life, and the age at which retirement is looming on the horizon. For some, the building of their personal influence takes even longer. The oldest person to assume the presidency is Joe Biden, who took the oath at the age of seventy-eight years, sixty-one days, on Inauguration Day. It was his third try for the highest office—he had also run in 1988 and 2008. His predecessor, Donald Trump, was seventy when he took office. Trump had made previous bids for the Oval Office in 2000 and briefly in 2012. Then in 2016, suddenly, he had tremendous influence, and he won the Republican nomination and then the presidency.

Because high-level networking based on relationship building, which continues to increase influence, takes time, you need to be *focused* in your intentions and your planning. You cannot fritter away your time. You need to have a goal and start working toward it *now*.

To gain perspective, you've got to look around at what's happening today and put that into historical context, and you also need to look at yourself and where you fit in.

Does this sound like a traditional SWOT test, where you assess your strengths, weaknesses, opportunities, and threats? Yes, it's very much like that. You've probably done this before—or I hope so! But each time you do it, your horizon should get larger. You should be able to look farther afield, both spatially and temporally. Instead of thinking about what can happen in your immediate neighborhood or market, you'll start planning for what may happen in markets you have yet to enter. Instead of thinking about what may happen tomorrow or next quarter, you'll start to think in terms of years. And instead of thinking only about the people you know today and how you can influence them, you'll think about people you've never met but who could become a part of your sphere of influence.

And most of all, you'll think not just about the opportunities that exist at present, and of which you're aware, but of the opportunities over the horizon, out of sight, or better yet, the opportunities that you can *create*.

Experience matters. The more you've seen of the world, the better you can put what you see into context. You can more accurately judge opportunities and what it will take to reach your goals. The author Malcolm Gladwell popularized the idea that it takes 10,000 hours of practice to become proficient in a skill— including, presumably, building and using influence. In fact, the 10,000-hours concept originated in a 1993 paper called "The Role of Deliberate Practice in the Acquisition of Expert Performance." Written by Anders Ericsson, a professor at the University of Colorado, the paper highlighted the work of a group of psychologists in Berlin, who had studied the practice habits of violin students in childhood, adolescence, and adulthood. Ericsson found that 10,000 hours was the *average* required to reach proficiency, and that depending upon innate talent and the focus of the practice, it could be more or less.

Building and using influence is not unlike any other skill that can be developed over time. You have to apply yourself and work toward your goal.

Motivation and focus are important qualities to have when forming relationships and building influence. Just putting a powerful engine in your ship is only half the answer—you need to know where you want to go. And to know where you want to go, you need a broad perspective. You need to see the big picture.

UNDERSTANDING THE POWER OF MEDIA

While the focus of this book is on personal influence—the kind you create one relationship at a time—it's necessary to acknowledge the tremendous power of electronic and digital media. Platforms ranging from feature films and television to Facebook and Twitter can do two things for you:

1. EXPOSURE

They can make you and your accomplishments known to vast numbers of people who otherwise would have little knowledge of you. In this book, I've talked about the Kardashians as products of media; their TV show made them household names and built the platform for their marketing machines. Countless performers and politicians have done the same thing, and not just in the digital era. By most accounts, the first media celebrity was the stage actress Sarah Bernhardt. Born in Paris in 1844, at the age of eighteen, she made her stage debut there. Through the power of newspapers, magazines, photography, and the telegraph, as a performer, she became a household name around the world, even among those who never actually saw her onstage. Tens of millions of people read about her in the cheap newspapers published in both morning and evening editions, and millions more saw her photographs reproduced in magazines and displayed in shop windows. Her relationship with the press was symbiotic. Stories about her exploits guaranteed sales, and readers bought whatever product she was associated with. When she took a short trip over Paris in a hot air balloon, the press breathlessly covered it for days. She was like Madonna, Angelina Jolie, Lady Gaga, and Beyoncé all rolled into one.

Despite being a household name, everyone agreed that the real Sarah Bernhardt was unknowable. Her public persona was a fabulous creation of her imagination. Which leads us to the next point.

2. CONNECTION WITH THE AUDIENCE

The media can make a mass audience composed of individual people each feel as though you are their friend and they know you, even if the media image you are feeding them is a carefully constructed fiction. In Hollywood, there are endless stories about Celebrity X, who has cultivated a public image or brand as being sweet, caring, and approachable, and yet the people who actually interact with the real Celebrity X say the person is a self-centered jerk who treats his or her staff like peasants.

Hopefully, you won't use the media as a way to fool people into thinking they know you when, in fact, you're someone quite different.

The media—and in particular social media—can also tear you down in an instant and quickly destroy your personal brand. Consider the highly unfortunate case of Lindsey Stone. In October 2012, while on a work-paid trip to Arlington National Cemetery, she and her co-worker Jamie went to the Tomb of the Unknown Soldier. Stone spotted a sign that read, "Silence and Respect," and as a joke, she stood next to the sign, gave the middle finger, and pretended to yell. (No respect, no silence…) Jamie took a photo of her and then, with Lindsey's consent, posted the picture to her Facebook page, and tagged Lindsey in it.

As Lindsey told *The Guardian*, they thought it was no big deal. Off-duty, she and Jamie had a quirky habit of taking irreverent photos, "smoking in front of a no smoking sign or posing in front of statues, mimicking the pose. We took dumb pictures all the time. And so at Arlington, we saw the Silence and Respect sign… and inspiration struck."

The photo went viral as online users hammered Stone for her really dumb insensitivity to the sacred spot. In a Facebook response, Stone attempted to quash the outrage. "Whoa whoa whoa… wait," she wrote. "This is just us… challenging authority in general. Much like the pic posted the night before, of me smoking right next to a no smoking sign. OBVIOUSLY, we meant NO disrespect to people that serve or have served our country."[23]

A Facebook group was formed called "Fire Lindsey Stone." The page demanded her resignation from her place of employment, Living Independently Forever, Inc. (LIFE), a nonprofit organization in Hyannis, Massachusetts, that assists adults with disabilities. Her bosses at LIFE learned of the controversy and placed Stone and her co-worker on unpaid leave pending an internal investigation.

They fired Lindsey. Her boss met her in the parking lot and told her to hand over her keys. "Literally overnight, everything I knew and loved was gone," she

---

23   *Huffington Post.* https://www.huffpost.com/entry/lindsey-stone-facebook-photo-arlington-national-cemetery-unpaid-leave_n_2166842

said. She fell into a depression, became an insomniac, and barely left home for a year. It was only after eighteen months that she was able to land another job.[24]

Be very careful with social media—it can make you or break you!

GAINING A PERSPECTIVE OF THE INFLUENCE LANDSCAPE

In order to navigate your way through the halls of influence and widen your sphere while avoiding blind turns, you need to have a broad perspective in general, and you also need specific knowledge of the influence landscape. This comes from experience and the desire to really pay attention to the information that's made available to you.

Think of your skills as resembling those of the ancient Polynesian sailors. The early people of the Pacific were intimately tied to the ocean. They sailed the sea hundreds of years before Europeans, using ocean going canoes crafted with stone tools from island materials. Without the aid of sextants or compasses, on voyages lasting weeks at a time, they traversed thousands of miles of open water between islands. They navigated their canoes by the stars and other signs they discerned from the ocean and sky. To them, it was an art learned over a lifetime, passed on verbally from one navigator to another over countless generations.

To this day, ancient Polynesian navigation relies heavily on two crucial activities:

1. CONSTANT OBSERVATION

Navigators who don't use instruments need to be keenly aware of their surroundings. Through unceasing observation, they're able to detect changes in the speed of their canoes, their heading, and the time of day or night. The sun is their most important guide, and they note its exact points as it rises and sets. Once the sun has set, they observe the rising and setting points of the stars. They watch the behavior of shorebirds that fly out into the open ocean to feed and the size and direction of the waves.

2. MEMORIZATION OF SETS OF FACTS

In addition to being keen observers—that is, *collectors of current data*—the Polynesian navigators must memorize huge amounts of historical data about the positions of stars in the sky relative to the sun, the horizon, and each other.

Each star has a specific declination, or distance in degrees above the night-time horizon, and provides a bearing for navigation as it rises or sets. Polynesian voyagers set their heading by sighting a particular star near the horizon, then

---

24   *The Guardian.* https://www.theguardian.com/technology/2015/feb/21/internet-shaming-lindsey-stone-jon-ronson

switch to a new one when the first rises too high. For each route from island to island, a specific sequence of stars must be memorized. Some star compass systems include as many as 150 stars with known bearings, which the navigator would know by heart.

Polynesian navigators know the patterns of waves and currents of wind and the behaviors of sea and shorebirds. When there are no stars because of a cloudy night or during daylight, a navigator uses the winds and swells as guides.[25]

Their vast knowledge of their environment gives context to the data collected by observation and turns it into *actionable information*. To an untrained eye, the sight of a white tern flying south at midday with a small fish in its beak means nothing. It is just a data point. But to the Polynesian seafarer, it's useful information: The tern is flying back to its island nest to feed its chicks, and land is, therefore, no more than forty miles away, due south.

TRAIN YOUR MEMORY

Just as Polynesian navigators commit to memory vast data points of environmental and historical information, you would be well served to train yourself to remember names and facts about the people you meet. This is for two reasons.

1. REMEMBER NAMES

You need to be quick on your feet and be able to connect names and job titles and other salient information about the influential people you meet or learn about. For example, one day, your business partner says, "I just learned that Ajax Company got the big contract from the government—can we partner with them? Whom do we know there?"

You need to instantly reply, "I know Jane Smith, the Ajax director of operations. She belongs to the Hilldale Country Club. Plays bridge there every Thursday. And Joe Jones, the Ajax finance director, went to my university. He graduated a year before me. I think we even lived in the same dorm. I can give them both a friendly call." Boom—a pathway for interaction is open.

2. PEOPLE LOVE IT WHEN YOU REMEMBER THEM

It makes them feel good. When you first meet someone, be sure to use their name a few times as you speak to them. Don't be obnoxious about it, or you'll sound like a salesman. Keep it natural. It will help you remember their name, and they'll be flattered. Then, when you meet them again, be sure to refer to some previous subject of conversation. Such as, "Hello, Sam. Good to see you

---

25   http://archive.hokulea.com/ike/hookele/on_wayfinding.html

again. Say, how's Junior doing at Harvard? The last time we spoke, he was thinking about majoring in anthropology."

Remember, people love it when you ask about what they're doing. But if they have a child, they *really* love it when you remember their child's name and ask about him or her. Truly influential people remember the birthdays of not only their business associates but their children and even grandchildren.

When you are invited to a social event, *after* you've accepted the invitation, inquire as to who else might be coming. Be upfront—tell the host you want to be able to chat with them. If there are people whom you don't know, find out some basic information, like where they work or the neighborhood they live in. Anything that will enable you to strike up a conversation.

Never ask anyone about their politics, sexual orientation, or religion. Be very careful when asking about spouses or children—you might step on an emotional land mine. Use only information that your acquaintance has already told you, like Junior's choice of major at Harvard.

The same rules apply when you go to an interview for a new job or a promotion. Before the interview, find out who will be there and something about their job description. Research the company or department and its recent projects. At the interview, your attitude should be like that of a person who *already works* on the team and is ready to collaborate with your colleagues.

CREATE A RELATIONSHIP NAVIGATION PLAN

Just like the Polynesian navigators memorize the star positions they'll need to guide them on their journey, you need a navigation plan to help you as you pursue high-level networking based on relationship building, thereby increasing your influence.

These four planning stages shown in *Figure 8.1*, correspond to the actual ones described by the International Maritime Organization, a specialized agency of the United Nations responsible for regulating shipping, in its Resolution A.893(21).

Your navigation plan will consist of four steps.

1. APPRAISAL

As the IMO puts it, "The navigator should develop a detailed mental model of how the entire voyage will proceed."

In the world of networking and relationship building, this means having a goal and planning how you're going to achieve it. It means having a clear idea of the *known* elements of your plan—that is to say, the people you need to meet and form relationships with. This may be within the corporate organization you

THE FOUR PLANNING STAGES OF A RELATIONSHIP NAVIGATION PLAN

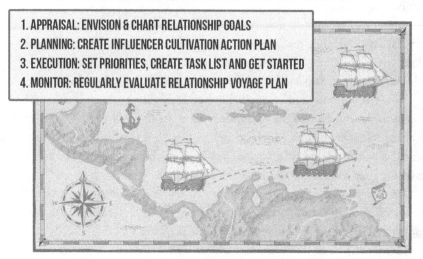

1. APPRAISAL: ENVISION & CHART RELATIONSHIP GOALS
2. PLANNING: CREATE INFLUENCER CULTIVATION ACTION PLAN
3. EXECUTION: SET PRIORITIES, CREATE TASK LIST AND GET STARTED
4. MONITOR: REGULARLY EVALUATE RELATIONSHIP VOYAGE PLAN

Figure 8.1

presently work for, in which case the people you need on your side are denoted by their job titles. But in a more fluid environment such as entrepreneurship or politics, the people you will need to build relationships with are not so clearly marked. They may be loud, vocal people with little influence, or they may be quiet, reclusive power brokers. People who have significant influence today may have no influence tomorrow.

While you must have a plan, you also must be willing to change that plan at a moment's notice. You must be continually engaged in the collection of human data and the synthesis of that data into useful information. Your task is to identify and evaluate those individuals and organizations that are truly influential and could be accessible to you.

Remember, appearances can be deceiving. You need people who wield influence and who can, if you develop a relationship with them, help you to achieve your goals. The people whom you meet, who *appear* to wield influence, will fall into three general categories.

A. THE POSEUR

This person is often a darling of the media and can be seen on cable news and infotainment programs expounding on some topic and assuming the air of a highly influential person. In fact, this person may have very little influence and may even be toxic. Stay on good terms with the poseur—there's nothing to be gained by angering or alienating them—but do not allow yourself to be identified with them, lest your personal brand suffer as a result.

B. THE ICON

Like the poseur, this person is highly visible in the media and is very comfortable being at the center of attention. But unlike the poseur, the icon has substantial, long-lasting influence, and if you are in this person's orbit, you'll be networking at the very highest levels and bolstering your own influence.

A good example of the icon is Bill Gates. He was never camera shy, but in June 2006, he announced he would be transitioning to a part-time role at Microsoft and full-time work at the Bill & Melinda Gates Foundation, the private charitable foundation that he and Melinda Gates established in 2000. Since then, he's been focused on his philanthropic endeavors, including climate change, global health and development, and education. He often appears in the media as a commentator or expert witness on those topics.

Gates has said that in becoming a philanthropist, he was influenced by the example of David Rockefeller. Gates and his father, Bill Gates, Sr., met with Rockefeller more than once, and their charity work is partly modeled on the Rockefeller family's philanthropic focus, dedicated to tackling the global problems that are ignored by governments and other organizations.

Gates knows he has influence, and he's careful about how he uses it. In 2011, he said, "If you gave me the choice between picking the next ten presidents or ensuring that energy is environmentally friendly and a quarter as costly, I'd pick the energy thing."[26]

C. THE SHADOW

The shadow is a person who wields tremendous influence within a certain sphere and yet avoids publicity. Most people would not know them by sight. They do not appear in the media, and you have to be "plugged in" to their circle to even know what they do.

Here's a person I'll wager that, unless you're a denizen of Silicon Valley, you've never heard of. His name is John Doerr. Ring a bell? Probably not. In fact, in the world of venture capital—the high-risk business of launching new companies—he's a superstar.

With a net worth estimated to be $11.5 billion, he's the chairman of Kleiner Perkins, which *The New York Times* has described as "perhaps Silicon Valley's most famous venture firm," while *The Wall Street Journal* called it one of the

---

26   *WIRED*. https://www.wired.com/2011/06/mf-qagates/

"largest and most established" venture capital firms. Doerr has directed the distribution of venture capital funding to some of the most successful technology companies in the world, including Compaq, Netscape, Symantec, Sun Microsystems, drugstore.com, Amazon.com, Intuit, Macromedia, and Google. He's backed some of the world's most successful entrepreneurs, including Larry Page, Sergey Brin, and Eric Schmidt of Google; Jeff Bezos of Amazon.com; and Scott Cook and William Campbell of Intuit.[27]

And if you thought that this book's story about a person landing in Metropolis with no job and no connections was fanciful, read what John Doerr says on the Kleiner Perkins website about his career path:

"I came to Silicon Valley in 1975 with no job and no place to live. I wanted to start a company with friends, just like my dad (and hero) Lou Doerr. I tried to get an internship with a VC firm. And well, they all turned me down. One of them told me about Intel, a new chip company. I cold-called and landed a job there just as they invented the 8-bit microchip.

"Five years later, I joined Kleiner Perkins. They promised to back me in my own startup—and did so, twice. I co-founded Silicon Compilers for chip design and @Home for broadband internet....

"I love working with social and policy entrepreneurs who are transforming healthcare, fighting the climate crisis, improving public education, and combating global poverty."[28]

2. PLANNING

As the IMO says in reference to undertaking a voyage, once information is gathered and considered, the navigator can begin the process of actually laying out the voyage. This involves taking known information and projecting various future events, including landfalls, narrow passages, and course changes expected during the voyage.

In your voyage of relationship building for professional and personal influence, once you have a sufficient grasp of the influential players in your industry or social circle (I say "sufficient grasp" because the process is never-ending), you need to prioritize them. As I've mentioned in this book, you need to do this because your time is not unlimited. The clock is ticking, and you need to follow a plan as you build your network of relationships with people who are more influential than you or who have a specialized influence that's useful to you as you pursue your goals.

---

27 Thrillist.com. https://www.thrillist.com/culture/
   the-most-influential-people-you-have-never-heard-of
28 Kleiner Perkins. https://www.kleinerperkins.com/people/john-doerr/

Let's say you want to meet Susan Smith, the CEO of a firm that you or your company could partner with. How do you get to know her? Of course, you could simply cold-call her, but to form a relationship based on trust, you'd want to engage with her in an outside setting, like in a group designed to foster such relationships.

To go back to our seafaring metaphor, it's like if you knew the course of her ship, you'd simply position your ship so that you were certain to pass each other. Greetings would be exchanged, a conversation would ensue, and—well, you know the rest.

3. EXECUTION

You know the old saying—"Talk is cheap."

There's another one, too: "Actions speak louder than words."

There are probably hundreds of such sayings and for a good reason. No plan, no amount of information, no ambitious intentions are worth a nickel unless they are turned into *action.*

Plans are meant to be acted upon. Plans that are not executed become sources of indecision. As Dale Carnegie said, "Inaction breeds doubt and fear. Action breeds confidence and courage. If you want to conquer fear, do not sit home and think about it. Go out and get busy."

As the IMO says about maritime navigating, be sure to list the tasks that need to be executed during the course of the voyage. It's the captain's—that is, your—responsibility to treat the plan as a "living document" and to review or change it in case of any special circumstances that should arise.

Take small, achievable steps. The biggest mistake you can make is to devise a grandiose plan, and jump into it, expecting it to produce instant results. This is bound to result in failure and disappointment.

The idea of taking positive steps was illustrated perfectly by the 2014 graduation speech Admiral William H. McRaven made at the University of Texas. In the speech—which has since become a bestselling book—McRaven explained why, in the armed services, the first task every recruit does in the morning is *make their bed.* Why is this so important? Because it's a simple task with a defined goal (the military's bed making directions are very precise), and when completed, it provides the recruit with a small victory. As McRaven said, "If you want to change the world, start off by making your bed. If you make your bed every morning, you will have accomplished the first task of the day. It will give you a small sense of pride, and it will encourage you to do another task, and another, and another. By the end of the day, that one task completed will have turned into many tasks completed."[29]

4. MONITORING

The fourth and final stage of voyage execution is the monitoring stage. Once the voyage has begun, the progress of the vessel along its planned route must be regularly checked. This requires that the ship's position be determined using standard methods, including dead reckoning, celestial navigation, pilotage, and electronic navigation.

The same rule applies to your progress in building a network of relationships that help you build influence. Set milestones for yourself. Periodically review those milestones and see if you've met them. What successes have you had? Are there problem areas or challenges?

Monitoring means not only looking backward but looking ahead. Sometimes you achieve a series of milestones that at one time seemed daunting, such as joining a business group and meeting certain people. At that point, you can create a new set of goals that previously seemed outlandish or impossible. Perhaps when you started, the idea of meeting and getting to know a particular CEO was beyond your imagination, but as you completed a set of steps, you found yourself sitting across the table from that CEO! Now it's time to re-evaluate your goals and take your game to the next level.

CREATE ACCOUNTABILITY PARTNERS

If we were all capable of perfect self-analysis, then we wouldn't need anyone else to help us stick to our plan and reach our goals. But we're human, and it can be difficult to be objective. We all need people around us to both cheer us on when the going gets tough and to remind us of goals that are yet unmet.

For many powerful people, their spouse or life partner is a key accountability partner. Carnegie Mellon University psychologists investigated how much difference this can make. A lot, as it turns out. published in *Personality and Social Psychology Bulletin*, researchers discovered that people with supportive spouses were more likely to take on potentially rewarding challenges, and that those who accepted the challenges experienced more personal growth, happiness, psychological well-being and better functioning relationships.[30]

Other leaders have mentors or spiritual advisers. In the modern era, the idea

---

29 McRaven. https://www.usatoday.com/story/life/books/2017/08/23/
    readers-follow-admiral-mcravens-order-make-your-bed/590145001/

30 CMU. https://www.cmu.edu/dietrich/news/news-stories/2017/
    august/supportive-spouses-brooke-feeny.html

goes back to the "Brain Trust," the expert advisers surrounding Franklin D. Roosevelt during his presidential administration. The core consisted of a group of professors from Columbia University who presented Roosevelt with its thinking on economic and social problems facing the nation and helped him weigh the alternatives of public policy that would be open to the president.

More recently, the use of the term has expanded beyond politics to encompass any specialized group of advisers aligned to a decision-maker.

SHARE AND REVIEW YOUR PLANS AND PROGRESS

For your accountability partners to be of real value to you, you need to be transparent with them. It may be one thing to "spin" a story to the public or to investors to present the best possible image of you or your company, but with your brain trust or mentor, honesty is required. They should expect honesty from you and should expect to be able to provide honest opinions and ideas. We have seen throughout history that surrounding yourself with "yes men" who simply parrot back what you say to them will result in certain disaster. Make your plan, execute your plan, review the results with your team, and revise your plan. Repeat, repeat, repeat!

SUCCESS ACTION ITEMS –
PREPARE AND PLAN FOR THE ULTIMATE JOURNEY

- Raise your sights. Be proactive and create new opportunities.
- Gain perspective. Research the marketplace for opportunities. Look around at what's happening today. Ask yourself where you fit in?
- Connect with new business influencers. Think about people you've never met but who could become a part of your sphere of influence.
- Look out at the horizon. Think not just about the opportunities that exist at present, but of the opportunities over the horizon, out of sight, or better yet, the opportunities that you can *create*.
- Practice makes perfect. To build and use influence, you have to apply yourself and work towards your goal.
- See the big picture by creating a vision and plan. You need to know where you want to go. You need a broad perspective.
- Use digital and social media in a very calculated way. It can make you or break you!
- Widen your sphere of influence. To navigate your way through the halls of influence and widen your sphere while avoiding blind turns, you need specific knowledge of the influence landscape.
- Navigate and monitor your business environment constantly to learn patterns in the marketplace. Be as the ancient Polynesians. Their vast knowledge of their environment gave context to the data collected by observation and turned it into *actionable information.*
- Create a navigation plan to help you pursue high-level networking based on relationship building and increase your influence. Your navigation plan will consist of four steps.

    1. Appraise. Develop a detailed mental model of how the entire relationship voyage will proceed.
    2. Plan. In your voyage of relationship building for influence, get a grasp on influential players then prioritize them.
    3. Execute. No plan, no amount of information, no ambitious intentions are worth a nickel unless they are turned into *action.*
    4. Monitor. Set milestones, then review those milestones to see if you've met them. What are your successes? Are there problem areas or challenges?

- Create accountability partners who will both cheer you on when the going gets tough and remind you of goals that are yet unmet.
- Share your plan. For your accountability partners to be of real value to you, you need to be transparent with them.
- Make your plan, execute your plan, review the results with your accountability partner, and revise your plan. Repeat, repeat, repeat!

ANU SHUKLA
CO-FOUNDER & EXECUTIVE CHAIRMAN BOTCO.AI

"Innovation is My Game"

WHAT MOTIVATES ME

THERE ARE MANY THINGS THAT motivate me, so I'm very happy with what I'm doing, where I'm going, and what I'm getting.

I grew up in the northern part of India. I moved to the United States for college. I earned my MBA at Youngstown State University, where I was the commencement speaker in 2008. Then I went to work in Silicon Valley, and I've been there ever since.

About twenty years ago I co-founded a marketing automation company called Rubric, which in eighteen months we sold for about $400 million.

More recently I've been working on a venture called Rewards Pay. I'm the founder and CEO. Customers can use their miles on United Airlines, for example, to shop on Amazon. We were doing fine. I had turned it into a profitable enterprise, and then COVID-19 hit. We sell virtual currency-based payments in the airline industry, and they suffered a lot during the pandemic. It reduced our business by 90 percent but we expect them to rebound.

The third company is Botco.ai, which I co-founded with my partner from Rubric in 2017. Botco.ai is a disruptive enterprise marketing automation platform powered by natural language artificial intelligence. The idea was that we would bootstrap it and we would make it a second gig, but it started to take off, so we went in as co-founders, started the company, raised money, and now we're building a demand generation machine and closing deals. Interestingly enough, our shared vision was a new marketing platform using artificial intelligence, chat, and messaging to engage with customers, and to start where Rubric had left off, which was email drip marketing campaign management. We were quite the pioneers back then. This is like the next generation, but adding the mobile intelligent chat with AI capabilities, in an easy-to-use form for marketers.

We wanted to go out and be part of this new marketing technology, but

189

because of COVID-19, we actually started to take off. We got calls from all kinds of healthcare companies including behavior addiction, senior living centers, physical therapy clinics, and urgent care centers. People called us and asked, "What do you have that helps me better my patient experience digitally? I need to do more remotely." We started working with those clients, and we quit our other jobs and started to focus on this full-time. We're selling to marketing people a better way to engage, a better patient experience, and a better patient journey.

Another project I'm involved in is angel investing through a group called TIE Angels in Silicon Valley. I've made a few investments and am enjoying the process of working with my angel group and investing in companies with un-derrepresented founders, including women, Latinx, and Black entrepreneurs. A venture firm approached me called elevate.vc, who happened to have a lot of crossover with Thai Angels. So I got to know the GPs and I joined them as a venture partner. I liked their mission to fund underrepresented founders. It's a $40 million fund. I get to scout around and find deals, I get to weigh in, I get to do due diligence, and I can be as active as I want to be. All our founders are Black and Latinx women. That's our mission, that's all we do. When the first fund was closed, we basically announced six companies and they were all funded. Five of them were Black women founders and the sixth one was Latinx.

I have all this new stuff going on and the whole startup grind which I love. I get to do my own startup, which is just getting beyond seed stage, raising a few million dollars and lots of revenue coming in. Working with a new CEO, I can guide my RewardsPay project.

MAKINGS OF A STARTUP

Rubric was not the most successful company I've had. There were many others, but starting up Rubric was very interesting. It was my first startup. I've been fortunate enough to be part of teams of startups that either got acquired for lots of money or they went public, so I had a positive outlook to a startup. For years I had been working in marketing as a B2B marketer. I was well known. In fact, there was an article in *Business 2.0*, which was a big magazine at that time. The article asked, "What is a dream team?" If you were in the B2B high-tech industry and you had to put together a dream team, who would you hire? So the article gave a CEO, a CFO, a CMO all from different companies. I was named as the CMO.

I was good at what I did, and it contributed to my success in B2B. I went to a VC who funded me, and he told me, "You know, when you look at B2B marketing and you look at the top three people, your name is there. That's why I'm going to fund you."

I was a successful B2B marketer, and I wanted to build a piece of software that did not yet exist, called enterprise marketing automation. VCs waited on funding us. They asked us, "Isn't that like an oxymoron? Can you really automate marketing?"

Later, marketing automation became a very well-known concept, which is now a multibillion-dollar industry, but we were the first ones. One of the concepts was this idea of drip marketing, or email nurturing. Unlike consumer marketing, in B2B you don't send out a communication, a direct mail or a letter, or an ad, and then expect another business to buy your product. The client may say to you, "Okay, I know about you now, and when I have a need I'll call you." What you want to do is be in front of the client because that identifies you. They are going to want your product someday. So you send them your white paper, you invite them to whatever. You are building and nurturing business relationships.

I put that into software, and at that time, delivery was just web pages and email. Today, with Botco.ai, we're delivering it through messaging and conversations. We're doing the same thing, we call it "intelligent chat nurturing." That was a very dear concept which I feel that I had perfected, and I built the first piece of software that captured it.

Most VCs thought we were crazy. They said, "You're trying to do something with marketing that nobody needs. It's been done for years. It's an art." And I replied, "No, it's a science." The question was, why should only salespeople get automation from Siebel Systems or salesforce.com? People never envisioned a need for marketing automation. At the time, it was all about sales automation. And so here was marketing, sitting there with the biggest discretionary cash budget, and it didn't have a scientific way to spend and be effective. So we focused on our own concepts and we were definitely very friendly with the other two legs of CRM. I called them sales and customer service. We were the ones who said marketing is a third leg.

We went to leaders who used our product in amazing ways and had great success with it. It was a really original idea that we built, and it was built from our experience. Before the 2000 crash hit, we were fortunate enough to have five companies trying to buy us. Now it's an essential part of everybody's CRM suite. We made a lot of mistakes, but it was very exciting. We were subject matter experts, so it was natural for us to talk about it.

We also learned from leaders like Tom Siebel, who started Siebel Systems. He always wanted to look larger than life, so he would pick a CRM show and get the biggest booth. People thought Siebel was so big before they actually were that big.

We tried to learn from them. We went to the same show. One year Tom Siebel was the keynote speaker. The next year, I was the keynote speaker. I had my posters all over the McCormick Center in Chicago. People thought we were so big, and we weren't. We were sharing rooms in the nearby hotels because we didn't have enough money for everybody to have their own room. So we had to learn from other people who came before us to show us how it is done.

STEPPING INTO A STRANGE CITY

If I found myself in a strange land and had to survive, I would first find some place to stay. If I had zero money, then I would probably go to a church or a social place where I could stay. I would take care of my short-term needs.

I would seek out people who could help me. I have skills, so I would find out the best places to get a job because I would need to sustain myself. I'm educated, so I would concentrate on finding a temporary job so I could be self-sufficient.

Then, knowing that I like to build businesses, I would go around and check out the needs for products and services that are missing from this environment, which I could perhaps get involved with to build.

I would find out if there were a local entrepreneurs' club or women's club. I would start networking like crazy, to find people and meet them and tell them about myself and what I'm doing. I would look for collaborators and people who could help me. I would work on an idea that would create some value in whatever field I saw was missing.

I'd look for sources of people who would give me input. Because I've started many companies and that's what I know how to do, I'd try to find the need, then validate the market, design the product, find people to collaborate with me, and find people to fund me so I could get this enterprise going. That's what I do well.

INFLUENCE

Influence to me is having the ability to make your opinions matter. It's your opinion or your educated idea of what a solution or direction is, and persuading people that you are right, and that they should follow you or be in agreement with you in order to make something happen. It's coming from a person who wants to make a positive change happen. It's having credibility, and people thinking you are qualified to have an opinion that they would be open to listening to.

INFLUENCER

I think in the right environment, when I walk in with a lot of experience, people tend to listen to me. So I would say "yes." Because of my experience and my position, and because I have learned how to persuasively express my ideas, I do tend to be an influencer in my environment.

STRATEGIC INFLUENCE

When you think of the word "strategic," you're taking action with a long-term view. They go hand in hand. If you are knowledgeable and experienced and wise on certain subjects, then you have a strategy to approach a problem, and you can take a long-term view.

To be a strategic influencer, you have to be relevant, and you have to be of a certain integrity and a certain caliber that is relevant to your brand. For example, you can't have an influencer hold up everybody's product, one after the other. Today it's the best lipstick, and tomorrow, something else. That's less credible to me because you're just promoting whatever products someone is paying you for.

Secondly, if a so-called influencer who's not an expert in makeup is telling me that this lipstick is good, why should I care? It's like the infomercial with a singer who is promoting the best slow cooker. Why do I care? You're a singer! Why are you an expert in slow cooking? I think it's more interesting when you see somebody who is fifty-five years old, and they look younger. For example, Cindy Crawford is fifty-five and she looks like she's twenty-five. I'm going to believe her.

People want to know your motivation for why you're involved, and why you're influencing and promoting a certain product. I think people can see authentic engagement versus something that's made up for the purposes of a commercial.

CENTER OF INFLUENCE

When I think of a center of influence, I think of a "super influencer" with a lot of followers. People hang on every word they say. They probably have more impact than many of the small influencers. They are the strategic center because they have authenticity and demonstrated usefulness that has led to people being influenced. Maybe they're an expert, like in the gaming world, PewDiePie. People just tune in to watch him play because he's so good.

The question is how to cultivate relationships with these centers of influence. We're facing that all the time in business. Let's say you're selling something to a networking company, and if you can get Cisco as a client, then a lot of people like Juniper Networks will follow.

It's similar to that on an individual basis. You know who's the influencer in your industry. You have to network like crazy and find out what they care about. You have to give them something they really care about for them to pay attention to you. You find out that your brand promise is interesting to them, or the excellence of your offering is something that's right up their alley, or you're doing something good for a cause they care about so they want to be involved. You find some common ground to stand above everyone else trying to get their attention.

DEEP DOWN HABITS

I have had startups that have not been successful. That's okay because I learned a lot from them. I'm not afraid of failing. You fail, you pivot, you learn. Sometimes there's no time to pivot, and it's time to move on.

The two important things are to try your best and don't make the same mistake twice.

For my whole life, whatever I've done, I always try to do things that I like to do. I think being happy doing what you're doing is one of the things that makes a person successful. I like to pursue my passions. Everything is like a passion project to me.

I also like to do a variety of things. I don't like to be stuck in a rut. I don't like to say, "I'm only the CEO, or I'm only the VP of marketing, and that's all I can be." No, I can be many things. I can be whatever you need me to be for that situation. Not having a big ego is really helpful. I ask myself, "Does doing this make me happy and productive, and does it help the company?"

Next, I don't give up. I say, "Okay, that didn't work, so let's try something else." I actually don't care what the end result is. I'm just making sure I'm enjoying the journey.

STARTING ALL OVER AGAIN

If I had to go back, there are not very many things I would do differently. I was not very good in terms of staying in touch with a lot of people because there was always something new to go after. But on the other hand, I have some very long-term relationships. For example, I started my current company, Botco.ai, with my co-founder from Rubric, which was twenty years ago. It's not like I'm not capable of having long-term relationships; rather, I just wish I could have had more of them.

It takes effort to stay in touch with people, and I've tended to apply that effort to people in my current environment. If I had a "do-over," I would apply more energy and time to keep those older relationships fresh because they were really lovely people. I'm still in touch with them, but I wish I was more engaged with them over a longer period of time.

In some ways, social media is a problem. When you use social media, you're "friends" with all these people, but you never talk to them or meet them in person. If you had a party, or you hiked somewhere, and then you posted a picture, then you'd feel like you were in touch with them because they saw what you did yesterday. You feel very comfortable thinking, "I'm in touch with these four thousand friends." But you are not. You're not being genuinely friendly with any of the four thousand. Our dependence on social media can destroy real friendships.

ONE DEFINING MOMENT

I would have to say founding Rubric was a very momentous occasion for me because it was the first time that I started something on my own. I was always part of somebody else's team, but this was really a leap of faith. And I said, "I think I can do this." I started a marketing automation thing, and had the guts to do that.

I took my trusted lieutenant, who had worked with me for a decade over three different jobs, and I grabbed him. He had kids and a family life, and I asked him to start this company with me. We did not have a single penny of funding. We didn't even know any venture capitalists. Then I told a friend I was looking for somebody to build this, and she introduced me to Chris. He was a researcher at Xerox Park, finishing up his PhD, and had never had a job in his life at that point. We liked him. So we're like, "Oh, you're from MIT. You must be smart. Come on, you can build this."

And he said, "Yeah, I think I can build it."

Back then, we didn't know any better, so we just kind of did it. *USA Today* did a four-thousand-word front-page article about our team. We were in Chris's loft in San Francisco, building an enterprise software company. Because we didn't have the money, we were hiring people and paying them as little as possible. It was so much fun and so risky, and we didn't even care. It was all about taking that leap of faith, and then eighteen months later selling it for four hundred million dollars. That was a momentous thing for us to give up our corporate careers, which we were very comfortable in and at the top of our game.

Doing this could have gone either way. The thing is, it's better to be doing something than not. We could have had our corporate careers and we would have missed the whole bubble, because if you were in the bubble at the right time and you exited at the right time, you did well. I like being part of something and riding the wave because luck is a big part of being successful. It's not just how smart you are, and even greater preparation will not help you if you don't have that one bit of luck. That's why I believe that if you're doing things, and you're out there, then you're likely to have a good outcome.

I think that Rubric experience shaped that idea in me, that we should be *doing* something versus *not doing* something. That keeps me interested in keeping going. It's kind of a lifelong value.

MY GREATEST INFLUENCE

This is a very tough question for me. I've had bosses from whom I've learned valuable things. There are people whom I admire and have spent time with, like Steve Jobs. I'm like a sponge. I try to learn from everybody. I'm constantly in a learning mode, so if you have an interaction with me, I'm trying to learn from you, and hopefully I'm giving something back as well.

I would say all the people in Silicon Valley whom I look up to certainly influence me: Tom Siebel, Larry Ellison, Bill Gates, Elon Musk. They're all amazing. I read everything about them, and I learn about them, and I've met most of them.

I've been influenced by their moves and what they're doing, but also by many great women leaders as well, such as Meg Whitman because they have great qualities and have overcome some bigger barriers. I'm influenced by everybody who came before me.

I do have to say that my parents were amazing, and if they didn't give me the values, I think I would be nowhere. If I were to put everybody and my dad in two buckets, I would say my dad influenced me the most. He mostly influenced me by making me believe that I could do anything, by really valuing education. He would give me these books to read, and we would discuss subjects like physics and dark matter. These are the kind of conversations we had at home. We had no television, so conversation was a big deal for us, as was engaging at that level on a variety of subjects from religion to politics to science. That's the way he influenced me. Of course, he was a very successful businessman, and he was an army officer. He fought for his country. For girls, our dads are like our heroes.

Anu is a serial entrepreneur with more than twenty-five years of high-tech industry experience. She is an active angel investor and venture partner with elevate.vc *personally supporting and investing in women and minority led enterprises. Anu has founded and exited several software companies: Fintech, RewardsPay, Tapjoy, MyBuys, and early marketing automation pioneer Rubric, Inc. She has successfully exited two startups with $600M enterprise value. Anu is the Co-Founder and Executive Chair of Botco.ai, an emerging player in the application of AI/NLP to enterprise marketing automation use cases. She serves on several nonprofit boards and has experience in SaaS, Adtech and Martech product companies. She has a Bachelor of Arts degree from St. Stephens College, and an MBA and Doctorate (Honorary) in Business Administration and Management from Youngstown State University.*

Website: www.botco.ai
LinkedIn: www.linkedin.com/in/anushukla/

SPHERE OF OPPORTUNITY

SUCCESS FACTOR 7:
ASSESS YOUR PERSONAL DRIVING FORCES

*"There is a powerful driving force inside every human being
that once unleashed can make any vision,
dream or desire a reality."*
—Anthony Robbins

WHEN CHRISTOPHER COLUMBUS FIRST SET sail for what he thought was the Far East, he made his daring expedition into the unknown for several powerful reasons.

He wanted the personal glory of being the first European explorer to sail west to China.

He was undoubtedly driven by a sincere desire to expand the knowledge of humankind about the uncharted areas of the Earth, about which little was known.

He wanted to reward his patrons, Ferdinand and Isabella, who had agreed to underwrite his project.

He also expressed a desire to establish Christianity in new territories. There was a practical reason for this. Under the Mongol Empire's hegemony over Asia, European traders had long been granted a safe land passage, via the Silk Road, to India, China, and other Asian regions. These were sources of valuable imports, including spices and silk. But with the takeover of Constantinople by the Ottoman Turks in 1453, the land route to Asia was closed to Christian traders. Hence, Europeans felt new pressure to find a sea route across the Atlantic.

Perhaps more than anything, though, Columbus also had a significant interest in building his personal power and wealth.

As Samuel Eliot Morison noted in *Admiral of the Ocean Sea: A Life of Christopher Columbus,* in the April 1492 agreement entitled "Capitulations of Santa Fe," King Ferdinand and Queen Isabella promised Columbus that if he succeeded in discovering unclaimed lands, he would be given the rank of Admiral of the Ocean Sea and appointed Viceroy and Governor of all the new lands he could claim for Spain. He had the right to nominate three persons, from whom the sovereigns would choose one, for any office in the new lands. He would be entitled to ten percent of all the revenues from the new lands in perpetuity. Additionally, he would also have the option of buying one-eighth interest in any commercial venture with the new lands and receive one-eighth of the profits.

Profit and power—two very motivating forces!

The same can be said for your personal journey to develop your influence. While you need to be focused on reaching your external goals—meeting people, forming relationships, entering into partnerships—you also need to look in the mirror on a regular basis, and take stock of what motivates you, and determine how you can best leverage that motivation for success.

I call these motivators your *personal driving forces*. They consist of those values or goals that are most important to you and that motivate you more than others. They are not the same thing as skills. We all know plenty of people who have an amazing skill at something, but because they lack sufficient driving forces, their skill languishes. They don't leverage it for the betterment of themselves or large numbers of people.

When you first landed in Metropolis, having few resources, you instinctively did those things you were good at. If you were a gregarious person who had no problem talking to strangers, that's probably how you got started on the road to building relationships. If you were more introverted but possessed a special skill, you used that skill to give your personal brand its value and to draw people to you. You just did whatever you were capable of doing to get ahead, and if you were smart and hardworking, it worked. (Hey, it brought you this far! That's good!)

Up until now, you have been developing your Personal Value, (covered in chapter one), by means of obtaining education, knowledge, expertise, and experience. Personal value gave you the necessary credibility to establish a strong reputation, to acquire strategic relationships, and to become a leader. You assumed the role of influencer and through association with strategic relationships, or centers of influence, you then gained a higher perspective of what it will take to expand your influence. Opportunity is on the horizon.

In as much as you have taken the time to prepare and plan for the ultimate journey, you are now ready to enter into the Sphere of Opportunity. You're using the influence you've built to not only respond to opportunities but to create them, the stakes are getting higher. It's like moving up the ladder from employee to manager to director, or from city councilor to mayor to member of Congress. At each step, the rewards and responsibilities grow. More is expected from you, and your growing influence means that what you choose to do impacts not only your own life but the lives of an increasingly wide circle of other people.

The further you go on your Success Factor journey, the more important your personal driving forces become. This is because you need them to be both broad and deep. When you first set foot in Metropolis, it may have been sufficient to have one or two personal driving forces to get you started. Let's say your first job in Metropolis was flipping burgers at a fast-food joint. At the time, your personal driving force was simply the desire to support yourself and avoid living in a homeless shelter. But as you made progress, and became the shift manager, then the store manager, and then a regional director in the corporate office, your personal driving forces needed to become more robust, and you needed to pay more attention to them.

EVALUATE YOUR PERSONAL DRIVING FORCES

The human personality is complicated, and much of what makes us who we are is formed early in life. We are shaped by genetics and by the circumstances of childhood. As an adult, you cannot simply re-invent yourself into an image you've chosen. It's difficult to suddenly care about things that, for your entire life, you haven't thought much about. While you can make an effort to improve or strengthen some aspect of your personality—for example, you can learn how to be a public speaker—your fundamental driving forces can be changed only very slowly.

Having said that, your personal driving forces can evolve over time. Human beings never stop growing and learning, and our values can change. For example, young people generally tolerate much more risk than older people, who, as they age, have more to lose. At every stage of your success journey, it's important to know your personal driving forces and how you can put them to work for you. To illustrate the concept, we'll use a sailing ship as a model to demonstrate personal influence growth as shown in *Figure 9.1*.

The ship's wheel, as has been portrayed throughout the book, represents the 6 spheres of strategic influence and the associated 10 success factors you have utilized to advance from one sphere to the next. The person at the wheel represents you as the leader and captain of the ship. The sails, represent the three growth elements of influence, beginning with the first sail labeled Personal Value (PV), as introduced in chapter one and illustrated here. Sail two is labeled Personal Driving Forces (PDF), representing your motivation or purpose, for seeking influence, leadership opportunities, and success. Sail three is labeled

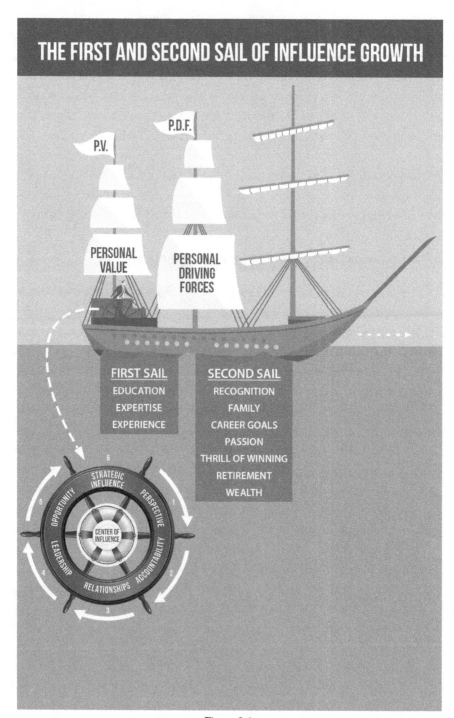

Figure 9.1

Personal Competitive Competencies (PCC). This is the third element of influence growth representing your leadership capability and potential, made possible through competitive assets you have developed. Competitive Competencies will be covered in the next chapter.

Here are seven common driving forces that propel leaders forward toward positions of influence. Let's imagine, for the time being, that every person possesses just one of these drivers. Of course, that's not the way real people are, but it makes understanding the concept much easier.

1. RECOGNITION

Human beings are social creatures, and the vast majority of us want and appreciate when our peers recognize and applaud our good deeds and intentions.

Recognition comes in three levels. The first level is the acknowledgment of our existence. We get this when people talk with us, listen to us, and take an interest in our thoughts, actions, and well-being. Without this basic type of recognition, we feel alone, and our sense of identity shrinks. At its extreme, prisoners in solitary confinement, deprived of even the most rudimentary recognition, can experience panic attacks, depression, and paranoia, and even hallucinations.

The next recognition is praise and reward, in which other people acknowledge our achievements and thereby encourage continued effort. Without this, we easily become demotivated and unsure of the real value of our work. Because human beings depend on each other for survival, as individuals, we seek signs of recognition from our peers and from those on whom we depend. We want to know that we're on the right track and are making a contribution to the growth and success of our culture.

The third level is respect—when we are truly valued for our contributions. This is the most satisfying because it's deeply felt.

2. FAMILY

Many people are motivated by the desire to have a family and then provide for their child or children. This is a healthy impulse that can provide purpose, drive, and satisfaction as you succeed in your business or profession while simultaneously sharing the fruits with your family.

The most successful family in American business is the Walton family, heirs to the Walmart company. As of early 2021, the three most prominent living members (Jim, Rob, and Alice Walton) have consistently been in the top twenty of the Forbes 400 list, as were John (died in 2005) and Helen (died in 2007) prior to their deaths. After his death, Christy Walton took her husband John's place in the ranking.

In 2018, the family sold some of their company's stock and now owns just under fifty percent. In July 2020, the annual *Sunday Times* Rich List reported the Walton family's net worth was estimated at $215 billion. Their collective fortune makes them the richest family in the United States and the richest family in the world. They are surprisingly harmonious, too—unlike the ultra-wealthy Koch brothers, you rarely read tabloid stories about conflicts within the Walton family.

3. CAREER GOALS

A powerful motivator can be career ambition and the desire to climb the ladder of success. A career path is usually well defined by society and visible to anyone. It's most often when you join a company and set your sights on rising through the ranks until you achieve the top executive position. As you climb upward, you can see your goal. Your leverage gradually increases as your influence relationship networking brings you into contact with more and more people who themselves have influence.

You can also build a career as a solo entrepreneur, like Sir Richard Branson. He began at the age of sixteen with a magazine called *Student*, and then he started a mail-order record business, and then he founded a chain of record stores. Today he presides over the Virgin Group, a vast global conglomerate that includes Virgin Galactic, a company that develops commercial spacecraft.

4. PASSION

Having a passion for something can be a powerful personal driving force, but you need to make that passion relevant to the wider community and to your quest to build your personal influence.

For example, in all of modern history, there is no one whom we regard as more passionate about his calling than the artist Vincent van Gogh. In the last decade of his short life, he dedicated himself to his art with an intensity that was unmatched. His passion was sincere, and it produced results: Today, many paintings by Van Gogh are considered among the world's great masterpieces. In 1990, his painting entitled *Portrait of Dr. Gauchet* sold at auction for a record $82.5 million.

While it seems inevitable that Van Gogh's work should be highly prized and influential long after his death, during his lifetime Van Gogh exerted very little influence on anybody. He labored in obscurity, and he sold only one painting—to another artist. He never experienced the influence he later created.

The goal of this book is to help you develop your influence while you're still alive and young enough to enjoy it!

Be passionate—but be sure to transform your passion into measurable results. Follow the lead of Yvon Chouinard, who in the late 1950s was an accomplished rock climber. Dissatisfied with the gear he was buying, in 1957, he began selling hand-forged mountain climbing gear through his company Chouinard Equipment. He worked alone, selling his devices from the back of his car until 1965, when he partnered with Tom Frost in order to improve his products and address the growing supply and demand issue he faced. The company grew, and today, Patagonia is an influential leader in outdoor clothing with annual revenues of over $200 million.

5. THE THRILL OF WINNING

Some people—maybe you—just like to *win*. They want to enter a competition and come out on top. Tiger Woods likes to win, and so does Tom Brady, Venus and Serena Williams, LeBron James, and other sports stars. But plenty of businesspeople like to win as well. Warren Buffett, the Oracle of Omaha, is a polite, mild-mannered person who likes to play bridge with his friends in the evening. But when it comes to investing, he likes to *win*. And win he does—as the chairman and CEO of Berkshire Hathaway, he's relentlessly focused on his strategy of value investing, and he's built his enterprise into a business that's worth nearly $500 billion.

In the investment community, Buffet has enormous influence. Each year, he writes an open letter to Berkshire Hathaway shareholders. Over the last forty years, these annual letters have become required reading across the investing world, providing insight into how Buffett and his team think about diverse subjects, including investment strategy, stock ownership, and company culture.

6. RETIREMENT

Most people, even some in their twenties and thirties, actively plan for retirement and focus their energy on building their retirement fund. To be able to enjoy a comfortable retirement has become an important goal for many because while people are living longer than ever, the age of retirement is still where it's been for decades. When Social Security was signed into law in 1935, the retirement age was set at sixty-five years old. Statistically, by the time most retirees hit seventy, they were dead. Retirement was designed to be a short period of time: You retired, spent a few years playing shuffleboard, and then you died. Times have changed, and now it's not uncommon for someone to retire at sixty-five or even sixty and then live another twenty or thirty years! That takes a lot of money, and you need to earn most of it when you're in the prime of life.

7. WEALTH

Wealth is a funny thing. If you asked people if they wanted to be wealthy, most would reply, "Are you crazy? Of course!" For some people, the acquisition of wealth for its own sake is a powerful personal driving force. They want all the trappings of extreme wealth—the private yachts, mansions, airplanes, club memberships. They work hard so they can get these things.

But for most people, wealth is a *byproduct* of their other personal driving forces. Of course, they want to make money, but they want to receive money for doing something they love to do and can make a difference. Think about people like Bill Gates, Mark Zuckerberg, and Jeff Bezos (who has become the wealthiest person in the world, with a fortune of $185 billion and counting). These entrepreneurs began with very little except an idea, which they didn't even know could be profitable. They wanted to succeed, but initially, they didn't know exactly what success would look like or bring them.

Sometimes the wealth is so great, it's embarrassing. In August 2010, forty of America's wealthiest people joined together in a commitment to give the majority of their assets to charity. Created by Bill and Melinda Gates and Warren Buffett, the Giving Pledge was born after a series of conversations with philanthropists around the world about how they could collectively set a new standard of generosity among the ultra-wealthy. The Giving Pledge is a simple concept: an open invitation for billionaires, or those who would be if not for their giving, to publicly commit to giving the majority of their wealth to philanthropic causes or organizations.

When you're ultra-wealthy, sometimes you can't unload your money fast enough! As *Business Insider* reported in August 2020, over seventy-five percent of the original signatories to the Giving Pledge had become richer than when they had signed in 2010, according to a report by the progressive think tank Institute for Policy Studies (IPS). The report suggested that many signatories were making money faster than they were giving it away. The net worth of nine of the original signatories, including Facebook's Mark Zuckerberg, Home Depot co-founder Ken Langone, and Salesforce's Marc Benioff, had grown by more than 200 percent.[31]

GOGETTER MENTALITY

Most people have a mix of personal driving forces, with varying levels of each one. Taken all together, they represent your GoGetter Mentality. This is your

---

31 https://bit.ly/3bTbUHW

unique combination of personal drivers that determines your individual path to Influence Relationship Authority, which I'll discuss in this chapter.

For example, Susan may care a great deal about recognition from her peers, the thrill of winning, and her passion for her work, while caring less about retirement, family, or wealth. In contrast, John might be focused on building wealth for his retirement and providing for his family, while caring little about recognition or the thrill of winning.

To chart your own GoGetter Mentality and see for yourself what's really important to you, complete this simple exercise. List the 7 Personal Driving Forces in order of importance to you.

But here's the special way to do it.

It's often easier to decide what you would *give up* rather than what you *want*. This is why you should start at the *bottom*. In other words, start by listing personal driving force #7, which you care the *least* about, and could afford to eliminate. Remember, it's not that you *dislike* the one you eliminate; it's what you would eliminate if you were *forced to*.

1. (Most Important)

2.

3.

4. (Somewhat Important)

5.

6.

7. (Least Important)

(I'm not going to give you a sample because I don't want to influence your choices.)

Then choose the next personal driving force that, if you had to, you would eliminate. This will be #6. Then you will have five left. Choose another to eliminate, and so on. Soon you will have only two left, and then just one.

This is your GoGetter Mentality, from 1 (most important) to 7 (least important). Can it change over time? Yes. It's logical that when you're twenty-five years old, retirement will be at #7, least important. Then by the time you reach seventy years of age, it will probably be near the top!

INFLUENCE RELATIONSHIP NETWORKING

At this point in your journey, you're ready to think in terms of Influence Relationship Networking.

It's quite simple, really.

The three terms are symbiotic. They depend upon each other for their growth and success.

1. The more influence you have, the more networking you can do, which creates relationships.

2. The more you network, the more relationships you create, which builds your influence.

3. The more relationships you have, the more you can network, which builds your influence.

As you can see, each of the three support and reinforce the other two. The net result is that your influence grows in proportion to your level of networking and the number of quality relationships you have.

Once you have a high level of influence, the networking and relationship-building pieces will begin to be self-fulfilling because people will be coming to you.

Consider anyone who's highly influential, such as Oprah Winfrey, Bill Gates, or the President of the United States. At their level, people are clamoring to meet them and form relationships with them. The problem faced by these high-level influencers is one of weeding out the trivial or even toxic potential relationships from the ones that are positive and valuable. There are two forces at work here:

1. There are only so many hours in the day, and if you're a high-level influencer with people lined up to meet you, you need to edit the line.

2. Unfortunately, high-level celebrity influencers attract people who are unstable or who have malicious intent. Security becomes an issue, and this serves to limit access to you. That's one reason why celebrities flock to events such as the Academy Awards in Hollywood or the annual World Economic Forum in Davos—there is safety in numbers.

INFLUENCE RELATIONSHIP AUTHORITY

Your Influence Relationship Networking is the key to building your Influence Relationship Authority. This is the culmination of everything you've done since landing in Metropolis (or being born, or graduating from college—take your pick) to establish your place in society and the economy, assume positions of leadership, and influence the thinking and activities of others.

Your Influence Relationship Authority is built on three pillars. The stronger these pillars are, the better.

PILLAR 1: ENTRUST

All great relationships begin with trust. It takes time to build and is hard to regain once it's lost. Without trust, relationships of every kind—business, personal, romantic, political—will fail.

To build trust, you need to be true to your word and follow through with your promises. Keeping your word shows others what you expect from them, and in turn, they'll be more likely to treat you with respect, developing further trust in the process.

Communication is key. Good communication includes being clear about what you have or have not committed to and what has been agreed upon. Poor communication can destroy a relationship.

Know that it takes time to build and earn trust. It doesn't happen overnight—building trust is a daily commitment.

Put trust in, and you will get trust in return.

Always be honest, even when it's difficult. If you are caught telling a lie, no matter how trivial, your trustworthiness will be diminished.

Everyone makes mistakes. If you attempt to hide your mistakes, people will sense that you are being dishonest. If you pretend that you never make mistakes, you'll make it difficult for others to trust you because they will know you aren't being truthful.

Don't always self-promote. Recognize and appreciate the efforts of others. This will show your capacity for teamwork and leadership and strengthen the trust others have in you.

How do you know when trust has been achieved? You know you trust each other when you feel safe, comfortable, open, close. It's reflected in your willingness to listen to the tough stuff—and learn from it.

PILLAR 2: ENGAGE

Trust will grow significantly only when each party of the relationship engages and practices trust by doing business together in some form, such as introductions to customers, partnering in various ways such as cross-promotion, bundling of products and services, or joint ventures.

In the workplace, build trust by seeing your colleagues as potential and synergistic business partners and by encouraging your team members to do the same. This means that in your relationships—and theirs too—you go beyond everyday cordiality and the ability to "get along" with each other, which are the bare minimum requirements for a successful enterprise. Look at it this way: If you've ever worked on an assembly line or in any other group setting with repetitive work, you know that the relationship bar is very low. All that is expected or necessary is that you do your job, keep up the pace, and behave like a normal human being. Influence is *not* part of the equation.

When you see your colleagues and stakeholders as potential partners, your interactions go to a much higher level. You're not just completing or managing work; you're creating work and planning for future projects. For that, you need a high level of influence. You should focus on influence-based engagement activities, including making personal introductions and creating activities where you and others can bond.

Engaging with someone can happen fast or very slowly. The question I'm often asked is, "Is it possible to fast-track a relationship?"

My answer is yes, if you can do these three things:

1. Be fully present in each personal contact (face to face, ear to ear, Zoom to Zoom). Remove all distractions, and focus on the person you are with.

2. Listen intently. This means listening with an active interest or active listening. As you do it, you should be listening for situations for which the other person needs help. Focus on learning one thing you can help resolve for this person with whom you want to build a new relationship of trust.

3. Be proactively helpful. Once you identify an opportunity to help this person, then proactively schedule a time to get it done.

These three steps will do more to help build a relationship and fast-track trust than months of shallow attempts to "get to know" the other person.

PILLAR 3: ENDORSE

Once a deep-rooted relationship evolves, then relationships of trust can endorse and promote each other.

This is synergy—the interaction or cooperation of two or more people, organizations, or other agents to produce a combined effect greater than the sum of their separate effects.

Relationships of mutual endorsement are based on co-creating outcomes. In these synergistic relationships, each person shares their opportunities with the other so that both benefit.

A simple example would be if Jack belonged to the exclusive Business Leaders Club, and Susan belonged to the equally exclusive Entrepreneurs Club. If each sponsored the other for membership in their respective clubs, then both would benefit. Remember, a key component of building influence is your ability and desire to provide something of value to another person, which is not only the basis for a relationship built on trust but also adds to your personal influence. When the other person reciprocates—which they almost certainly will, eventually—then you will acquire something of value that you didn't have before.

Build strong relationships by consistently providing value to your network—things as simple as responding to inquiries in a timely manner, offering advice when solicited, and making industry connections for others. If you think two of your professional colleagues could benefit from each other's expertise, then introduce them. This simple gesture will be remembered, and you'll be the first to come to mind when they can return the favor.

Here's an important point to remember: While your influence is determined by how abundantly you place other people's interests first, you should never be anyone's doormat.

The world is full of "takers," who seek to take advantage of every opportunity without giving anything in return. Such people are toxic and should be avoided. You'll find out about them by painful experience, but consider the lesson to be valuable.

Periodically evaluate your relationships to ensure that they continue to be mutually beneficial. Always look to ensure that you're feeling the reciprocity over time.

SUCCESS ACTION ITEMS –
ASSESS YOUR PERSONAL DRIVING FORCES

- Assess your personal driving forces. While you focus on meeting people, forming relationships, entering into partnerships—look in the mirror on a regular basis, and take stock of what motivates you.
- Consider which of the seven driving forces apply to you and create your own list and prioritize

  1. Recognition. Your peers recognize and applaud your good deeds.
  2. Family. Provide for your family and share the fruits of your success.
  3. Career goals. Achieve your ambition and the desire to climb the ladder of success.
  4. Passion. Have a passion relevant to your quest to build your personal influence.
  5. Thrill of winning. Enjoy the winning for its own sake.
  6. Retirement. Enjoy a comfortable retirement.
  7. Wealth. Focus on making a difference.

- Cultivate a Go-getter mentality. This is your unique set of personal drivers that determines your path to Influence Relationship Authority.
- Embrace the power of Influence relationship networking. The three terms are symbiotic. Your influence grows in proportion to the level of networking and number of quality relationships you have.
- Use these three pillars to build your Influence Relationship Authority.

  ○ Pillar 1: Entrust. All great relationships begin with trust. It takes time to build and is hard to regain once it's lost.
  ○ Pillar 2: Engage. Trust will grow significantly only when each party of the relationship engages and practices trust.
  ○ Pillar 3: Endorse. Once a deep-rooted relationship evolves, then relationships of trust can endorse and promote each other.

- Build strong relationships by providing value to your network.
- Refuse to be anyone's doormat. While influence is determined by how abundantly you place other people's interests first, you should never be anyone's doormat. Periodically evaluate relationships.

GARY KENNEDY
MANAGING PARTNER,
DOUBLE EAGLE VENTURES,
FORMER PRESIDENT OF ORACLE USA

"Making a Difference"
MY PERSPECTIVE

N 1993, I WAS CALLED on by my church to serve full-time for three years as a mission president for the Church of Jesus Christ of Latter-Day Saints in Sao Paulo, Brazil. When I was preparing to be a mission president, the church sent a large quantity of information to me, including a guide.

I read the guide, and in the very first paragraph, they asked this question: "What is the most important characteristic of a successful mission president?"

I thought through a few possible answers but none of them was correct. Instead, the right answer was that those mission presidents who succeeded *genuinely believed they could make a difference.*

In my family, my business career, and my philanthropic activities I have found this to be a universally true principle. The importance of this principle may not be obvious to everyone. Please understand that I am not saying that everyone who believes they can make a real, tangible, measurable difference will do so. I am saying that a leader who does not believe they will make a difference will never do so.

This is always the first piece of advice that I give to everyone who asks me for guidance. It takes a lot of courage to step into a new situation where we have a less than perfect knowledge of the state of the organization and boldly declare, at least to ourselves, that we believe we can make a difference. Courage is essential because if we do not make a tangible difference then we feel as though we have failed. It is much easier to tip toe into a new institution and then see what happens. Leaders who take the passive approach are often fond of saying "oh well, it is what it is." *Wrong! It is what you make of it.*

I have seen many situations where talented people get into a difficult situation, and when they realize that they are not making a difference, they turn their energy toward finding someone or something to blame. In other words, they look for a soft place to land. When the situation does not change, they effectively give up. Sadly, their attitude always determines their altitude.

I don't take on any responsibility unless I feel I can make a real, tangible, measurable, difference. With this kind of attitude, I take on challenges knowing that I will make a difference by resolving them. I would not suggest that I have made a significant difference in all cases and it was not easy for me to accept that. In many other cases I have made a real, tangible, and measurable difference and I am certain, that would not have happened unless I approached the problem with the attitude that *I can make a difference*. As an aside, it has never been difficult for me to know if I made a difference. When one has made a significant difference, I will always know that. Once I took on the CEO role in an existing company. Naturally, I was confident that I could make a difference. The company's revenues were declining 20% year over year and our backlog had declined by 50% in the months before I started. I spent two years there. Our revenue and profits were roughly the same as when I joined but at least we stemmed the bleeding and the year over year revenue decline. I completely revamped the Executive Team by replacing 10 out of 12 members. Most importantly we began to win a large number of long-term contracts. Our contractual backlog grew four times over what it was when I started. I left due to complications from a major surgery. The company's backlog of contracts began to turn into significantly higher revenues and profits in the next few years. Even though traditional measures like revenue and profits had not improved, I knew that we had met the company's most important needs, booking new contracts and upgrading the talent level on the executive team.

LANDING IN A STRANGE LAND

If I stepped off the dock into the strange city of Metropolis, and I had to survive, I could find ways to live on the street. I'm okay eating from garbage cans for a few days if I have to. That's just reality: You arrive somewhere, you see what's there, and you accept it. And then you accept the responsibility to do something about it. If you are willing to make yourself vulnerable, and you genuinely believe you can make a difference…you will.

INFLUENCERS

Influence is important. I realize it's broader than this, but for me, influence has a positive connotation. I know there are people who can influence you in a bad way, but I don't even think about them, and I want to avoid them at all costs. Influence should be a positive thing, and it shines from somebody who doesn't have an ego as far as helping others is concerned. If the actions of others help make you look ten times better than they are, then great! Sign me up.

I remember once I was having lunch with Larry Ellison (Co-Founder of Oracle Corporation), and I said, "I interviewed a man this morning. He's unbelievable, and we're going to hire him. Someday we may all be working for him."

Larry smiled and said, "You know, you said that about the last five or six guys you hired, and yet they're all still working for you." Why is that? My reply was "if their performance pushes me up then it is a win for all parties. If they are good enough to take my job then that is an excellent problem to have. If they are better than I am then I will gladly work for them.

In my mind an influencer is anyone—subordinate, peer, or superior—who is in a position to make a difference. Ideally, they really understand the problem and can provide the context-based advice you need to succeed. So, if you'll share the context with them, they will give you advice within that domain. If you don't share context, they'll give you advice, but it's possible that the lack of context renders their advice of little value. Few people care enough about the advice they give you to take the time to learn about the domain so that the advice you are giving them is most relevant.

You know the saying, "It's not *what* you know, but *who* you know?" That used to be the case when there were a lot of intermediaries between you and someone who would influence you. Unfortunately, the message was often lost by the intermediaries. One of the subtle, but significant benefits of the internet and the tsunami of data it yields is that people can give advice from a perfect context. It used to be if you knew somebody who was a vice president, you could call them, and they could arrange a time for an under-the-radar interview. No one else even knew there was an opening. Today, everyone can find anyone they choose to. If you know someone important today, you should use that relationship if you are able, but in a few more years, the option may no longer be available to you.

STRATEGIC INFLUENCER

The funnel of all influencers is wide, but it grows narrower if you want someone who is willing to help. I call these people *strategic influencers*.

I've talked about influencers or people who can be influential, then progressed to people who could be helpful, who could introduce you to the right kind of person while they have an important strategic perspective regarding your business.

STRATEGIC RELATIONSHIP INFLUENCER

Many companies want to get strategic about influencers because they want influencers to have some perspective and an ongoing relationship and, if possible, have relevant industry experience that can make a difference.

Most influencers today have no relationship whatsoever with the companies who hire them. You hire them, they'll post something for you on social media, but you never meet them, and you never talk to them. They do it for a fee, and most of them are not strategic. For example, a celebrity has millions of followers, and just the mere mention by them about your company or product might help you at least temporarily, but not in the long-term. Someone who is strategic will be more aligned with your company values, your team, and the people who know, use, and love your product.

For a strategic influencer to be effective, they must have a perspective in the industry you compete in or the markets you want to move into. They need to be willing to spend the time to build a good strategic and working relationship and not just offer short-term advice on every transaction. They only want to be involved in a business relationship in things that are strategic.

CENTER OF INFLUENCE

Next are centers of influence, which means that your circle of potential influencers is a certain size, and if you cut that down to just strategic influencers, it's a smaller subset. If you're looking for an ongoing relationship with a strategic influencer, that's a harder ask because people who have something unique to offer and a relevant context from which to offer it, are often swamped and can hardly justify committing to spend time counseling just anyone who approaches them. If they think they're signing themselves up for a lot of time, they'll hesitate while they worry that you're going to overwhelm them with questions every five minutes. As a result, they are often slow to grant you time in the first place.

There is a bit of a dichotomy between people who want a strategic influencer and people who just want advice on an ongoing basis. In some situations, these two qualities can conflict with each other since the person who has the skill and inclination to help is often busy while another person has plenty time and in inclination to offer advice, little of which is useful.

The center of influence, especially someone who strategically wants a relationship, must be a win-win relationship. For example, if you can help them become established into new circles, that would provide significant value to them. If you are able to help them untie a Gordian Knot of a problem, then they're going to want to interact with you again. If you can find some way to help them, then you have the raw material for a positive long-term relationship. If you think that someone's going to badger you every time they have a problem, you're not going to want an ongoing relationship with them.

I think I'm a center of influence. Being at the center of it means that through me, the people whom I'm influencing can get to other people who are not even in their circle, so to speak. The idea is that eventually, the link between me or the influencer and the original people who wanted the relationship will be so strong, they'll no longer need me to be involved. That, to me, is what's necessary.

MY DEEP-DOWN HABITS OF SUCCESS

There are a few deep-down habits or characteristics that have helped me succeed in my career. One of the most important is that I am willing to take risks. Most people have low tolerance for risk, especially if they enjoy sleeping well at night. When I left Intel, a fine established company, to become the twelfth full-time employee of a flaky little software company called Oracle, that was a major risk. I estimated that there was a 25% chance that Oracle would be successful. Since the benefit of establishing a successful company in a new segment of the market was well worth the relatively low probability of success in that segment, it was an easy decision to join Oracle. As I joined Oracle, the risk it presented was largely centered around whether we were able to convince mainstream companies to adopt a relational database management. It was clear that the intelligence agencies of the US Government had to have a relational DBMS but it was not quite so clear why commercial enterprises needed RDBMS. It seemed clear to me that if we could figure out the value proposition for buying RDBMS as opposed to network and hierarchical systems that Oracle would become a very successful company.

I consciously seek out opportunities where there is a high return that is concomitant to the risk. I then look to see if my skills are such that I can mitigate the risk while maintaining the return. In other situations, the risks I took were more than I could overcome. I was knocked down by the pain of the failure. While it hit me hard, I was eventually able to pick myself up, dust myself off, and jump back into the fray.

It is also important to give credit to others. I know that for me to make a significant difference it would require assistance from many other people. When I went to work for Oracle, there were only twelve full-time people in the company. It was tiny! I had lunch with Larry two or three times before he convinced me to leave Intel and take a job at Oracle. In the end, the reason I decided to join was that I was convinced that I could make a difference at Oracle.

WOULD I DO IT AGAIN?

Recently I asked my father, "If you could go back and live your life again, would you do it again?" He said, "Yeah, I would." And then he asked me what my choice would be? I said, "No. No way. I obviously could have done many things better, but there is also a significant risk that things would turn out worse.

LARRY ELLISON, A GAME-CHANGING CONNECTION

Meeting Larry Ellison was a game-changing connection for me. My friend, Bruce Scott, was the fourth employee at Oracle (aka Relational Software Inc). He was always talking about Larry Ellison. He kept saying, "You have to meet Larry. When are you free to meet Larry?" Larry had a profound sense of Oracle's destiny. During our first interview, he said relational database management systems will replace all other data management methodologies, and Oracle will become the dominant provider of relational database systems. I left Oracle in 1990, after almost ten years. At that time, Oracle had over 60% share of the relational marketplace. I do not know how much of the database market had converted to relational in 1990. However, it was clear that 100% of the market would eventually convert to relational since no one was buying new database management systems that were not relational.

Larry gave me responsibility, possibly too much responsibility given my age and experience. When I was thirty-five, I was President of Oracle USA, which accounted for roughly sixty percent of all of our revenue. I mean, he faced significant risk giving me so much responsibility. As our business grew, he continued to give me more responsibility until I reached the level of my incompetence, and then he let me go. It was a hard day for him and an even harder day for me. He offered me several jobs that were a step down from President of Oracle USA. He said, "Gary, this is just too much responsibility for you. We have thousands of investors who are depending on us. We need to make a change".

I said, "Have you considered the possibility that things are going to go from bad to worse?"

He said, "We have, and that is a risk we have to take."

As I look back, it may have been the right thing. After one or two hiring mistakes, he hired a partner at Booz Allen Hamilton who took over the position of President of Oracle USA. Most considered him successful, but after a few years, he and Larry could not get along, or perhaps he reached his own level of incompetence.

Mr. Kennedy is the managing partner of Double Eagle Ventures, a private venture fund targeting early-stage investments. Double Eagle Ventures has been the first investor in TenFold, Overstock.com, American School Academy, Remedy Informatics, and AIM Technology as well as an early investor in January.ai, iDirect, Neumont University, Kanab Hills LLC and Imagine Learning. From December 2003 to October 2014, he was the Founder and Chief Executive Officer of Remedy Informatics, the leading provider of registries for Life Sciences Research and Healthcare Delivery organizations.

He served as President, and Chief Executive Officer of TenFold Corporation a software applications developer. From 1993 to 1996 Mr. Kennedy served as Mission President for the Church of Jesus Christ of Latter-Day Saints in Sao Paulo, Brazil. He served as President, Chief Executive Officer and Chairman of PRC, Inc., a systems integration company.

Prior to joining PRC, Mr. Kennedy served in various management and executive positions at Oracle Corporation from 1982 until 1990. His positions included National Sales Manager, Senior Vice-President Oracle Corporation and President of Oracle USA. He was one of the first handful of professional employees of Oracle. Prior to joining Oracle, Mr. Kennedy served as a Marketing Manager for Intel Corporation. Mr. Kennedy holds a B.A. in finance from the University of Utah and a Masters Degree in Business Administration from Northwestern University's Kellogg Graduate School of Management.

Email: garydkennedy@gmail.com
LinkedIn: www.linkedin.com/in/gary-kennedy-424910/

SUCCESS FACTOR 8: IDENTIFY AND LEVERAGE YOUR COMPETITIVE COMPETENCIES

"Knowing your superpowers changes everything!"
—*Nadalie Bardo*

I
N THE PREVIOUS CHAPTER, WE discussed the personal driving forces of Christopher Columbus and how they came together to make him, and not someone else, succeed at becoming the first modern European to plan, fund, and complete a westward voyage to what turned out to be the New World. Just like Columbus and countless other highly influential people, you'll need your own personal driving forces to inspire you and motivate you to make your way up the ladder of influence and reach your goal.

This chapter is about the last part of the equation: your competitive competencies.

To move to the next performance level of influence and success, you need to possess a credible amount of personal value, purposeful personal driving forces, *and* a robust set of competitive competencies. For maximum opportunity, you cannot have just one of them.

For example, if you have credible personal value such as a college education and some work experience but no motivating driving forces or established competencies, your ability to connect with influential people or create a strategic partnership will be severely limited. On the other hand, if you have a powerful driving force but no education, no expertise, and no competencies, you'll forever be the pushy, annoying person whom everyone avoids at parties. You'll have nothing to contribute. Your eagerness to be influential without having the requisite knowledge and competencies will make people think you're just an empty egotist.

If you have competencies but no driving force, you'll spend your days frittering away your time on pointless activities that aren't productive. People will say, "She's so smart, but I don't understand why she doesn't make something of herself!"

If you think you have no competencies or insufficient competencies, I have good news: Competencies can be learned. Unlike personal driving forces, which are baked into your personality, perhaps even from childhood, and which take a long time to evolve, competencies can range from being fairly superficial (at least at the everyday level we're talking about) to very deeply learned. And yes, once you get to a certain level, your value, competencies, and personal driving forces become fused together into one powerful and efficient package. Consider public speaking, for example. It's definitely a skill that you can learn, and anybody can become a competent public speaker. But the greatest speakers rise above the ordinary because their personal driving force becomes indistinguishable from their skill, and they use their competency to achieve a greater purpose.

Competencies can be learned—but how do you measure your proficiency? How do you know you're good at something, or qualified for certain tasks or positions?

Competencies fall into two categories: Those that can be objectively measurable by a third party, and those that are "soft," meaning they can't be easily measured.

OBJECTIVE COMPETENCIES

If you traveled to Metropolis on a ship, and you had no money, perhaps you worked your way across as a member of the crew. Ships are highly organized workplaces with a long tradition of rigid hierarchies of authority and responsibility.

Let's say you boarded your ship with no prior experience and no maritime competencies. You had to start at the bottom of the ladder. The crews of modern ships are organized into four "departments"—deck, engineering, steward, and others. Let's say you were hired to work on deck. Here's how you would have progressed up the ladder according to your measurable competencies and experience:

1. Ordinary seaman (or, if you had *zero* experience on a ship, a lowly "landsman"). You'd do things like swab the decks, scrape rust, and stand watch. Few competencies were required, and you had no influence on how the ship was handled.

2. Able seaman. On most merchant ships, to serve as an able seaman you'd need more than two years of experience at sea and be considered a person "well acquainted with his [or her] duty." An able seaman has had some advanced training, including lifeboatman certification.

3. Boatswain. This crewmember is the most senior "rate" of the deck department and is responsible for the overall condition of the ship. On a sailing vessel, the boatswain is the officer responsible for the care of the rigging, cordage, anchors, sails, boats, flags, and other stores.

4. Third officer / Third mate. Among other duties, he or she directs the bridge team as they maneuver the vessel, keeping it safe and on course. On a scale of influence, the third officer would be at about the middle—say, a five out of ten.

5. Second officer / Second mate. Their primary duty is navigational, which includes updating charts and publications, keeping them current, making passage plans, and all aspects of ship navigation.

6. Chief officer / Chief mate. This person is capable of assuming command of the entire ship in the absence or incapacitation of the master. Influence scale? Nine out of ten.

7. Captain / Master. He or she is the most highly skilled mariner on the vessel. In the old days, when ships sailed for months at a time across uncharted seas, the captain's word was law. While the captain, like Christopher Columbus, was ultimately accountable to the ship's owner or patron, when the ship was under way, he had complete and total influence over the very lives of his crew. Times have changed; these days, even while at sea, captains are accountable to higher military or civilian authorities.

The ranks of crewmembers on a vessel at sea resemble those of any other professional or trade career: doctors, police officers, plumbers, electricians, accountants. Nearly every profession or trade has a state certification requirement, where you have to prove that you possess the required competencies to do the job.

For example, in the state of Utah, to practice law you need to complete several well-defined steps. You need to earn your undergraduate degree, take the LSAT, attend an accredited law school, take the Utah State Bar Exam, be admitted to the Bar, and complete a mandatory New Lawyer Training Program (NLTP).

This type of verifiable, third-party skills-building takes time and planning. For example, if you want to become a doctor—a general practitioner—you need to earn your bachelor's degree (four years), go to medical school (four years), then complete a residency (three or more years). If you then want to become a specialist, such as a surgeon, you'll need another five to eight years of training.

There is measurable value in acquiring objective competencies. Generally, the more degrees you have, the higher your income and your influence authority. According to the US Bureau of Labor statistics 2019 figures, annual earnings are:

- High school diploma: $38,792.
- Associate degree: $46,124.
- Bachelor's degree: $64,896.
- Masters' degree: $77,844.
- Professional degree: $96,772.
- Doctoral degree: $97,916.

This is how you build your influence authority step by step, slowly and methodically. The advantage to this method is that while it's perhaps unimaginative, it's virtually guaranteed to get you where you want to go. If you don't screw up along the way, and keep your nose to the grindstone, and pass all your exams, then you will achieve an expected level of professional stature in the community. This will open doors for you. You'll have access to professional associations and exclusive clubs, where you'll meet influential people and be admitted into their orbits. You'll be welcomed into an influence-building networking group. Whether you take advantage of these opportunities is entirely up to you. There are plenty of doctors and lawyers who are content to do their jobs, go home at night, and take two weeks every year for a cruise around the Caribbean. Others—perhaps you—want more. You want to take part in shaping the future of your community or even your nation, and to do that you need to demonstrate exceptional competencies.

If you were a doctor and were seeking to become highly influential, you could do this in one of two ways:

The first is to become exceptionally skilled in some cutting-edge aspect of medicine. Back in 1967, Dr. Christiaan Barnard vaulted into the limelight when he performed the first successful heart transplant.

The second way is to attain a position of influence and prestige. If you're a doctor, one of the most prestigious jobs you can have is surgeon general of the United States, who is appointed by the president. He or she is the operational head of the US Public Health Service Commissioned Corps, and thus the leading spokesperson on matters of public health in the federal government of the United States.

Other doctors combine their medical training with leadership skills. For example, Rod Hochman, M.D., who earned his medical degree at Boston University, is the president and CEO of Providence St. Joseph Health, the third-largest not-for-profit health system in the United States. The system employs 119,000 caregivers in fifty-one hospitals, nearly 1,000 clinics, and hundreds of programs and services across the western United States. To be a successful health system leader, you need multiple competencies, including your medical degree, business knowledge, ability to manage thousands of employees, and your effectiveness at working with powerful and influential stakeholders, such as your board of directors and, in the case of a nonprofit hospital, wealthy donors.

SOFT COMPETENCIES

Many influential people have subjective or "soft" competencies that they've acquired by experience or self-development and which cannot be measured. Soft competencies include people competencies, social competencies, communication competencies, character or personality traits, attitudes, mindsets, career attributes, social intelligence, and emotional intelligence.

The ability to make an *emotional connection* with others is a soft competency possessed by many influential people. How many times have you heard someone say about another person, "He's so amazing! When you talk to him, you feel like there's no one else in the room. He really pays attention to what you have to say." The ability to focus on the person you're talking to is incredibly important when building your influence. Recall the story of Susan and Tom, who attend a social gathering at a local business club. Both Susan and Tom are new in town and don't know many people. They are both introduced to Robert, who's president of the First National Bank in town.

Tom doesn't seize the opportunity to make a connection. Perhaps he feels that Robert won't be interested in him. "He's a bank president," Tom tells himself, "and I'm just an insurance broker. Why would he want to talk to me?" Sounds familiar, right? Aside from lacking confidence in himself, Tom is forgetting that Robert is a human being, and he has many more interests than his job at the bank.

Susan, who has more self-confidence, is ready to make a connection. So, she engages Robert on a safe, non-controversial topic (that is, neither politics nor religion!). Let's say it snowed the previous night. The weather is always a good, reliable topic to use to break the ice. So, Susan asks, "What do you think of the snow? Are you a skier?"

Robert can respond in one of two ways:

1. "Yes, I love to ski. We're going to the mountain this weekend."

2. "Not for me, thanks. I'm a summer guy. Can't wait to put the boat in the water this spring."

Bingo! Susan has made a connection. Now the ball is in her court. It doesn't matter what her personal preferences are, because she can engage Robert either way.

If Robert replies that he likes to ski, Susan can respond with either one of these:

1. "I'm a bit of a skier myself. Which resort do you go to?"
2. "I can't say I've ever been skiing. I should probably try. How long did it take you to learn?"

If Robert replies that he does not like the snow and wants to sail his boat, Susan can say either:

1. "Oh, my family had a boat! I have such great memories of sailing with my dad. What kind of boat do you have?"
2. "I'm a landlubber, but I've thought about buying a boat. What kind do you have?"

Note that each of Susan's responses consists of two parts. First, she repeats the premise of the conversation. This lets Robert know that she's been listening to him. She might offer a little comment, but then she immediately shows an interest in Robert by asking him a question about himself. She does *not* drone on about herself. A conversation with a new acquaintance—particularly someone influential with whom you're endeavoring to connect—should be like a friendly game of tennis. You politely volley the ball back and forth. You don't hog the ball and you don't smash a 100-mph overhand.

And—this is very important—you also give your new acquaintance the opportunity to escape. The worst thing Susan could do is think, "Wow! I've got the president of the bank talking to me! I'm not going to let him go! I'm going to impress him with my brilliance!" Don't pressure your acquaintance. Keep it light.

Above all, *have confidence in yourself.* This means that Robert—or whoever—will find you interesting and pleasant to be around, and not overbearing or creepy. Treat the other person as you would want to be treated.

In our culture, if you're a man and you're meeting a woman executive for the first time, you must be certain that you behave appropriately. If you harbor any "old-school" beliefs about the "gals" in the workforce, do yourself a favor and rid yourself of them now. If you need sensitivity training or counseling in this area, which will enable you to improve your interpersonal competencies and bring them into the twenty-first century, then don't hesitate to get it.

Another highly valued skill is the ability to see a new solution to a vexing problem and the willingness to take action to solve it. This skill cannot be taught in school and cannot be measured with a test. What was it that set the personality of Christopher Columbus apart from his peers? In those days, there were plenty of European sea captains with knowledge of the continents and their surrounding oceans. In fact, while Columbus was sailing west, other skilled commanders including Vasco de Gama, were working to establish sea routes to the east, around the southern tip of Africa at the Cape of Good Hope. These explorers were meeting with success, and it was commonly accepted that you could reach India and then China—well-known destinations for merchants traveling overland—by sailing around Africa. Columbus could have easily joined the crowd heading east, but he alone took the opposite direction.

Columbus showed an entrepreneurial spirit. Business entrepreneurs are people who defy convention and seek to solve problems in unconventional ways. Some entrepreneurs begin their careers with minimal objective competencies, and instead of looking for a job requiring a set of measurable qualifications, they "make their own job" by starting their own company. The list of highly successful and influential college dropouts is long and includes Bill Gates (Microsoft), Steve Jobs (Apple), Mark Zuckerberg (Facebook), Rachael Ray (TV chef), Russell Simmons (Def Jam), and many more.

THE TEN COMPETITIVE COMPETENCIES

In the previous chapter we introduced a ship model with three sails, which we named personal value, personal driving forces, and personal competitive competencies. While each element or sail individually has the ability to propel our ship forward towards a higher and more strategic form of influence, when we open a second or third sail, and allow the winds of influence to be combined, the rate of influence growth accelerates and provides maximum power for propelling our influence ship. The synergistic effect can be extremely impactful, giving us the potential at some point to become a center of influence, which we will cover in the next chapter.

In this chapter we'll complete the power capacity of the ship by discussing the third and largest sail, which represents the key element of influence growth—*competitive competencies*. When combined with personal value and motivational driving forces, this element affords you the ability to differentiate your value, accentuate your motivation, and stand out from the crowd. This is possible because when you master and then possess certain expert competencies, they in turn can act as your superpowers, giving you an edge to compete and lead at the highest levels. *Figure 10.1* illustrates this scenario.

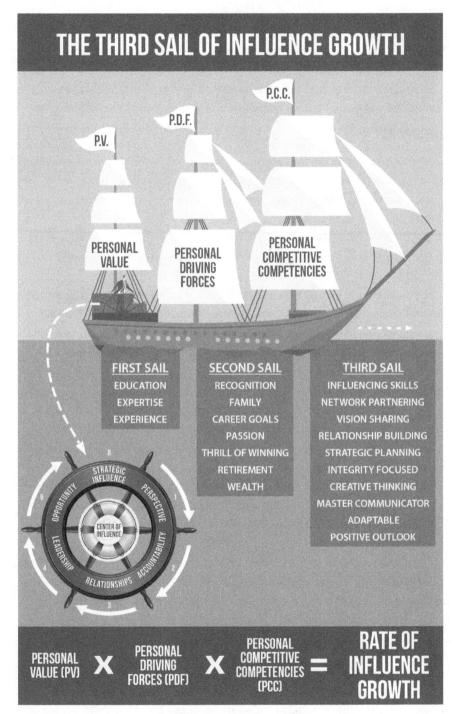

Figure 10.1

THE 10 COMPETITIVE COMPETENCIES OF INFLUENTIAL LEADERSHIP

As we discussed in the driving forces section, it's a tall order to expect a leader to master all ten competencies. That is why they surround themselves with smart, talented and resource minded employees and partnerships. With that said, the best leaders will score high on many of these and reasonably well on the rest.

1. INFLUENCING

Some people enjoy being in a position of influence. Other people don't—they'd rather just do their thing quietly, in the background. This book is for those people who like having influence because they want to use it to make the world a better place for everyone.

And remember, like any other competency, the ability to influence others can be learned. You don't have to be born with this superpower—you can develop it!

Someone with this competency will be happy to assume the role of leader and influencer. They are described as inspirational, charismatic, likeable, and magnetic. When in a position of leadership, they don't just issue commands and expect to be blindly obeyed. They persuade, inspire, and encourage. They tap into the knowledge and competencies of the group, point individuals toward a common goal, and draw out a commitment to achieve results.

They know that most organizations have two sides. There's the formal structure described on the organizational chart, and then there's the informal structure, which more often represents how things really get done. Leaders skilled in the art of influence understand both.

An important skill is trust-building, and the way to build trust is to lead by example. Be a role model, and do what you say you will. When you're a center of influence, all eyes are on you, and those following you look for evidence of your leadership skills. For example, in the US Marine Corps, "Officers Eat Last" is the rule during field training and in certain combat environments. The most senior leaders of the organization actually eat after the regular soldiers when the unit has a meal together. It's a time-honored practice that promotes the idea of servant leadership.

2. NETWORKING AND PARTNERING

In the business world, networking is a foundational component of building influence. Put simply, your efforts to meet people who would be willing to engage in exchanges of value is called networking. It's the act of creating a set of personal connections who will provide support, resources, business referrals, feedback, insight, and information. If you want to build and use influence, this superpower is a requirement.

This book introduces a new, next-generation approach to strategic business networking. It builds upon the central theme of positive influence combined with strategic relationship building.

The golden rule in networking, which makes it a positive experience, is this: Give more than you get. Offer to assist your new contact in some way, even if it's just a casual conversation where you can provide information on a topic of mutual interest. Telling your new contact all about yourself does *not* qualify as "giving." Sharing your expertise in a way that can benefit the other person does qualify.

Strategic networking happens in two arenas:

The first arena is networking with the goal of a future relationship. The person you meet may not have a direct connection to anything you're doing now, but down the road, they might!

The second arena is when you and others are engaged in high-level planning of projects and initiatives that have long-term ramifications.

In addition to networking within the upper echelons of a corporation or at the board level, you can meet people very effectively by joining a structured business networking or community service group. Joint ventures are often preceded by personal networking and the nurturing of relationships that are non-competitive, and where the products or services perfectly align and complement each other.

3. VISION SHARING

If you're embarking on a long voyage, your destination is over the horizon. You cannot see it. But you must be able to envision it. You must be able to visualize it in your mind's eye, so that it can inspire you to reach it and—this is helpful—you'll recognize when you arrive!

A vision for your life, your business, your relationships, and your health will provide a roadmap for your decisions, thereby enabling you to align your choices with your best interests.

Sharing a vision is a central role of a leader. To influence others—the crew of your ship, for example—you need to be able to describe to them the destination. You must be able to get them excited and eager to do the work necessary to get where you want to go.

Effective leaders are inclusive and create a shared vision. This may mean listening to others and taking into account their hopes and dreams, too. For example, if you're a CEO who has no children, in your own life you may not think too much about issues of childcare, because you don't need it. But the vision your employees have for the company may include childcare, and to be an effective leader, you need to be empathetic and responsive to their aspirations.

Don't just be a "leaf in the wind." Conscious responsibility for your life means living intentionally and deliberately making the best choices to move ahead toward manifesting your vision. If necessary, create a life, relationships, and business vision statement which will provide a roadmap for your decisions and to align your choices with your best interests.

Needless to say, "Making lots of money" is not a sufficient vision, either for you or for your organization. The best vision—a real superpower—focuses on making the world a better place for others.

4. RELATIONSHIP BUILDING AMBASSADOR

In your voyage of relationship building for professional and personal influence, once you have a sufficient grasp of the influential players in your industry or social circle (I say "sufficient grasp" because the process is never-ending), you need to prioritize them. You need a navigation plan to help you as you pursue high-level networking based on relationship building, thereby increasing your influence.

Because high-level networking based on relationship building (which continues to increase influence) takes time, you need to be focused on your intentions and your planning. Nothing happens overnight, and it's easy to either become impatient or lose sight of your vision for success. Take Christopher Columbus, for example. He first proposed a mission to sail west to Asia in 1484, when he lobbied King John II of Portugal. Rejected, he then went to Queen Isabella of Spain, and even tried to interest King Henry VII of England. Finally, in 1492, after exercising every bit of influence he had, he got the go-ahead from Queen Isabella. His patience and shrewd networking paid off!

Like Columbus, when you have a great connection with someone whom you value, it adds to or enhances your personal value. It also makes it possible to influence others to join you in a project or mission. Relationship-building competencies will help you be a good coach and build a strong team with the right talent, foster mutual trust, and inspire high performance with the expectation of high rewards. It's all about having the ability to connect people who can work well with each other and can add value to each other.

RELATIONSHIP BUILDING SKILLS

Here are five skills you should use when building relationships.

I. SEEK OUT PEOPLE WHO SHARE YOUR VISION OF SUCCESS

Unless you're entering into a purely transactional relationship (such as, you're going to sell them something and then walk away), spend your valuable time only with people who are oriented towards success and who want to get things done. Don't become identified with people who are unmotivated or who are looking for a get-rich-quick scheme.

II. SHOW GENUINE INTEREST IN THEIR BUSINESS

Before you meet with someone, take the time to research their company. Find out who they are, what they do, and what they've posted on social media. Get to know their business as if it were your own.

Having a genuine interest and passion for their company shows that you don't care about ingratiating yourself with them or selling them something, but that you care about offering them something of value and creating results.

III. GIVE BEFORE TAKING

People will come to you because they want help in your area of specialization. Share your valuable lessons and pass on expert advice to your colleagues. If you can prove you know something that will help their business, you will elevate yourself to a valuable partner rather than simply a grip-and-grin person at the Rotary Club lunch meeting.

IV. CELEBRATE WHAT MAKES YOU DIFFERENT

You have your own point of view, your own skill set, and your own personal drivers. While it may seem to be safer to remain in the herd, the herd is full of people who aren't going to rise very far. As new challenges emerge—the pace of disruptive innovation is accelerating, not slowing down—the people who offer fresh solutions are the ones who will become influential.

V. DON'T BE AFRAID TO CHALLENGE THE STATUS QUO

Just because people or businesses have always done things a certain way in the past doesn't mean it's the best way today. Come to the table with new ideas, emerging opportunities, and fresh viewpoints your colleagues haven't realized even existed.

Saying "yes" to the same old thing isn't going to gain you any influence. It's only going to reveal you to be a milquetoast manager who doesn't appreciate innovation.

5. STRATEGIC THINKING/PLANNING

When you set sail on your long voyage, you need to engage in strategic planning. You need to calculate your course, plan your route, acquire the correct provisions, instruct and inspire your crew. This is a formal process with inputs, activities, outputs, and forecasted outcomes.

(When Columbus first approached King John II of Portugal, the court turned him down because they thought—correctly, as it turned out—that Columbus's estimate of 2,400 nautical miles to Japan was a gross underestimation. They didn't like his strategic plan!)

Long-term strategic planning is important and needs to be done carefully. Questions to be answered include:

> **Where are we now?** You cannot create a plan without knowing where you are now. This requires honesty. If your company is currently losing money, don't sugarcoat reality.

> **Where do we want to be?** After accurately determining where you are now, then you need to decide where you want to be. This is basic goal setting.

> **How do we get there?** This is your action plan. Goals are reached incrementally, one step at a time. Measure your progress every day, week, month, and year. Along the way, use strategic influencers. Seek out and align yourself with trusted strategic partnerships and joint ventures.

Focus on solving problems. The strategic planning process will help you uncover ways to improve performance and spark insights about how to restructure your organization so that it can reach its full potential. This superpower gives you a better awareness of your strengths and weaknesses and where you stand in the market, both individually and in relation to competitors. Strategic planning is an opportunity for you and your stakeholders to exchange ideas and develop new solutions.

6. INTEGRITY FOCUSED

Personal integrity is a foundation of true, lasting influence. It's about always doing the right thing, even when no one is looking, and even when the choice isn't easy. It's about staying true to yourself and your values, even when you're faced with serious consequences for the choices that you're making—perhaps even losing your job.

The influential leader accepts personal responsibility. He or she is accountable and answerable. As the old saying goes, "The buck stops here." It's all part of setting a good example, because if you're the leader, then you want everyone who works for you to be accountable for what they do. If your employees or followers see you dodging responsibility, then they'll conclude they should too.

Always do what you say you'll do. The foundation of a good reputation is integrity, and you build your integrity by having a history of making good on positive intentions. To establish a reputation of integrity, you need to have a history of making good on positive intentions. This means that you have to make good on your promises over and over again.

Trust and integrity are essential to strong, meaningful relationships. People want to work with others about whom they never have to think twice about in terms of integrity or honesty. When we have integrity, we gain the trust of our leaders, our colleagues and our team; and from trust comes influence.

Integrity is a cornerstone of ethical leadership. Clients, coworkers, companies, stakeholders, communities, churches, and families want leaders they can trust, and when you demonstrate integrity, you show everyone you can be trusted and respected.

7. CREATIVE THINKING

Creative thinking is our ability to look at a problem and find new alternatives that solve it. This superpower is important because it helps you look at situations from a fresh perspective. It's a way to develop novel or innovative solutions that do not depend on past or current solutions, and to employ strategies to clear your mind so that your thoughts and ideas can transcend the limitations of a problem.

It's linked to an ability to envision the future. By thinking creatively, you can envision and plan your own destiny. You can embrace it, change it, improve it, make your mark upon it. It makes you more willing—even eager—to navigate uncharted waters and take visionary risks.

But creative thinking needs to be focused, and allowed to flourish as long as the idea has a strategic purpose and benefits the players involved. It's good to have a leading or cutting-edge focus while staying away from reckless, bleeding-edge strategies.

It thrives on innovating, doing the seemingly impossible, and being the first to accomplish something. Elon Musk is a great example of innovator, whether it's with Tesla or his SpaceX rocket program. He sees enormous opportunities that previously were unthinkable and undoable. He then assembles a team of talented, innovative team members who are single minded and are up to the task.

As Elon Musk has shown, creative thinking helps you become more confident and self-reliant. You can think on your own without depending on others to make you a stronger, truly happy person. By thinking creatively, you become true to yourself. You can discover and embrace who you are without worrying about other peoples' judgments.

8. MASTER COMMUNICATOR

In the world of influence, communication is a true superpower. While you can have plenty of communication with no influence, you cannot possibly hope to have influence without being a skilled communicator.

The ability to communicate with influence has never been so important. Businesses are moving away from traditional hierarchies in favor of matrix structures, in which quality communication skills and the ability to influence stakeholders and colleagues have become vital components in the journey to success. This is because in a matrix organization, to achieve results and deliver your outcomes, you may find yourself relying on people you've never met, or over whom you have no real authority.

Good communication includes being clear about what you have or have not committed to and what has been agreed upon. Poor communication can destroy a relationship. When it comes to influencing, leaders who haven't earned trust, built relationships, or gained credibility will be at a disadvantage. Here are a few ways you can communicate with influence:

Inspire: Get people excited about your idea. They will respond if you show enthusiasm yourself, or even appeal to their values and beliefs in your message.

Build trust and credibility: If you've helped others in the past, you've developed trust, which can be returned. If you've got credibility from previous successful collaborations, people are more likely to return the favor and help you with yours.

Use reason: Use logic to explain the importance of your ideas or projects to your audience in meetings and conversations.

Consult and collaborate: To create an attachment to your idea, ask for help or involve others as much as you can. If your proposal benefits others, make sure your message makes that very clear.

9. AGILE AND ADAPTABLE

To be agile is to be quick and alert. To be adaptable is to be willing and able to change. Together, they form a powerful superpower.

As your work and environment change on an increasingly rapid basis, you need to be open to shifting, getting feedback, and beginning again. With disruption being the only constant in today's business environment, agility allows you to release the need for absolute certainty and lead with confidence in the face of ambiguity.

As a leader, your ability to adapt quickly and put the team at the center to solve problems will keep your organization nimble and competitive. The organization that moves faster to solve a problem, create a product, or respond to a need will be one that wins.

The need to be adaptable is more important every day. This is not just a slogan, it is literally true. The pace of innovation in our society is accelerating. The rate of change is getting faster. Discomfort is the new normal. Agile leaders adapt to current conditions, even if doing so makes them feel uncomfortable.

An agile and adaptable leader is always listening to their stakeholders, their markets, employees, clients, and even competitors. It requires being present in each moment. Being present brings greater awareness, which is necessary in addressing the challenges facing your team.

A knowledge of history is a good thing, and so is a knowledge of past solutions. But to solve tomorrow's problems, the agile and adaptable leader won't rely on what worked yesterday. Leaders should always use their experience as a resource, but not rely on it solely to solve problems. Agile leaders don't worry about their egos; instead, they take pride in being resilient and creative in their approach, and in using their influence quietly, behind the scenes.

10. POSITIVE OUTLOOK

The desire to make life better is itself a source of great happiness and positive energy, and gives us a good reason to get out of bed in the morning. Having a positive viewpoint is healthy, and can bring you happiness even during challenging times. Studies have shown a direct link between having a positive outlook and health benefits like better weight control, lower blood pressure, less heart disease, and healthier blood sugar levels. In fact, Johns Hopkins expert Lisa R. Yanek, M.P.H., and her colleagues found that people with a family history of heart disease who also had a positive outlook were one-third less likely to have a heart attack or other cardiovascular event within five to 25 years than those with a more negative outlook.[32]

Instead of complaining about a situation, the leader with a positive outlook will ask themselves, "What is the opportunity here? What can I learn from this?" This is the true value of the law of attraction: you always look for the positive energy that can supersede the negative energy. Hope and positivity are a super-

---

32 https://www.hopkinsmedicine.org/health/wellness-and-prevention/
    the-power-of-positive-thinking

power that helps people make better health and life decisions and focus more on long-term goals.

Mary Barra, the CEO of General Motors, is an example of a person who saw her life unfolding in positive terms, took responsibility, and focused not on obstacles but on opportunities.

You gain influence by helping others to reach their goals and keeping a positive attitude. Whether positive or negative, a leader's disposition affects their stakeholders. Therefore it's important to commit to a consistent positive attitude. Not only is it better for your mental health, it will have a marked influence on your team.

When you are positive, it's easier to build a network of advocates and champions. Positive people are like magnets, and they don't need to struggle to attract others to their vision. When your "can-do" outlook engenders trust and confidence, others will be happy to be on your team.

TAKE STOCK OF YOUR PEER GROUP

When piloting a ship across the ocean, the navigator must, on a regular basis, determine the ship's location relative to various known landmarks, such as certain stars or the moon. Similarly, you need to regularly look around and see how your skills compare to others in your industry. Do you have competitive qualifications and experience? Are there new industry trends that you need to be comfortable with and leverage to your advantage?

Trade associations and influence-building groups are excellent places to not only meet new people but to stay abreast of innovations and changing standards in your industry. Attend them regularly, and then rate yourself (on a 1 to 10 scale, for example) how competitive your skill sets are to others in your industry. Find a way to capitalize on the areas where you're ahead and strengthen the areas in which you may be behind.

SUCCESS ACTION ITEMS –
IDENTIFY AND LEVERAGE YOUR COMPETITIVE COMPETENCIES

- Succeed by identifying and leveraging personal driving forces and competitive competencies.
- Separate and prioritize your competencies into two categories: Those objectively measured by a third party and "soft skills," which can't be easily measured.
- Learn and master the following ten competitive competencies.
  1. Embrace the role of influencing others. Take the role of leadership and being influential seriously. Build trust by leading by example. Do what you say you will do.
  2. Learn the value of networking and partnering on a strategic level to build and use influence. Give more than you get.
  3. Envision your future and create a shared vision. Have a relationship navigation plan to help you pursue high-level networking opportunities based upon relationship building.
  4. Become a Relationship Building Expert. Relationships are formed by connecting with people and are solidified when you're able to solve problems and create opportunities together. Here are five skills you should use when building relationships.
     ◦ Seek out people who share your same vision of success.
     ◦ Show genuine interest in their business.
     ◦ Give before taking. Elevate yourself as a potential partner by offering knowledge or help to solve a business problem.
     ◦ Celebrate what makes you different. Be open to new ideas.
     ◦ Don't be afraid to challenge the status quo.
  5. Think and plan strategically. Long-term planning includes asking, "Where are we now? Where do we want to be? And, how do we get there?" Focus on solving problems which in turn will provide insights into new opportunities.
  6. Be integrity focused. Personal integrity is about doing the right thing, even when no one is looking, or the choice is not easy.
  7. Think creatively, but be focused so your idea has a strategic purpose and benefits all the players involved.
  8. Use good communication methods to create trust, credibility and to build relationships. Inspire, be clear, and collaborate.
  9. Be agile and adaptable. This means you are willing and able to make change, and adapt quickly when needed.
  10. Have a positive outlook. When problems arise ask, "What is the opportunity here? What can I/we learn from this?"
- Take stock of your peer groups. Regularly review how your skills compare to others in your industry. How competitive are you?

GLO GORDON
CEO & BOARD MEMBER MATRIXX SOFTWARE

"Mastering Your Pitch"

MY SUCCESS STORY

GREW UP IN JAMAICA, WEST Indies. I was there through elementary and middle school, and in the eighth grade we moved to Lafayette, California. Academically I had been in a British schooling system, and the California school wanted to move me up a grade after some testing, but thankfully my mom agreed with me that it was a bit too much, especially given the immersion and associated social pressure I would be dealing with.

My sister and I were a year apart. We went to Stanley Middle School. She was in seventh grade and I was in eighth. It was sink or swim, figuring out how to survive, asking questions, as simple as how you push the "walk" button to cross the street when you've never seen one before. Then you watch somebody else do it, and you figure it out. We went through things like that, which was disruptive to settling in a new place because you're often off-kilter.

After graduating from high school, I didn't really want to go to college, but my parents said I had to go, and it had to be a college in the University of California system. So I picked one on the beach, UC Santa Barbara. I majored in sociology, checked that college degree box, making me eligible to interview for some of the jobs I would be interested in.

I didn't know exactly what I was going to do but I ended up in sales, which was really fun. I worked at Xerox for twenty years. It was a great foundation and I learned so much. I was really into it, knocking on doors and saying, "Hi, do you want to buy a copier?" I was assigned zip codes, and I was cold-calling, knocking on doors and learning the game of odds.

I had been a waitress in college, where I also excelled, as there was a selling aspect that I really enjoyed. Working for Xerox felt like a continuation of that customer experience, with a career path beyond my sights. After twenty years, I asked myself, "If I were to come out of college today, where would I want to go? The past doesn't dictate my future. Where's the real challenge of today?"

I took a year off and then decided to go into software. My sister had been selling software, was successful and we were close. She was at Peoplesoft and convinced somebody there to take a chance on talking to me. They had a strong team who needed leadership and prioritized leadership over software knowledge for this hire. I moved to Laguna Beach and took on running this sales team. I stayed in Laguna for 10 years and loved it.

When PeopleSoft was acquired by Oracle, I was recruited by SAP where I focused on Communications. SAP's culture wasn't a good match for me and I left within 2 years. Oracle started talking to me about coming back. By that point the complexities with the acquisition had settled down so I went back, and I took my second Communications focused leadership role. Being successful there meant you had to perform to thrive. I loved that as there was nowhere to hide. At Oracle, you're working with some really talented people, you've got to be aggressive and have a voice. You develop strong communication and persuasion skills, you also sharpen your skills on each other. I progressed to Group VP of World-Wide Communications sales, which was my last role before I left in 2014. It was time for a new challenge.

One of the leaders on my Oracle team left to join a Silicon Valley IoT startup company called Jasper. He said to me, "You've got to come over here. We have a CRO job opening and we are actively evaluating candidates, just come meet our CEO." So I met Jahangir Mohammed, Founder and CEO. To me, he was like a prophet; I was intrigued, then moved and ultimately compelled. I learned so much over the next 2 years as their CRO, and then we were acquired by Cisco. Cisco was a great experience; however, after helping with the transition of Jasper into Cisco, it was time for a new challenge, staying on the pure software path.

I found this new challenge as the new CRO for a company called Uptake. The technology is artificial intelligence (AI), which was the next, natural progression of IoT, leveraging my prior experience. The CEO/Founder was the co-founder of Groupon, and the main investors of Groupon were the main investors of Uptake. I worked for the CEO, who is super creative, and the challenge of building an Enterprise software business was exciting for him. This was a great opportunity, great market, but we agreed I was brought in too early. We had an amicable parting, I had a few colleagues who had joined me, some are still there and having fun. I learned a lot through that experience.

After I left, I wanted to be on boards. I met with a company named MATRIXX Software, where I had some relationships. This eventually led to a board role and after a year of being a Board member, we decided it was time to pivot MATRIXX from technology focus to a commercial focus. The prior CEO/ Co-Founder is now Chief Scientist and Chairman of the Board. I am currently MATRIXX's CEO.

I'm a salesperson at heart, and as a CEO my focus and strength is go-to-market. I make sure I have talented people around me who are strong in the areas where I don't have much experience. I believe in advisors and their experience to help us stay focused and to execute.

HOW I WOULD SURVIVE IN A STRANGE CITY

If I were dropped off in a strange city, with no connections, I imagine it would be a tropical location. I would find a dive shop because I'm a diver, and I'd see if there were something I could do there.

I'd also go to a high-end restaurant to see if I could be hired on as a server, and make connections for future employment opportunities, and find a room to rent.

In my conversations, I would be more open than I usually am. I'd try to immediately find work that I could do at night or part-time while looking for other work. I would try to get access to a computer to do some research on the top economy for that area, where I might be able to find a full-time role, leveraging my experience.

If I only had a little bit of money, I'd conserve it because I would need to cover the basics. I would go to the commercial areas frequented by people with whom I might be able to strike up a meaningful conversation that could lead to opportunities. I would focus on the very basic things that need to be taken care of immediately, so I could settle down and focus on the bigger picture.

SPHERE OF INFLUENCE

To me, influence means leadership. It doesn't necessarily mean that you have a title of a leader, but you have leadership skills. You can probably persuade people to go out of their way for you, like being able to influence someone to keep me healthy (such as food, water, shelter), give me a job, introduce me to others, whatever I need at that time. A sphere of influence might mean a cross-section of all of those things.

STRATEGIC INFLUENCER

To me, strategic means a really thoughtful and deliberate set of steps where you're trying to get to a higher order outcome. It means having a long-term goal in mind while using strategic influence to focus on the immediate or more tactical needs.

There's the short game and the long game. To be strategic, I'm usually thinking of the long game, and anybody I'd surround myself with or keep in my circle of influence, would need to share my values. You want to work with people you never have to think twice about in terms of integrity or honesty. They must have a strong personal brand. Of course, I'd eventually be looking for the people I can connect with who are going to share the kinds of values I have, otherwise it's short-term. So, it's like a leapfrog—in getting to that place you might meet some people who share some of your values, and have a different belief system. We may cross paths and help with each other's short-term goals. A fork in the road may lead us each to a different long-term vision.

INFLUENCE VS. SOCIAL MEDIA

I am not on social media outside of LinkedIn. I'm not on Facebook or Instagram or any other sites where I used to be. To me, it felt transactional, and influenced by pattern recognition. You might think somebody is having some kind of experience when their real world is very different. I'm not a big fan of social media. I think there are positives to it, but I think there's also a downside, so I don't personally participate.

STRATEGIC RELATIONSHIP INFLUENCE

There are people you meet with whom you click, and it becomes more personal. Then you start wanting to connect and work on more initiatives. Relationship to me is knowing somebody beyond those brief encounters and single initiatives. You may have many strategic initiatives going with that person over time, so they become part of your circle, and that to me is different than a transactional relationship.

TRUSTED PARTNERS

I think there are people about whom you learn, over time, that you can absolutely trust, and they have your back. You're on a professional journey together through life and you navigate things in a way where you help each other.

Liking someone is also important. There might be influential people you don't really care for too much. You don't really like their communication style, or they're just abrasive. But then there are people whom you naturally like. You like the way they deal with people and how they make people feel while accomplishing the same goal. You don't have to like everyone you work with; however, people who like working together tend to follow each other, go faster and take on new challenges together. Diversity of thought is important here to maintain an important balance.

CENTERS OF INFLUENCE

A center of influence is a group of people like your personal board, who travel with you through different challenges. Together you have found that you really love working together as a group and you're willing to take on new challenges and take on risks together.

I'm thinking of a group that has followed me into different companies. There's influence across the group because there's a bi-directional respect regardless of title. It's like a brand that you're creating with your own personal board of directors, and you like to take on new challenges together— a well-respected cohort. I'm extremely honored and flattered when people I respect take a chance with me when they have so many options available to them. We've seen each other in really tough situations. We are battle tested. When in the trenches going through hard times, it reveals who we are.

Regarding people who are centers of influence in my life, I do have a handful of people whom I call on for advice. These are people whom I respect, like Jahangir Mohammed, Founder and CEO of Jasper. He's moved on to a different company, an early-stage startup in India. From time-to-time I have called him for his advice on things, and I highly value it. I do it very sparingly.

I'M A CENTER OF INFLUENCE

I consider myself to be a center of influence. I would never go out there and say that about myself, but based on the activity and the behavior and the patterns around me, I'd have to agree that the indicators are there.

The first time I realized I had influence was when I went from one group to a startup group within a big company. Many had just left the startup group and I was asked to come in and turn it around. I was surprised at the number of people who wanted to join me to help with that turnaround. That's when I realized I had a small following. Because we were in a male dominated industry of technology, it was really encouraging to me that a lot of women were also up for this challenge. We did really well and a lot of us have stayed together since then.

Part of what makes some people fun to follow is that they are not all about themselves. It's not about their ego; it's about taking care of each other. I have some influence on people who follow me, and although they may not agree with some of my decisions, they understand my thought process in arriving at those decisions. I have become predictable to them due to a consistent experience over time.

My team also responsibly makes me aware of challenges that wouldn't be visible to me until they get much bigger. This helps me help our employees, our shareholders and our customers with early course correction. Ultimately, we take care of each other in the spirit of doing what's right.

DEEP DOWN HABITS

I'm very driven and very committed. I would never ask anyone to do anything I'm not willing to do myself. I have done some of the roles reporting to me, so at times, I can speak firsthand and can relate.

I feel like I'm relatable and I have other people's back. They know how I'm going to respond to something because I'm consistent and I think that comes from knowing your north star and your values.

We're all in it together, and if they need me to be there with them for a tough meeting, I'm happy to join. I don't shy away from that. I am a person of my word. If I say I'm going to do something, I do it. If you ask people about me, they would say that when Glo says she's going to do something, you can count on it. Her word is her bond.

IF I COULD GO BACK TO THE BEGINNING...

I might have networked more. I figured out networking midway through my career when people would go out of their way to take things on for me that they didn't have to. I would show appreciation, send them their favorite wine, food, flowers, etc., and acknowledge what they did for me or the person I was representing. I have always remembered this and I work to pay it forward. But I would say, earlier in my career, I should have networked more and nurtured some of those relationships. The older you get, the smaller the community becomes, and sometimes people from the past show up with influence over decisions that matter to us. Bottom line: network more, show gratitude and pay it forward.

A DEFINING MOMENT

I had a short stint at Gartner Group in 1996. I was there for a year during my twenty years at Xerox. I was a sales manager for an advanced-systems team at Xerox, and was recruited to be a sales specialist, at Gartner. I wanted to see if I could still do it. They paid more and I wanted to get my life back. I wanted to be able to work out and sleep in my own bed. I took this new role with Gartner, and in a regional meeting the RVP said, "Hey, we have a new sales pitch. Does anybody want to volunteer to give that pitch at the next all-hands meeting?" I raised my hand.

I learned that pitch inside and out, and came back to deliver it a month later to a standing ovation. That year, I achieved the Rookie of the Year award, and proved to myself that I still had it. The greater lesson I learned from that experience was the importance of that pitch. After I learned it, it helped me so much in my job. I knew that thing cold and I wanted to deliver it everywhere! It was a good pitch. From that point forward, when I took on a sales leadership role, we would have a standard pitch. We certify all reps on a pitch before they can customize it as their own. That was a moment of discipline that changed everything. I knew it was necessary from personal experience for a sales organization. After a year at Gartner, I returned to Xerox and picked up where I left off with a new sense of purpose.

THE ONE PERSON WHO'S MADE AN IMPACT

My dad, rest in peace, had a big influence on me. He worked really hard. He was at Kaiser for thirty-plus years. He worked for one company his whole life. He demanded four years in college, and he demanded from us, a career after college. I had other opportunities besides Xerox, and I actually did accept one.

I was supposed to be the tennis coach at a brand new, prestigious tennis facility nearby. The hiring manager kept increasing the offer, and I still said "no." Xerox was just taking so long, so I finally said "yes." Then Xerox called and I was supposed to start the coaching job that next week, so I told Xerox, "No thanks, I can't. I've already taken another job."

I told my dad and he said, "No, you need to call back right now. You tell Xerox that you're coming for that interview, and you tell the other place to wait, or you're not coming." I ended up at Xerox.

My dad was a work hard, play hard kind of guy. He retired at sixty-two. I'm getting closer to that number every day, so that's on my radar. He retired at sixty-two and he just played. He bought a beach house and a fishing boat. He was on the beach and just had a great time. He seemed like a different person when he retired. He was relaxed and generous. The drinks were flowing and the music was playing and he liked to just fish and have a really good time with his friends and family. He was somebody who kept me serious, kept me focused, demanded more, and then showed me there's a lighter side, once you have worked hard and paid those dues. You can have fun along the way, you have a lot of fun after that too. He was hugely influential at the very critical stages in my life. He made sure I stayed on the right path because I could have definitely made some other choices at those forks in the road, no question about it. I'm so thankful to my parents, mentors and loved ones for all of the good things in my life.

Glo Gordon is a senior global executive leader and board member with more than twenty years of experience providing business operation strategy and senior sales experience to large multinational technology companies including Cisco, Oracle, SAP and Xerox. She held P&L responsibility for Cisco, the leading provider of Internet of Things (IoT) through acquisition and integration. Known for transforming underperforming organizations into high-performing environments by improving technology, processes, sales culture and relationship management, Glo consistently surpasses targets and achieves double-digit growth. She is highly qualified to deliver board and business value by exploring high-tech solutions and SaaS to transition from a product company to a service business.

Currently, Glo is CEO and Board Member for MATRIXX, a leading 5G Digital Commerce company in the Silicon Valley.

SPHERE OF
STRATEGIC INFLUENCE

STRATEGIC
INFLUENCE

OPPORTUNITY

PERSPECTIVE

LEADERSHIP

ACCOUNTABILITY

RELATIONSHIPS

CENTER OF
INFLUENCE

SUCCESS FACTOR 9:
BECOME A CENTER OF INFLUENCE

*"Position yourself as a strategic influencer.
The one who knows the movers and shakers. People will re-
spond to that, and you'll soon become what you project."*
—John David Mann

C ONGRATULATIONS!

It's been a long journey, but since stepping off the boat onto the dock in Metropolis, you've worked your way from being an outsider, with no connections and no influence, to forming relationships, then entering into profitable partnerships, and then becoming an influencer, and now you're seen by your peers and stakeholders as a Center of Influence.

You'll note that I said you're *seen* as a center of influence. This is a position that others bestow upon you. You cannot proclaim yourself to be influential. You only become influential by establishing trust over a long period of time, and you establish trust by helping others solve their problems. You don't have to do this for free; of course, you should be fairly compensated for your products or services. But you must establish your personal brand as being one of integrity and value, focused on elevating and assisting others.

WITH INFLUENCE COMES RESPONSIBILITY

When you become a center of influence—a CEO, industry leader, media celebrity—the things you do and say, and the decisions you make, can have a real impact on people's lives. You can use your influence to benefit yourself alone or to benefit your family, community, or nation.

We've all heard the saying, "With great power comes great responsibility." You can substitute the word "influence" for "power," because in many ways, influence is the indirect application of power.

In business, there are people—perhaps even yourself—who wield tremendous power by their direct managerial control of a company or organization. In the 1990s, Jack Welch, the CEO of General Electric, directly used his authority to reshape the company and alter the lives of many of its employees.

Other people may not have that kind of direct authority but instead have tremendous influence. For example, Warren Buffett, widely regarded as the world's most successful investor, generally declines to get involved in the management of the companies he owns through Berkshire Hathaway. Company management is just not something he's interested in doing. As one of the most powerful business leaders and influencers in the world, investors, bankers, and salesmen endlessly study his reports for clues on how he does it. Buffett has the power to be very aggressive in his approach to acquiring a company, but he chooses not to do hostile takeovers. He trusts the management team in place. If he doesn't like the company, he simply passes on it.

"The trick in investing is just to sit there and watch pitch after pitch go by and wait for the one right in your sweet spot," Buffett said in the HBO documentary *Becoming Warren Buffett*. "And if people are yelling, 'Swing, you bum!' ignore them."[33] The balance of power and responsibility is not a new idea.

The phrase bears a close resemblance to the Bible verse in Luke 12:48: "From everyone who has been given much, much will be demanded; and from the one who has been entrusted with much, much more will be asked."

It appears centuries later in the French National Convention in 1793, the first French government organized as a republic: "They [the Representatives] must contemplate that a great responsibility is the inseparable result of a great power."

In 1817, British Member of Parliament William Lamb was recorded saying, "The possession of great power necessarily implies great responsibility."

And in 1906, Winston Churchill, who was then under-secretary of the Colonial Office, said, "Where there is great power, there is great responsibility."

THE FIVE GUARDRAILS OF ETHICAL INFLUENCE

Because temptation is everywhere, it may take a conscious effort to use your influence wisely and ethically. Here are the Five Guardrails of Ethical Influence that will keep you from succumbing to unwise impulses.

1. LISTEN

Too often, people in power love to hear themselves talk. They think that listening to others is a sign of weakness. Nothing could be further from the truth.

---

33 Insurancebusinessmag. https://www.insurancebusinessmag.com/us/news/
breaking-news/warren-buffett-walks-away-from-deal-for-unilever-60746.aspx

If you don't listen to others, especially the subject matter experts (such as your doctor or your accountant) who are charged with reporting to you the facts, then you'll just listen to your own "echo chamber." You'll tell yourself what you want to hear, and you'll resent or reject the world when it doesn't conform to your expectations. This will result in your making decisions that are not based in reality—and which can therefore be very damaging.

Check your ego at the door. As Steve Jobs once said, "It doesn't make sense to hire smart people and tell them what to do; we hire smart people so they can tell us what to do."

Everyone, even a center of influence needs an *accountability partner* who has the authority to say, "Stop and listen," without fear of your retribution. Serving in that role should be a person who genuinely cares about your success and has nothing to gain or lose from it. You might start with your mother or father and then look for a mentor, or even a fishing buddy—anyone to whom you can speak honestly and who will give you their honest answer.

Proactively seek feedback, not just from people you want to impress, but from all levels. This goes beyond simply having an "open-door policy." In your organization, you must have processes in place to regularly and systematically gather feedback across all levels of the organization.

2. ACCEPT RESPONSIBILITY

Nothing is more infuriating to employees and other stakeholders than a leader who allows a project or action to move forward, and then when it fails, the leader avoids responsibility and points the finger at others. Your ability to influence others will diminish if you're unable to accept responsibility not only for your decisions but the decisions of the subordinates who act in your name.

Responsibility works in 360 degrees. With subordinates, responsible behavior means a willingness to take charge and not shirk from decisions that may be unpopular. The responsible manager ensures the group successfully achieves results that will benefit everyone in the organization. With superiors, it means accepting criticism for mistakes and fixing the problems. The responsible manager acts as a buffer from pressures that come from above and informs those at higher levels of needed resources and performance shortfalls.

When you say you're going to do something, then be sure you deliver it successfully and on time. Both your direct reports and your superiors need to believe that you are pulling your weight. Don't be cavalier with your words and promises. Track every commitment you make, no matter how trivial. If necessary, break them down into bite-sized tasks, or delegate them to a trusted subordinate.

3. MAINTAIN YOUR PERSONAL INTEGRITY

From personal integrity spring steadiness and dependability. If you live according to a moral code and a set of unchanging values, then those around you will be able to trust your judgment and have faith that you're acting in their best interest. The opposite of ethical leadership is the cult of personality, where the leader makes decisions based solely on some hidden personal agenda, and his or her followers are expected to follow along even in the absence of a rational plan. This is the worst misuse of influence and always comes to a bad end for everyone involved.

4. EMBRACE THE BIG PICTURE

To use your influence wisely, you need to see and embrace the big picture and how the various components of a project contribute to a common goal. The story of the three stonecutters perfectly illustrates the power of knowing how many small tasks work together to create more than the sum of the parts.

One day a traveler came across three stonecutters working in a quarry. Each was busy cutting a block of stone. Interested in finding out what they were working on, he asked the first stonecutter what he was doing. "I am cutting a stone!" Still no wiser, the traveler turned to the second stonecutter and asked him what he was doing. "I am cutting this block of stone to make sure that it's square and its dimensions are uniform so that it will fit exactly in its place in a wall." A bit closer to finding out what the stonecutters were working on but still unclear, the traveler turned to the third stonecutter. He seemed to be the happiest of the three, and when asked what he was doing, he replied: "I am building a cathedral."

If you can appreciate the big picture like the third stonecutter, then your decisions will reflect that overarching goal. You'll ask, "What is the cathedral going to look like, and how will it serve the people who come to it? How are we going to finance it? How is each stone going to fit into the building plan? How much should we pay for the stone? How should we get the stone to the building site?" To properly answer these questions, you need relationships and partnerships with others who have influence and can get things done. And you'll need to use your influence, not to line your own pockets but to achieve the common goal.

You also need to understand that your people—all of your stonecutters and other workers—are human beings with their own hopes and dreams, and if you help them to see the big picture too, they'll be more engaged and productive.

5. BE GENEROUS

There's an old saying in business—and in life—that goes, "Pass the credit, take the blame."

Leadership generosity means more than approving fat paychecks (although those are pleasant, too!). It means stepping back and allowing others to shine. Leaders who misuse their influence to grab the spotlight and extoll their own virtues find themselves isolated and with their influence waning.

The power of generous leadership was best captured by Lao Tzu: "A leader is best when people barely know he exists, when his work is done, and his aim fulfilled; and his followers will say: we did it ourselves." This is the art of leadership at its best.

Or, as Nelson Mandela said: "It is better to lead from behind and to put others in front, especially when you celebrate victory when nice things occur. You take the front line when there is danger. Then people will appreciate your leadership."

BE A ROLE MODEL

When you're a center of influence, all eyes are on you—from both above and below, and inside and outside the organization.

Your subordinates will be watching to see if you "walk the walk" and if your talk about ethics and honor is for real. Having personal integrity means turning away from the easy score or the desire to shortchange the organization. If you leave work for long lunches at the club, or you take off early to go play golf, or you use company funds to fix your house, your subordinates and teammates will see this, and the effect will be corrosive. They will think, "Hey, it's every man for himself around here! I'd better grab what I can get while the gravy train is running."

Your superiors—the board of directors, perhaps—will want to see that you are a good and effective steward of the organization and that you're honestly and fairly working to get a robust return for the company's investors.

Outside analysts and investors will want to know the direction of the company and if, under your direction, investor funds are being used appropriately and for the good of the company.

Don't let them down. Be the role model they expect and deserve.

Remember, with great power comes great responsibility.

ASSOCIATE WITH LIKE-MINDED COIS

"You will move in the direction of the people that you associate with," said Warren Buffett in a speech at Columbia University. "You want to associate with people who are the kind of person you'd like to be… It's important to associate with people that are better than yourself."[34]

As you become a center of influence, you need to keep your standards high and your relationships secure. While you constantly strive to expand your sphere of influence and meet new people, you must also maintain your relationships with your peers. Do not just be a taker, but also be a giver. If you attend parties or social gatherings at the homes of other influencers, be sure to reciprocate by being a host yourself. Join clubs or associations where you can mingle with people who share your views (and maybe even a few who don't!). Within such settings, you can exchange ideas and further expand your relationship circle. Such associations are both a reward for your hard work and progress and also a vehicle for learning about new opportunities.

One of the benefits of joining a professional networking group or a business club is that all the members have been vetted already and bring value to the table. Such an environment can act as a force multiplier, where the time you spend there is made more productive because your peer group has been pre-selected for compatibility with you.

MANAGE AND LEVERAGE YOUR PERSONAL BRAND

Your personal brand is who you are, what you stand for, the values you embrace, and the way in which you express those values. Just as a company's brand helps to communicate its value to customers and stand out from the competition, your personal brand does the same for you, helping to communicate a unique identity and clear value to potential employers, clients, and partners. It should establish your reputation, highlight your strengths, build trust, and communicate the unique attributes that you bring to your industry.

You can, and must, control your brand—the version of yourself that you show to the public. To others, your brand is not what you wish it to be or think it is, but what others have actually seen from you. Remember what Longfellow said: "We judge ourselves by what we feel capable of doing, while others judge us by what we have already done."

The more relationships you form—and the more value you can provide in your interactions—the more likely it is your personal brand will be recognized. Remember, your personal brand is cultivated everywhere you go: in intimate environments with just a few people, conferences with hundreds or thousands of people, and social media with untold numbers of people. Focus on authenticity

---

34   CNBC. https://www.cnbc.com/2017/02/08/why-bill-gates-and-warren-buffett-say-your-friends-are-crucial-to-your-career.html

and generosity, and be sure those carry over into how you conduct yourself every day.

SOME PEOPLE CAN TAKE THE SHORT ROAD

This book is based on the idea that you—and presumably everyone else—has landed on the strange shores of Metropolis, without connections or any advantages; and your job is to establish yourself, form relationships, enter into partnerships, and gradually widen your spheres of influence until you yourself become a center of influence. In real life, some people are born and raised in Metropolis, and so have a built-in advantage over you. Some are even born into positions of great influence and don't have to lift a finger to earn it. This was common back in the days when nations were ruled by hereditary monarchs. If you were king, your kid would become king, too, regardless of whether he deserved it. It happens today, too—just ask members of the Walton family in Bentonville, Arkansas, who inherited the empire that Grandpa Sam built.

I don't know at which point in your life, or under what conditions, you started your journey to build your personal influence. Some people are granted access to the short road, so to speak, while others are destined for the long road.

If your parents sent you to a prestigious private school, and then you got accepted into an Ivy League university, this would be the short road, giving you the *opportunity* to build your influence much more quickly than someone taking the long road. Some privileged people grab the opportunity, while others don't. When a door is opened for you, whether by virtue of your birth or your own hard work, choosing to walk through that door is your decision. The fact that you are reading this book, and are nearing its conclusion, is evidence that you're ready and willing to walk through those doors that are open and take advantage of the opportunities in front of you.

And yes, even on the short road, there are shortcuts! For example, if you attend Yale, you're already in a sphere of influence. But if you stand out among your fellow students, you may be asked to join one of the "Big Three" three secret societies—Skull and Bones, Scroll and Key, and the Wolf's Head Society.

The most well-known—or notorious, if you prefer—is Skull and Bones. Founded in 1832, the first extended description of Skull and Bones, published in 1871 by Lyman Hotchkiss Bagg in his book *Four Years at Yale*, noted that "the mystery now attending its existence forms the one great enigma which college gossip never tires of discussing."[35]

---

35   Bagg, Lyman Hotchkiss (1871). Four Years at Yale.
New Haven, C.C. Chatfield & Co.

Since 1982, the society has published no official rosters, and membership for later years is speculative. Some news organizations refer to Bonesmen (and, since 1992, women) as a "power elite." Current membership reportedly includes former President George W. Bush, US Secretary of State John Kerry, former CEO and Chairman of Sears Holdings Corporation Edward S. Lampert, US Treasury Secretary Steven Mnuchin, United States District Court for the District of Columbia Judge James Emanuel Boasberg, and others in business, politics, and entertainment.

Scroll and Key is reportedly the wealthiest of the Yale Big Three. Like Skull and Bones, only fifteen juniors are tapped (literally, it seems, on the shoulder) for membership during their senior year. So they're only members on campus for one year before they head off into the world. They stay in touch through their society's alumni organization and, perhaps, through other means that are secret to outsiders. According to Lyman Hotchkiss Bagg, when Scroll and Key members write letters to each other, they add "YiT" at the bottom. We're not sure how this works in the age of email.

Notable Scroll and Key members have included former Mayor of New York John Lindsay, author Calvin Trillin, and CNN commentator Fareed Zakaria.

Not to be overlooked, Wolf's Head Society members reportedly include 2020 presidential candidate Tom Steyer, media personality Christopher Lydon, and American young adult and fantasy author Leigh Bardugo.

Most colleges have clubs and societies, ranging from Greek letter fraternities and sororities to special interest groups. These exist to bind their members together into trusting relationships that are meant to last a lifetime. With more than 336,000 lifetime members, the largest Greek letter organization is Sigma Alpha Epsilon. Founded in 1856 at the University of Alabama, SAE has approximately 13,500 undergraduate/collegiate members and counts alumni such as President William McKinley, NFL quarterback Troy Aikman, actor Nick Lachey, author William Faulkner, and actor Beau Bridges. There are ethnic and cultural fraternities, too, such as the nation's first African American intercollegiate Greek-lettered fraternity, Alpha Phi Alpha. Founded in 1906 at Cornell University, APA's membership has included Dr. Martin Luther King, Jr. and NAACP founder W. E. B. Du Bois.

The biggest women's fraternal organization is Chi Omega. Founded in 1895 at the University of Arkansas, it boasts an estimated 335,000 lifetime members. It describes itself as an "intergenerational women's organization" whose mission is "friendship, personal integrity, service to others, academic excellence and intellectual pursuits, community and campus involvement and personal and career development." The organization stresses personal integrity and admonishes its members, "the message of 'personal responsibility' cannot be shared enough. Each member's choices and actions affect the entire chapter and our national organization."[36]

Once you graduate from college and enter adult life, you can join any one of hundreds of membership organizations and affinity groups that are designed to build relationships and achieve some social mission. They run the gamut from Freemasonry (George Washington was a member) to the Junior League (educational women's volunteer organization), to the Union Club in New York City, regarded as the most exclusive club in America. If you have to ask how you can join… then you're not going to be a member.

To be honest, some of these organizations—particularly the secret ones— have an unsavory odor about them. They are exclusionary. (Why, for example, should the Skull and Bones and the others limit themselves to fifteen new members a year? What if #16 was someone who worked hard and could make a strong contribution?) Many others are dedicated more to socializing than anything else. What the world needs is an organization focused solely on helping its members foster meaningful relationships with influencers so that they themselves can build their own influence. But more about that later.

THE LONG ROAD

Some people are fated to start their journey to influence on the long road, without the benefit of connections or access to those who have influence. To become a center of influence after having arrived in Metropolis with neither relationships nor partnerships is difficult but not impossible. In fact, it happens more often than you might think.

Born in 1973 in Moscow, in what was then the Soviet Union, Sergey Mikhaylovich Brin emigrated to the United States with his mother and father in 1979. During their transition, the Brin family received support and assistance from the Hebrew Immigrant Aid Society. His father, Mikhail Brin, had secured a teaching position at the University of Maryland, and the family settled in Adelphi, Maryland. After graduating in 1993 from the University of Maryland with honors, he headed to Stanford University, where he met Larry Page. Together they formed a partnership and founded Google—and the rest is history.

Jan Koum was born on February 24, 1976, in Kyiv, Ukraine, which was then in the Soviet Union. In 1992, he moved with his mother and grandmother to Mountain View, California, where a social support program helped the family

---

36 ChiOmega. https://chiomega.com/what-we-stand-for/

to get a small two-bedroom apartment. His father stayed behind and died there in 1997. In California, the family had very little; Koum's mother worked as a babysitter, while he worked as a cleaner at a grocery store.

After high school, Koum enrolled at San Jose State University while working at Ernst & Young as a security tester. In 1997, Koum was hired by Yahoo! as an infrastructure engineer.

For the next decade, he bounced around from job to job. Then in January 2009, he bought an iPhone and realized that the newly created App Store had huge potential. He visited his friend Alex Fishman, and together they invented WhatsApp because it sounded like "what's up."

WhatsApp gained a large user base, and on February 9, 2014, Mark Zuckerberg asked Koum to have dinner at his home and formally proposed Koum a deal to join the Facebook board. Ten days later, Facebook announced that it was acquiring WhatsApp for $19 billion.

It's safe to say that in a little over twenty years, Jan Koum went from being a kid with zero influence to a true center of influence with a fortune in the bank and a seat on the Facebook board.

Here's one more inspiring example of a person who literally landed in America with no influence and no connections—but with an admittedly powerful asset.

Arnold Alois Schwarzenegger was born in Thal, Austria, on July 30, 1947. Inspired by movie idols, including Johnny Weissmuller and Steve Reeves, at the age of fourteen, he took up bodybuilding. At home, he was subjected to child abuse, which was fairly normal there; he told the *Edinburgh Evening News*, "I was one who did not conform, and whose will could not be broken. Therefore, I became a rebel. Every time I got hit, and every time someone said, 'You can't do this,' I said, 'This is not going to be for much longer because I'm going to move out of here. I want to be rich. I want to be somebody.'"[37]

After winning several bodybuilding titles in London, at the age of twenty-one, he flew to Los Angeles. He later said, "I finally arrived here in 1968. What a special day it was. I remember I arrived here with empty pockets but full of dreams, full of determination, full of desire… America gave me opportunities, and my immigrant dreams came true."[38]

He was relentlessly ambitious, and even as he was winning bodybuilding titles, he dreamed of becoming a famous actor, like the men he had seen in the movies as a kid. He pursued his education at Santa Monica College in California (including English classes) and the University of California, Los Angeles. In May

---

37   http://news.scotsman.com/arnoldschwarzenegger/Arnie-I-was-abused-as.2551492.jp

38   CNN. https://www.cnn.com/2004/ALLPOLI-TICS/08/31/gop.schwarzenegger.transcript/

1980, he received his bachelor's degree in business administration and marketing. Three years later, he got his United States citizenship.

By all accounts, he was a friendly, gregarious person whom people wanted to help. He was also a savvy businessman. By the age of thirty—well before his career as an actor started—his success as an entrepreneur with a series of lucrative business ventures and investments had made Arnold a wealthy man. They included a bricklaying business, which he then used to fund a mail-order business (this was before the internet), selling bodybuilding and fitness-related equipment and instructional tapes. Those profits he plowed into his first real estate investment venture: an apartment building he purchased for just $10,000. Over the years, he invested his earnings in an array of stocks, bonds, privately controlled companies, and real estate holdings.

His acting career was far from assured. "It was very difficult for me in the beginning," he said. "I was told by agents and casting people that my body was 'too weird,' that I had a funny accent, and that my name was too long. You name it, and they told me I had to change it. Basically, everywhere I turned, I was told that I had no chance."[39]

You know the rest of the story. By forming relationships and then partnerships with film industry people, Arnold built a new career in movies that brought him to the very top—in 1993, the National Association of Theatre Owners named him the "International Star of the Decade." Then politics called, and on October 7, 2003, in a special election to recall California Governor Gray Davis, Arnold won with 48.6% of the vote. As the second foreign-born governor of California after Irish-born Governor John G. Downey in 1862, he took the reins of a state which, if it were an independent nation, would have the fifth-largest gross domestic product (GDP) in the world, trailing only the United States, China, Japan, and Germany. In 2006, he was re-elected. Were it not for the fact that the US Constitution prohibits foreign-born people from running, he most certainly would have taken a shot at being president of the United States.

A CAUTIONARY TALE

We all have human weaknesses, and even the strongest among us can succumb to the temptation to abuse our hard-earned influence.

Can you become a center of influence by lying or cheating? Yes—but it will not last long. The day of reckoning will come, and it will be harsh. Just review the Bernie Madoff story.

In 1960, he founded Bernard L. Madoff Investment Securities LLC. After

---

39 Ask Arnold. http://www.schwarzenegger.com/en/news/askarnold/
news_askarnold_eng_legacy_444.asp?sec=news&subsec=askarnold

forty-one years as a sole proprietorship, the firm incorporated in 2001 as a limited liability company with Madoff as the sole shareholder. The firm's legitimate business model was to bypass exchange specialist firms by directly executing orders over the counter from retail brokers. At one point, Madoff Securities was the largest market maker at the NASDAQ, and in 2008 was the sixth-largest market maker on Wall Street. The firm also had an investment management and advisory division, which it did not publicize, and which was the center of the decades-long fraud.

Madoff and his family were highly influential. He was active in the National Association of Securities Dealers (NASD), serving as chairman of its board of directors and as a member of its board of governors. He served on the board of directors of the Securities Industry Association, a precursor of the Securities Industry and Financial Markets Association (SIFMA), the primary securities industry organization, and was chairman of its trading committee.

He was a founding board member of the International Securities Clearing Corporation, the London subsidiary of the Depository Trust & Clearing Corporation.

A prominent philanthropist, Madoff served on the boards of several non-profit institutions. He served as the chairman of the board of directors of the Sy Syms School of Business at Yeshiva University and as treasurer of its board of trustees. He also served on the Board of New York City Center, a member of New York City's Cultural Institutions Group (CIG). He and his wife undertook charity work for the Gift of Life Bone Marrow Foundation and made philanthropic gifts through the Madoff Family Foundation.

Madoff was well known and well liked. In a June 17, 2009, interview with the *New York Daily News*, he said that Securities & Exchange Commission chairperson Mary Schapiro was a "dear friend," and SEC Commissioner Elisse Walter was a "terrific lady" whom he knew "pretty well."[40]

Of course, we now know that Madoff and his accomplices were running a vast Ponzi scheme that took money from trusting investors and then told those investors they had made huge profits when, in fact, Madoff had simply put the cash in the bank. The size of the fraud has been calculated at anywhere from $10 billion to $65 billion, depending on how you calculate it. Madoff was arrested on December 11, 2008, and on June 29, 2009, Judge Denny Chin sentenced Madoff to the maximum sentence of 150 years in federal prison.

Of course, you're no Bernie Madoff, and in all of your relationships and partnerships with others, you'll conduct yourself with the highest level of integrity.

---

40 *NY Daily News*. Gendar, Alison (October 31, 2009). *"Bernie Madoff baffled by SEC blunders; compares agency's bumbling actions to Lt. Colombo,"*

SUCCESS ACTION ITEMS —BECOME A CENTER OF INFLUENCE

- Become a Center of Influence. This is a position that others bestow upon you. You cannot proclaim yourself to be influential. You only become influential by establishing trust over a long period of time, and you establish trust by helping others solve their problems.
- Take the role of influencer seriously. When you become a center of influence— a CEO, industry leader, media celebrity—the things you do and say, can have a real impact on peoples' lives.
- Use your influence wisely and ethically. Here are Five Guardrails of Ethical Influence.
  1. Ability to listen. Listen to others who are charged with reporting to you the facts.
     - Everyone, even a center of influence, needs an accountability partner who has the authority to say, "Stop and listen," without fear of your retribution.
     - Proactively seek feedback, not just from people you want to impress, but from all levels.
  2. Accept Responsibility. When you say you're going to do something, then deliver it successfully and on time.
  3. Maintain your personal integrity. If you live according to a moral code and a set of unchanging values, then those around you will be able to trust your judgment and have faith that you're acting in their best interest.
  4. Embrace the big picture. Use your influence, not to line your own pockets but to achieve the common goal.
  5. Be generous. Leadership generosity means more than approving fat. It means stepping back and allowing others to shine.
- Be a role model. When you're a center of influence, all eyes are on you. Don't let them down. Be the role model they expect and deserve. Remember, with great power comes great responsibility.
- Associate with like-minded COIs.
- Manage and leverage your personal brand. Your personal brand is who you are, what you stand for, the values you embrace, and the way in which you express those values.
- Use your influence cautiously and responsibly. We all have human weaknesses, and even the strongest among us can succumb to the temptation to abuse our hard-earned influence.

JOHN HEWITT
CEO LOYALTY BRANDS
CO-FOUNDER OF JACKSON HEWITT
FOUNDER OF LIBERTY TAX

"I Never Look Back"

A RISK WORTH TAKING

W HEN I WAS YOUNG, IN college at the University of Buffalo, I started at H&R Block, and I loved it. In my second season, my manager asked me if I would quit school and run ten H&R Block offices. So at twenty-one years old, I was running over 10,000 tax returns and ten offices, with a staff of about eighty. The guy who hired me was the regional director, and I said to myself, I want to set a goal to be an H&R Block regional director. Ten years later, they called me up, interviewed me, and made me a Block regional director.

I was incredibly successful at a young age. Out of about forty regional directors in the country, I was fourth-best in growth, and I went into the toughest region in the country where they had had fourteen regional directors in thirteen years. And out of my sixteen district managers, I had eight new rookies who had never gone through a tax season; and in spite of that, I had a great year.

Then my dad interceded. He was CFO of a public company, and around 1980 he told me he liked the little Apple computer he had bought by mail better than the mainframe that was running his public company. He said, "John, let's computerize taxes." It took him a long time, about six months, but he convinced me to leave H&R Block, where I was incredibly happy. So he tore me out of my job, and he left his job too. In 1981 we developed the first tax software for an Apple computer. That was the biggest point in my career.

ARRIVING IN A STRANGE LAND

I can identify with the traveler who arrives in Metropolis as a stranger with no influence and not even a friend. In 1963, when I was fourteen years old, my mom was driving myself and my four siblings in a small AMC Gremlin through

Canada from Buffalo to Detroit. My sister was in the back seat, singing, and it was horrible. So I told my mom, "Tell her to shut up!"

We were going fifty-five miles an hour. I was riding shotgun. I opened the door, and my mom came screeching to a halt. She dropped me off by the side of the road in Canada and then took off. She was so mad, she just drove away.

I often joke that if she hadn't come back for me, within ten or fifteen years, I would have owned Canada.

In my whole life, I never doubted I was going to be successful. In the book called *I Choose Peace: Raw Stories of Real People Finding Contentment and Happiness*, by Doug Bender, one of the chapters is entitled "Bliss." It's about Kathie Lee Gifford. Her theory was that when we're children, we think we can do anything. We can be president, we can go to the moon, we can be Superman or Batman—we can do anything. And then everyone beats us down. Not just our enemies, but our teachers and our parents and everyone in our life says, "Oh, you'll never be able to do that."

All of us are born with an innate confidence that we can do anything, but when others start imposing limits and boundaries, we lose it along the way. Successful people ignore that self-limiting behavior. Each one of us can have success if we don't limit ourselves, our thinking, our behavior, or our potential.

About fifteen years ago, I heard Doug Bender on the radio, and I had an epiphany. One of the differences between me and other people was they never beat me down. I was always cocky. I always knew I could do it, and even to the extent that I thought I'd make a few million dollars and retire. But I learned that's no fun, because what would I do after I had retired? Just sit by the pool all day, or play golf? No thanks.

I learned it was the *journey* that was fun.

There was no question in my mind that I would be successful.

In any new situation I was in, the first thing to do was gather information. I interviewed a dozen people and got as much information as I could, and looked for opportunities. I didn't know what the right opportunity was. So it would be the same thing as if I took over a company in a different industry.

Let's pretend I took over a restaurant. I would go and interview all the staff because I believe that there's gold in them thar hills. I would do intensive gathering of information, and then I would start off in a chosen direction. You don't want to start out in a direction and be going the wrong way.

INFLUENCERS

Let's talk about influencers. Most people, when they talk about influencer marketing, my first thought goes to the ultimate customer. My experience is a little bit different. The best achievements that I've had with influencer marketing are *internal,* with franchisees and master branches. When you have a hundred franchises, among them, there are five or seven superstars and fifteen or twenty low achievers. The other seventy to eighty are between the two groups.

I teach my people that you're never going to help the superstars; they are way above your help. They are the go-getters, they're the achievers, and they are going to win. And the fifteen or twenty low achievers just aren't going to listen and succeed.

The five or seven superstars are the influencers. Our work is with the big middle group of seventy, and I use the influencers to help. I go to them and say, "You are an expert at training taxes, so we'd like you to teach our other franchises." Believe it or not, I could be up there with fifty-one years of experience, and I could have an influencer/co-franchisee with two years of experience, and the one needing help is going to listen to the franchisee more than they listen to me.

I consider myself to be an influencer because I have to be! I've brought in five thousand franchises in my career. I don't know anyone else who has done that. I've won all kinds of accolades, like Entrepreneur of the Year from the International Franchise Association. I was also named one of the Top 100 Most Influential People in Accounting by *Accounting Today* for fourteen years in a row, so there's no question about it.

STRATEGIC INFLUENCE

I think the implication or inference of *strategic* is that it's positive and that you change people in a positive way. I think that if you're strategic, you've actually had success, and you've changed people's lives.

I've had the opportunity to help change many people's lives. I think just having influence is good, but if you don't get others to improve, if they do what they've always done, then they get what they've always got. I've made a hundred millionaires from people listening to me give them strategic advice on their situations. One of the reasons I believe I am incredibly successful in business, not just in franchising, but in *business,* is that I always want what's best for the other person. At the end of the day, I want what's best for each and every person. That's what I think is strategic to me. If it's not valuable, then it's not strategic.

Being a strategic influencer means looking out for the best of each person that you're dealing with. It's a win-win situation—they see added value by you being involved, and you also see value, or you wouldn't do it.

STRATEGIC RELATIONSHIP INFLUENCER

In my business, I personally don't have much interaction with the ultimate customer—for example, the person for whom we file taxes. My relationships are with my employees, my franchisees, and with my area representatives of my master franchises.

For example, when I was at Liberty Tax, we had a sign on the wall that read, "Happy Successful Franchisees." I would ask my people to define what the relationship is with a franchisee.

It has to be integrated, meaning they have to have involvement with the franchisee, there has to be a proven way to succeed, and the franchisor has to provide a road map for success.

It comes down to the customer. It's family, it's a team, it's a partnership. And at the end of the day, it's about the relationship. Most of my career people have said, "John, you have a family of relationships." This included the franchisees. I had an eight-bedroom beach house, and in my twenty years with Liberty franchisees, they spent thousands of nights at my house. I'm a very accessible CEO. When I go on the road, I typically have a dozen or more people for dinner. I am always accessible to them. I always answer their emails or texts. It comes down to that: team, family, customer.

My new company name actually says that: "Loyalty Brands." I'm loyal, and I try to be the kind of leader to whom people feel comfortable telling things because I reciprocate, and I try to help people before they even ask for it.

One of our things is you get loyalty by giving loyalty. I have ten people who have been with me over twenty years—two of them for thirty and one of them for fifty years.

CENTER OF INFLUENCE

You have to set an example. An employee once asked me this question: "I am about to have my first child. What are the one or two most important things I should do?"

I said, number one, you introduce them to God. And number two, you set a good example.

You know, talk is so cheap. I think the key is this: honesty is rare, and integrity is rare, but do you know the difference between honesty and integrity? Honesty is talking about the past, and integrity is about the future. If I say to you that I'm going to do something, then I'll become fanatically committed to that. I have found that most people, when they say, "I am going to do this or that," few of them actually meet their goals. Most of them don't even meet half their goals. They have no integrity. If you do what you say you're going to do, you will always be successful. If someone asked me what the key to success is, I'd say, "Do what you say you're going to do."

THE 4 HABITS OF SUCCESS

The deep-down habits that have helped me become successful are:

1. Integrity.

2. Drive. In the prologue of his book, *Made in America,* Sam Walton wrote, "If you asked me why I'm different, the only thing I can think of is I'm driven, and part of my drive is the ability to compete."

3. Desire to compete. The name of the book I wrote was called *I Compete.* I live to compete, and so do many others. At the very least, we all need to do what we say we're going to do. It's drive. It's competition.

4. Perseverance. You have to have perseverance. And again, as I said earlier, it's about trying to help the other person be all they can be. I'll even tell a person, "If you're not going to be extraordinary with me, then go find somewhere else to be extraordinary, and I'll even help you get there."

LOOKING FORWARD, NOT BACK

I'm different from many other people my age because I never ever go back and say, "What if?" It's just a waste of time! I've made so many mistakes, and when I look back, I see things I should have done differently, but then that path goes off a tree of different paths, and so who knows? I've made mistakes. I'm sorry for my mistakes, and I wish I hadn't made them, but you have to learn by them and get better. I've never spent one second thinking about that. I don't think it's a good idea to dwell on the past.

MY GREATEST INFLUENCERS

My dad and Jesus Christ.

John T. Hewitt is an American entrepreneur, CEO of Loyalty Brands, Co-Founder of Jackson Hewitt, and Sole Founder of Liberty Tax Service. Together these companies account for more than 10,000 tax-preparation offices in the United States and Canada. John was a pioneer in the development and use of specialized tax-preparation software, which is now the industry's standard practice.

John Hewitt is the only person who has launched and founded two highly successful, national tax-preparation brands, and is on his way to doing it again with his new Loyalty Brands company.

Website: www.loyaltybrands.com
LinkedIn: www.linkedin.com/company/loyaltybrandsinc/

SUCCESS FACTOR 10:
GIVE BACK!

"From what we get, we can make a living;
what we give however, makes a life."
—*Winston Churchill*

ELCOME TO THE TENTH AND final Success Factor of the Sphere of Strategic Influence-Give Back! On your life's journey, if you have passed through the first eleven and have arrived here, then congratulations on becoming a member of a very exclusive club: the people who are in a very secure position and can materially benefit their fellow citizens, not just once in a while but on a consistent and significant basis.

These are the few people who no longer have to worry about a paycheck. They live comfortably on passive income from wealth-producing assets they own—typically, industrial stocks or real estate. For the most part, they are immune to the vagaries of the economy. A recession doesn't affect them, or if they lose a little, it's no matter. Does Bill Gates care that from 1995 to 2007, he was the wealthiest person in the world, but in 2008 he was knocked off his perch by his pal Warren Buffett? In 2009, Gates regained the crown, only to be superseded the following year by Carlos Slim Helú. In 2014 Gates was back on top, and then in 2018, he was deposed by Jeff Bezos, who claimed the title until Elon Musk took over in 2021. At this level, what's a few billion among friends?

If, like most people, you're still building your spheres of influence, then this chapter will give you something to look forward to and aspire to. Many of its precepts you can begin to practice at any time on a scale that works for you. If you have a dollar in your pocket and you give ten cents to a food bank, then you have performed an act of great generosity. Anyone and everyone should be able to make a small contribution of time, talent, or money to a worthy cause, even if they are still forming relationships, looking for partnerships, or even dreaming of becoming a center of influence. There's an old saying that goes, "If you want to be somebody in the future, start being that person *now!*"

Obviously, if you're just starting your journey and you're earning a minimum wage, while you may *aspire* to be a center of influence in the future, you aren't one *now*. You're not going to be invited to join the board of trustees of the Museum of Modern Art in New York. We know that. But you can see yourself as being one day worthy of that position. You can share the values and interests of people who support the museum and other influential organizations. You can go to the museum (if you belong to one of various groups, you can even attend for free) and learn about the artists on display. You need to see yourself as worthy of being part of the group you want to join; only it's not yet the right time to actually take the plunge. Someday, but not quite yet.

If you're in business, imagine yourself as the future CEO or board chair of your company, and you're on the path that will take you there.

INFLUENCE HERO

For the purposes of this book about influence, using your time, abilities, resources and connections to help another person can make a tremendous impact. Giving back is like paying it forward. You help a person inasmuch as others have helped you and because you are fortunate enough to do so. The attitude of wanting to give, and more importantly, choosing to act on your intentions to give, will elevate you to a new level of hero status for some people in certain circumstances. As a result, if you do give back, if you help a person in need, if you make an important and influential connection for someone, if you help solve a problem, or even if you just say hello and smile for someone who desperately needs some kindness, you will have attained the title of *Influence Hero*!

THE LAW OF ATTRACTION ON A BIGGER SCALE

In the First Success Factor, we talked about the law of attraction, which in its most extreme form suggests that if you focus your mind on something, it will appear in your life. The method cites a three-step process: ask, believe, and receive. Some people extend this to include physical objects such as money and new cars, and that if you envision something strongly enough, it will appear in your life. Poof! Just like that.

While that may be a stretch, the law of attraction is undeniably effective in putting your mind into alignment with future success. Let's go back to that quintessential American success story, Arnold Schwarzenegger. From an early age, he saw himself as an immense success—a champion. In his mind, there was no question about it. He imagined himself as physically transformed, and he set his mind on making his goal a reality:

"When I was just a fifteen-year-old kid starting out, I visualized myself looking like [bodybuilder] Reg Park, only better. I kept telling myself that I could and would develop my body until I could beat my idol. I told myself before and after every workout that I was going to be the best. I went to bed at night and formed a mental picture of myself winning the Mr. Universe title. I wrote down the measurements I wanted to have when I won.... I never had the slightest doubt that I'd someday be the world's greatest bodybuilder. Some people may call that arrogance; I call it supreme confidence developed from using the full power of the mind."[41]

You may be wondering why, in the very last chapter of the book, I'm talking about using the power of your mind to transform yourself. You might think that should be a topic that would apply to a much earlier chapter. After all, Arnold was describing what he did when he was a young man, at the very beginning of his journey, even before he emigrated from Austria to the United States. You'd be correct, in as much as when Arnold was a teenager in Austria, he had no power or influence over anything *except his own body*. That was the one thing his overbearing father and the oppressive schools could not control. To Arnold, being a champion bodybuilder was a goal he latched onto because it was something he could do. He could envision a *future state* in his mind and then *take action* to achieve it.

As Earl Nightingale said, "Picture yourself in your mind's eye as having already achieved this goal. See yourself doing the things you'll be doing when you've reached your goal."[42]

You can use your mind to attract anything you want... but your mental focus must be supported by decisive, sustained action. When he was a teenager, Arnold did what he could do. As he grew older and more successful, his sphere of influence widened and kept getting bigger.

What happens when you've reached the level when you've expanded your influence beyond the limits of your own body... beyond your local area...

---

41   Ask Arnold. https://www.bodybuilding.com/fun/arnold-a-to-z-ask-arnold-wisdom-of-the-austrian-oak.html

42   https://www.awakenthegreatnesswithin.com/50-inspirational-earl-nightingale-quotes-on-success/

beyond your region... and even beyond your nation? How does the law of attraction work then?

It works the same way it always has! But now, you have a much more expansive canvas on which to project your dreams. Instead of trying to enlarge your biceps, or get to know a regional bank president, or form a partnership with another corporation, you can imagine innovations on a global scale.

What could be more exciting—or more heavy with responsibility?

THE GO-GIVER ATTITUDE

The vast majority of successful people have a "go-getter" mentality. It's pretty easy to understand why they do because life is highly competitive. The race to build influence and wealth is exciting and, for people born with little, represents an incredible opportunity to lift themselves from an ordinary existence.

Having a go-getter attitude has no relation to your economic level when you were growing up. Some people with great wealth and influence, such as Bill Gates, Elon Musk, and Jeff Bezos, were raised in comfortable circumstances. These people have never known the sting of poverty, and yet they have the inner drive to excel. But others have come a very long way to get to the top. Oprah Winfrey, Howard Schultz, Ralph Lauren, Larry Ellison, J.K. Rowling, and many other wealthy and influential people grew up in harsh circumstances. They were not unlike the person stepping off the boat and onto the dock in Metropolis— they had little to work with besides their own vision of a better future.

But all the people in both of these groups made it to positions of great success and influence. And once they arrived, many of them made the transition from go-getter to "go-giver." This is someone who makes the rational recognition that he or she now possesses fabulous wealth—more wealth than any person could possibly use—and therefore, for moral reasons, some of that wealth should be reinvested into the community in the form of charitable giving or public service.

ANDREW CARNEGIE

In the United States, the idea is not new. In the late nineteenth century, at the height of the Industrial Revolution, America produced its first group of super-wealthy people. They included Cornelius Vanderbilt (shipping, railroads), John Jacob Astor (real estate), John D. Rockefeller (oil), and Andrew Carnegie (steel).

Possibly the greatest "go-giver" of that era was Andrew Carnegie. Born in 1835 to a poor weaver's family in Dunfermline, Fife, Scotland, Andrew was thirteen years old when the family crossed the Atlantic and settled in Allegheny, Pennsylvania. There, both father and son found work at a cotton mill. The following year, in 1849, Andrew got his first break when he was hired to be a telegraph messenger boy in the Pittsburgh Office of the Ohio Telegraph Company. A hard worker, he memorized all of the locations of Pittsburgh's businesses and the faces of important men. More promotions followed, and influential people, seeing his potential, opened doors for him. He got into the iron and steel business, and during the Civil War, his company played a significant role in the Union's munitions manufacturing, as well as its telegraph service.

By the late 1880s, Carnegie was the largest manufacturer of pig iron, steel rails, and coke in the world. In 1902, he merged the huge Carnegie Steel Company into the United States Steel Company and took a payout worth over $300 million (about $7 billion today) in addition to his existing fortune. He retired from business, and until his death, he devoted himself to establishing philan-

Andrew Carnegie

thropic organizations and making direct contributions to many educational, cultural, and research institutions. They included the Carnegie Library, Carnegie Institution for Science, Carnegie Endowment for International Peace, Carnegie Mellon University, Carnegie Trust for the Universities of Scotland, and the Carnegie Hero Fund. His final and largest project was the Carnegie Corporation of New York, founded in 1911 with a $25 million endowment, later enlarged to $135 million. In all, he gave away $350 million, or ninety percent of his fortune.

At his death in 1919, aside from provisions for his widow and daughter, his last $30 million was given to foundations, charities, and to pensioners.

LEGACY

Today, over a century after the death of Andrew Carnegie, the Carnegie legacy lives on. With good reason, he's often referred to as the "father of modern philanthropy." Even as a young man, before he earned the immense fortune that made him the world's wealthiest person, Carnegie pledged that he would give away all of his money before dying. He later codified this pledge as a set of recommendations in his essay "The Gospel of Wealth"—its central message, "the man who dies thus rich dies disgraced."

One of the most tangible examples of Andrew Carnegie's philanthropy was the founding of 2,509 libraries in the late nineteenth and early twentieth centuries. Of these libraries, 1,679 were built in the United States. Carnegie spent over $55 million of his wealth on libraries alone, and he is often referred to as the "Patron Saint of Libraries."[43]

The biggest component of the Carnegie legacy is the Carnegie Corporation of New York, which has a very broad scope with respect to its grantmaking. Its accomplishments include everything from providing support for the research behind the drug insulin to helping launch PBS television and its mainstay children's program *Sesame Street*.

The Corporation, a 501(c)(3) nonprofit charity, works to promote democracy, education, and peace across the globe, advancing knowledge and understanding in these areas of central importance. For example, in education, the Corporation makes grants "to ensure that American public education prepares all students with the knowledge, skills, and dispositions they need to fully participate in democracy and thrive in the global economy." In the area of international peace and security, the Corporation seeks to "build a more secure, peaceful, and prosperous world through independent analysis and action addressing critical global challenges."[44]

Andrew Carnegie, in his mature years, after having attained a level of influence enjoyed by few others, carefully planned his legacy and brought it to life. He knew that after his death, his wealth would pass into the hands of others, who would assume responsibility for it. Instead of setting down strict rules that might hamstring his administrative heir, he made it clear that changing conditions would warrant changing strategies: "Conditions upon the earth inevitably change," he wrote in the Deed of Gift to the Corporation, "hence no wise man will bind Trustees forever to certain paths, causes or institutions.... They shall best conform to my wishes by using their own judgment."[45]

Your monetary legacy probably won't be as large as Andrew Carnegie's. But every person leaves *something* behind—a record of hard work, of being a good influence, a child who has learned from his or her parent. It's never too late to think about how your life and work might influence others, both in the present and in the future. As Stephen Covey said, "We do make a difference—one way or the other. We are responsible for the impact of our lives. Whatever we do with whatever we have, we leave behind us a legacy for those who follow."[46]

---

43   Carnegie Corporation of New York.
      https://www.carnegie.org/interactives/foundersstory/#!/
44   Carnegie Corporation of New York. https://www.carnegie.org/programs/
45   Ibid.
46   Libquotes. https://libquotes.com/stephen-covey/quote/lbr7y5l

DOLLY PARTON

Country music legend Dolly Parton is one of those rare philanthropists who does her work quietly, without much fanfare. It's only when you take the time to explore the astonishing depth and breadth of her charitable giving that you can appreciate the full impact of her generosity.

It's no exaggeration to say that after sixty years of success in the entertainment industry, Dolly Parton should be a billionaire. In fact, she's worth a reported $600 million, which is a lot of money, but since the mid-1980s she's given away hundreds of millions of dollars to a wide variety of worthy causes, particularly in the area of literacy, primarily through her Dollywood Foundation.

Formed in 1988, the Dollywood Foundation originally launched to help decrease high school dropout rates in Sevier County, Tennessee, where Parton grew up. In the early 1990s, she promised every seventh-grade and eighth-grade student she would personally give them $500 if they graduated from high school. This effort, called the Buddy Program, decreased the dropout rate to just 6 percent.

The Foundation also offers five scholarships of $15,000 each to the county's high school seniors to help further their education at any accredited university.

She created Dolly Parton's Imagination Library, a book gifting program that mails free, high-quality books to children from birth to age five, no matter their family's income. Launched in 1995, books were initially distributed to children living in Sevier County.

In 2014, Dolly told *Southern Living* magazine that the Imagination Library was "one of the things I'm proudest of, of anything I've ever done.... You can't educate enough children. A lot of that came from the fact that a lot of my own relatives didn't get to go to school because we were mountain people. You have to get out and work and help feed the family. My own dad couldn't read and write. And my dad was very proud of me. He got to live long enough to see the Imagination Library do well, so he felt like he had done something good too—that he was the inspiration for it."[47]

The Imagination Library became such a success that in 2000, it went national. By 2003, the Imagination Library had mailed one million books. In 2020, the number had reached 150 million. The Imagination Library is no longer just Dolly's project; it has become tremendously influential and is supported by many other like-minded people.

On November 28, 2016, massive fires swept through Sevier County, de-

---

47   https://theboot.com/dolly-parton-charity-work/

stroying the homes of over 1,000 families. Dolly asked the Foundation to spearhead the effort to distribute $1,000 per month for six months to the families who had lost their primary residence. In two weeks, the Foundation created the My People Fund, designed the distribution process, and implemented the distribution.[48]

With the help of a cavalcade of country and pop music stars who were persuaded by Dolly's stature in the music industry, the telethon, *Smoky Mountains Rise: A Benefit for the My People Fund*, raised more than $13 million.

As the program wound down, the My People Fund gave recipients a check for $5,000 and donated $8.9 million directly to families in need.

In December 2006, Dolly pledged $500,000 toward a proposed $90 million hospital and cancer center to be constructed in Sevierville in the name of Robert F. Thomas, the physician who delivered her. She has been a generous donor to Vanderbilt University School of Medicine (VUMC). In April 2020, in response to the COVID-19 pandemic, she donated $1 million towards research at Vanderbilt University Medical Center and encouraged those who could afford it to make similar donations.[49]

The list goes on…. Suffice to say that Dolly Parton has successfully and generously leveraged her influence and wealth to help improve the lives of millions of people.

THE GIVING PLEDGE

While plenty of people became wealthy in the decades following the Gilded Age of Andrew Carnegie and his fellow industrial tycoons, the next big group of super-rich people emerged at the beginning of the twentieth century, as a result of the maturing of the Digital Revolution. Many of those at the top of the "Forbes Billionaires" list derived their wealth either directly or indirectly from digital technology, including Jeff Bezos (Amazon), Bill Gates (Microsoft), Larry Ellison (Oracle), Mark Zuckerberg (Facebook), Steve Ballmer (Microsoft), Larry Page and Sergey Brin (Google/Alphabet), and Jack Ma (Alibaba).

Occupying their own solar system are the heirs to the Walmart empire, including Jim, Alice, Rob, and Lukas Walton, who collectively boast a net worth of $247 billion, making them the richest family on earth.

And of course, we need to mention highly influential investor Warren Buf-

---

48   https://imaginationlibrary.com/the-dollywood-foundation/

49   https://www.wjhl.com/local-coronavirus-coverage/dolly-parton-announces-she-will-donate-1-million-to-vanderbilt-for-covid-19-research/

fett (Berkshire Hathaway), also known as the "Oracle of Omaha," who in 2020 ranked #4 on the Forbes list, behind Jeff Bezos, Bill Gates, and Bernard Arnault.

Among this group of super-wealthy and highly influential people, some are concerned with using their influence for good today, while leaving a positive legacy for tomorrow. Following in the footsteps of Andrew Carnegie are Bill and Melinda Gates.

Like Carnegie, as an entrepreneur Bill Gates made a pile of money and then resolved to give much of it away. His career as a philanthropist began in 1994 when he asked his father, William H. Gates Sr., to help improve reproductive and child health in the developing world by establishing the William H. Gates Foundation. In 2000, it merged with the Gates Learning Foundation to create the Bill & Melinda Gates Foundation. The primary goals of the foundation are to enhance healthcare and reduce extreme poverty across the globe, and expand educational opportunities and access to information technology in the US. The foundation is controlled by its three trustees: Bill Gates, Melinda Gates, and their friend Warren Buffett.

In June 2006, Gates announced that he would be transitioning to a part-time role at Microsoft and full-time work at the Bill & Melinda Gates Foundation. He was then just fifty-one years old. Then in February 2014, he stepped down as chairman of Microsoft. Six years later, in March 2020, Gates left his board positions at both Microsoft and Berkshire Hathaway to focus on his philanthropic work. At that point he was sixty-five years old, which meant that statistically he could look forward to a decade or more solely devoted to giving away his money.

In July 2010, Gates and Warren Buffett—who are well known to play bridge together—announced the formation of The Giving Pledge, an informal organization with this premise:

"The Giving Pledge is a simple concept: an open invitation for billionaires, or those who would be if not for their giving, to publicly commit to giving the majority of their wealth to philanthropy. It is inspired by the example set by millions of people at all income levels who give generously—and often at great personal sacrifice—to make the world better. Envisioned as a multi-generational effort, the Giving Pledge aims over time to help shift the social norms of philanthropy among the world's wealthiest people and inspire people to give more, establish their giving plans sooner, and give in smarter ways."[50]

Within a month, forty billionaires had signed the pledge, and by early 2021, the number had swelled to more than 200 of the world's wealthiest individuals,

---

50   The Giving Pledge. https://givingpledge.org/About.aspx

couples, and families. Their collective worth has been estimated at $734 billion. Names on the list—which anyone can see at givingpledge.org—include Lynne and Marc Benioff, Sara Blakely, Michael R. Bloomberg, Barry Diller and Diane von Furstenberg, Barron Hilton, Elon Musk, David Rockefeller, Ted Turner, Mark Zuckerberg and Priscilla Chan, and many more.

As for Bill and Melinda Gates, their promises have been backed up by action. Since 1994, CNBC reported, citing the *Chronicle of Philanthropy*, the Gates have given $45.5 billion to charitable causes, including the eponymously named Bill & Melinda Gates Foundation. In 2019, they donated $589 million to charity, making them the seventh most philanthropic people of that year.

In 2020, the year of the COVID-19 pandemic, the world's wealthiest people gave away a lot of money. According to the *Chronicle of Philanthropy*, the biggest donor was Jeff Bezos, who put up $10 billion to launch the Bezos Earth Fund. Bezos, who on February 2, 2021, announced he was stepping down as Amazon CEO to devote more time to philanthropy and to his Blue Origin spaceflight program, also contributed $100 million to Feeding America, the organization that supplies more than 200 food banks. In his letter to Amazon employees, he wrote, "Invention is the root of our success. Keep inventing, and don't despair when, at first, the idea looks crazy. Remember to wander. Let curiosity be your compass."[51]

Number two on the list was Bezos's ex-wife, MacKenzie Scott, who had received $35.5 billion in her 2019 divorce, making her one of the world's wealthiest women. In that same year, she signed the Giving Pledge and willingly committed to give away most of her wealth to charity over her lifetime or in her will, though her pledge—like all the others—was legally non-binding. The next year she gave $5.7 billion by asking community leaders to help identify 512 organizations for seven- and eight-figure gifts, including food banks, human-service organizations, and racial-justice charities.

Number three on the list was Michael Bloomberg, who gave away $1.6 billion, followed by Phil and Penelope Knight with $1.36 billion, and Jack Dorsey, at $1.09 billion. [52]

To be fair, it must be pointed out that many very wealthy people enjoy passive incomes that keep the money rolling in faster than they can give it away. For example, in 2020, despite the US entering its worst economic downturn since the Great Depression, Jeff Bezos saw his fortune gain $74 billion, to hit a record

---

51   Space.com. https://www.space.com/jeff-bezos-steps-down-amazon-ceo
52   https://bit.ly/2RGrRuc

$189.3 billion. This means that despite donating $10 billion to the Bezos Earth Fund, his net worth continued to swell.

While the marriage of Bill and Melinda Gates did not stand the test of time, they have both committed to work together and to remain active in their philanthropic work with the Foundation.

CHUCK FEENEY: THE MAN WHO GAVE IT ALL AWAY

There are a few very wealthy and influential people who have truly given away their fortunes before they died.

Charles F. Feeney was born in Elizabeth, New Jersey, in 1931, during the Great Depression.

His mother worked as a hospital nurse, and his father was an insurance underwriter. He graduated from Elizabeth's St. Mary of the Assumption High School in 1949; he has credited his charitable spirit to his education at St. Mary. During the Korean War, he served as a US Air Force radio operator, and in the 1950s, began his career selling duty-free liquor to US naval personnel at Mediterranean ports. His business evolved into DFS ("DFS Group"), a Hong Kong-based travel retailer of luxury products, including duty-free stores in major airports and city and resort locations.

In 1982, Feeney created The Atlantic Philanthropies, and two years later secretly transferred his entire 38.75% stake in DFS, then worth about $500 million, to the foundation. The foundation's main areas of interest were health, education, reconciliation, and human rights.

Through Atlantic, he began making donations in secret. Over time, the largest single beneficiary of Feeney's giving was his alma mater Cornell University, which received nearly $1 billion in direct and Atlantic gifts.

In February 2011, Feeney signed The Giving Pledge. In his letter to Bill Gates and Warren Buffett, he wrote, "I cannot think of a more personally rewarding and appropriate use of wealth than to give while one is living—to personally devote oneself to meaningful efforts to improve the human condition. More importantly, today's needs are so great and varied that intelligent philanthropic support and positive interventions can have greater value and impact today than if they are delayed when the needs are greater."[53]

About his personal philosophy of philanthropy, which Feeney called "Giv-

---

53   Atlantic Philanthropies. https://www.atlanticphilanthropies.
      org/news/the-atlantic-philanthropies-signs-off

ing While Living," he said, "It's a lot more fun to give while you're alive than to give while you're dead."[54]

On September 14, 2020, with the last grants having been made, during an online ceremony that included a congratulatory video message from Bill Gates, Feeney signed the documents to officially close The Atlantic Philanthropies.

Feeney provided for his five children (four daughters and one son) with funds through their mother, his first wife. As of March 2021, Feeney was living in a two-bedroom apartment in San Francisco with his wife, Helga. According to biographer Conor O'Clery, Chuck Feeney is "very happy" that he completed his almost forty-year mission and celebrated the milestone with Helga.[55]

GLOBAL ALLIANCES TO BENEFIT OTHERS

In our global economy, where raw materials and products are routinely shipped from one continent to another, it's difficult to affect positive change if you're only capable of acting regionally or even nationally. Your nation may have laws and standards governing labor, safety, and the environment, but the other nation may not. The story of international trade has long been made more difficult and complicated by the variations in cultural norms and the tolerance for abuse from one nation to another.

One answer has been Fair Trade USA. The Fair Trade movement dates back to the late 1940s, when Edna Ruth Byler, an American businesswoman, resolved to support the women artisans she had encountered along her global travels. To help them earn a living, she began selling their handmade textiles to her friends and neighbors. Out of this grew Ten Thousand Villages and a global Fair Trade movement.

Today, Fair Trade is "a global movement made up of a diverse network of producers, companies, consumers, advocates, and organizations putting people and planet first."[56] Fair Trade Certified products earn the title by following a robust system relying on independent, third-party evaluation and certification to hold businesses accountable to their fair trade commitments.

Across a wide range of products and industries, the network of global collaborations is impressive. To provide a more stable income for smallholder farmers in Latin America, Fair Trade USA partners with the Sustainable Food, Agriculture and Environment (SAFE) platform of the Inter-American Development Bank, Oikocredit, Keurig Green Mountain, and Catholic Relief Services.

---

54   Atlantic Philanthropies. https://www.atlanticphilanthropies.org/giving-while-living

55   BBC. https://bbc.in/34m5dKc

56   Fair Trade. https://www.fairtradecertified.org/about-us

It's quite a diverse group, held together by mutual trust and a common goal—a theme that we have seen throughout this book, but now on a global scale.

For the apparel and footwear manufacturing sector, there is the Social and Labor Convergence Project, which, together with the Sustainable Apparel Coalition, is a collective agreement between brands, retailers, and industry groups to improve working conditions.

In seafood, the Conservation Alliance for Seafood Solutions connects leading conservation groups that work with businesses to solve sustainable seafood's biggest challenges. The Alliance's Global Hub is an international community of organizations and subject area experts working to improve the responsibility and sustainability of seafood supply chains. Global Hub members work to connect, build capacity, and effectively leverage tools, approaches, and experience in order to advance the sustainability and responsibility of wild fisheries and aquaculture production.

As a trusted collaborator, Fair Trade USA shares the goal of improving ocean health and ensuring a long-term supply of seafood.

All of these partnerships, and many more, are the result of influential people reaching out to one another, often across continents and oceans, to form trusted partnerships designed to make the world a better place.

There could be no higher aspiration or more worthy goal.

ONE MORE STORY

While this book—and this last chapter—have focused on how to build your personal influence to the point where you could think and act globally, like Bill Gates and Warren Buffett, it's good to remember that anyone can have influence at any stage of their journey. You don't need a billion dollars in the bank to make a difference in someone's life. And you never know what the ripple effects will be!

It was 5:30 in the morning at the 130 Diner in Delran, New Jersey. As the usual early-morning crowd filed in looking for a good breakfast to start their workdays, server Liz Woodward noticed two men who appeared to be exhausted from a long night. She greeted them, and Tim Young and Paul Hullings told her they were firefighters who had been up all night battling a massive warehouse blaze.

"I had been following the New Brunswick fire on the news," Liz later told TODAY.com. "This was their first meal in over twenty-four hours."

After enjoying their breakfasts, Tim and Paul called for the check. Liz handed it to them. On it, she had written this:

"Your breakfast is on me today—Thank you for all that you do; for serving others & for running into the places everyone else runs away from. No matter your role, you are courageous, brave, and strong... Thank you for being bold... every day! Fueled by fire and driven by courage—what an example you are. Get some rest."

The surprised and grateful firefighters thanked her and went on their way.

It's a lovely story, isn't it? It's heartwarming that Liz—who probably didn't make much money—acted with such generosity.

But the story didn't end there.

Through social media, Tim and Paul discovered that Liz's father was a quadriplegic, and she was trying to raise money to buy him a wheelchair-accessible van.

"Turns out, the young lady who gave us a free meal is really the one that could use the help," Tim wrote in a Facebook post, highlighting the GoFundMe campaign Liz had started a few months earlier. At that point, the campaign wasn't going very well. But when the two firefighters spread the word, the community stepped up, and quickly they raised $67,000—well over the goal. Soon, Liz's father was able to get around town in his very own van.

"People from all over the world have heard our story," said Liz, "and from it, they're recognizing opportunities to do something little or big for someone else.... This is just one example of how so many people in this world have incredible hearts, and they pay it forward, so the circle keeps on moving."[57]

Helping others and paying it forward, in ways small or large, is something you can do at any time while you're on your way to massive global influence!

---

57   Today.com. https://on.today.com/3wsFCLE

SUCCESS ACTION ITEMS – GIVE BACK!

- Begin giving back now. Anyone can practice giving back. If, like most people, you're still building your spheres of influence, then this chapter will give you something to aspire to. Even so, you can begin to practice at any time, on a scale that works for you.
- Focus on the present. If becoming a center of influence is important to you, then there's an old saying that goes, "If you want to be somebody in the future, start being that person now!"
- Give back, if you help a person in need, if you make an important and influential connection for someone, if you help solve a problem, or even if you just say hello and smile for someone who desperately needs some kindness, you will have attained the title of *Influence Hero!*
- Use the law of attraction on a larger scale. You can use your mind to attract anything you want… but your mental focus must be supported by decisive, sustained action.
- Have a go-giver attitude. When you arrive at a position of success and influence, make the conscious decision to transition from a go-getter to a "go-giver."
- Give the go-giver role a try. It's never too late to become a go-giver. Whether or not you become a local, regional, national, or a center of influence like Andrew Carnegie and other legendary tycoons, there is nothing stopping you from using your example and influence to leave a legacy of helping others as a go-giver.
- Remember that anyone can have influence at any stage of their journey.
- Help others and pay it forward, in ways small or large. You can do it at any time while you're on your way to massive global influence!

LARRY NAMER
CEO METAN GLOBAL ENTERTAINMENT
CO-FOUNDER E! ENTERTAINMENT TELEVISION

"Gift of Honesty and Transparency"

THE STORY BEHIND E! ENTERTAINMENT

I N 1984, MY FRIEND ALAN Mruvka and I started kicking around ideas. We wanted to do something for ourselves. Alan was actually a real estate guy and his group had bought a movie studio, the old Francis Ford Coppola truck studios, and he had gotten the entertainment bug. I was trying to figure out what my next act was, and we were kicking around ideas. We then said, "If you look at cable TV, it really is an electronic newspaper. CNN is the headlines, ESPN is the sports, the Home Shopping network is the ads section." But what was missing, the second most-read paid pages out of any Sunday newspaper, was the entertainment section. So we said, "We're going to create the entertainment part of the electronic newspaper!"

We thought we were brilliant, so we wrote a business plan. At that time, to build a cable network, you needed somewhere between sixty and a hundred million dollars. We wrote a plan and figured, this is a great idea, people will give us money to start a TV network. We didn't realize that nobody ever thought that people like us could wake up in the morning and start a TV network. The comments we got were, "Well Larry, that's an interesting idea, but you're not Rupert Murdoch. You're not Ted Turner."

But Alan and I believed in it so much and we thought it was just so logical. People love Hollywood gossip! We kept at it, and after three and a half years of people telling us, "Good idea, but no, we're not giving you any money," we met a guy on an airplane who worked for Warner Communications. He was doing acquisitions and divestitures, and he said, "Tell me more." So we told him about it, and he said, "Oh that's a really good idea. I know somebody who will give you the money."

We were like, yeah right. But we ended up going to New York and we met with a gentleman. He had just started being the head of investment banking for a traditional bond house. We walked in the office, and he had movie posters on the wall. Alan and I looked at each other and said, "What the heck is this?"

"Oh, I love this," he said. "I used to be the entertainment reporter for my college newspaper."

"Yeah, okay, but we need sixty million dollars."

"Well, I'm new," he said, "and I'm only allowed to sign for two and a half million dollars."

So we asked ourselves, "What can we do with two and a half million dollars?" But then we looked at each and said, "We're in!"

He got us that money. His name was Jeffrey Pollack, and he worked with another gentleman named Chip Barnes. And so we had two and a half million dollars. Now we had to figure out how to make it work.

We started putting a team together. I contacted a friend who taught radio and film at a college in Austin, Texas. He worked for me when I was at Valley Cable. He was my head of programming. So I called him up and I said, "Brian, I'm doing this thing. Do you have any kids who need internships?"

And he said, "Yeah, I've got a whole bunch of them. We couldn't place many kids this summer. How many do you want?"

"All you've got."

So he sent us thirty-one interns. We rented apartments in Hollywood, got mattresses, and started the company with thirty-one interns and eleven employees.

We launched on July 31, 1987. We put it on the air. We bought old industrial equipment. We rented the old Hollywood freight railroad station and turned it into a studio. Our voiceover booth was the clothes closet in the conference room, so if you needed to use the voiceover booth you had to walk through the conference room during a meeting. We just had to figure it out, how to make it work with what we had. It was a good testament that when your back is up against the wall, you get really inventive. Because we didn't have a lot of money we just said, "We don't make movies, so we really need to be different. We have no control over the movie theater, so when we show the movies, they're going to be what they are. But we do have control over whom we pick as hosts."

We started using the MTV format, with a green screen, and we said, "If you can stand someone up in front of a green screen when Madonna has a new record, why not put a guy in front of a green screen when Schwarzenegger has a new movie? It's exactly the same thing."

Even now, people say we were very lucky that we had all those great hosts, but none of our original hosts were ever on TV before. We hired Julie Moran, who went on to be the first woman ever to do *Wide World of Sports* and then did *Entertainment Tonight.* Katie Wagner went on to do *Lifestyles of the Rich and Famous,* and Richard Blade went on to be the top DJ in L.A, then VH1. People would see our program and say, "We've never seen anything like this before." Even to the point where we started getting movie clips and we would have our host introduce the movie clips, and we got those from the movie studios.

Greg Kinnear started with us. Greg was an assistant at a company that was making low-budget monster movies. We went in to pitch his company on advertising. And he said, "Well, who's going be the host?"

And we said, "Well, we're interviewing."

"I can do that," he said.

"Eileen is the person putting people on tape," I told him. "Next Tuesday at two o'clock, just go see Eileen."

We got back to the office and I said, "Eileen, this guy's coming in at two o'clock on Tuesday. We're trying to sell some advertising to him, so just be nice to him. I don't even care if you turn on the camera."

Tuesday comes and Eileen comes in and says, "Oh, that guy Greg is here, he'd like to say hello to you."

"Eileen, I'm trying to figure out how to make payroll this week," I said. "I'm really busy. I just don't have the time. I'm really jammed," I said. "Just go to the studio and tell him I'm sorry, I can't meet with him."

She comes back five minutes later, and says, "We're ready to go in the studio. He'd like to just stick his head in and say hello."

"I'm really busy Eileen! What doesn't he understand?"

Then she gets in the studio, and she comes back in and says Larry, we're starting to work with that guy. We think you should come in."

So literally she grabs me by the ear, and suddenly I'm going to the studio. Now by this time we had put more than 5,000 people on tape, and we had *not chosen even one host.* We didn't like any of them.

As we were walking down the hall, I was mumbling, "Eileen, I can't believe you are doing this. You're a bother, I don't know how I'm going to pay you on Friday. Why are you making me do this?"

"Larry, just shut up and come into the studio."

We entered the studio, and she cued him. I looked up and said, "Oh, my God! He's a star! Hire him!" And so Greg was the centerpiece, and we knew it from day one.

We started getting a few letters from women: "I saw that Greg Kinnear, and he's so cute!" And the next week, we got ten letters. "Oh, when he makes a mistake and he raises his eyebrows, he's the cutest guy!" The next week it was fifty letters. And we thought, this is crazy. And then we started getting *hundreds* of letters.

I just love Greg. And he's an absolutely sweetheart. We were doing a reunion years ago, and Greg was doing a movie in London, and he actually flew in for the reunion dinner. I guess it was 2015, it was like the 28-year reunion. And you know, he's just a sweet guy, really down to earth sweet guy, family man, and a great actor.

Then we started thinking about doing original productions.

We applied for credentials to go to the Oscars. The reaction we got was, "Are you cable guys nuts? You're not getting any passes to the Oscars. Go away!" We weren't from ABC, NBC, CBS, or Fox. So one of our producers named Jay said, "Larry, I checked it out. Why don't we just go climb over the fence?"

"Will they shoot us?" I asked.

He said, "No, they won't shoot us. If they catch us, they'll just throw us out."

To get inside the first Oscars that we ever covered, we climbed over the fence with our camera equipment. Our stuff looked very pirated, since it was old, and it made it look like we were not supposed to be there. But when we aired the footage, it was the first time our audience felt like they were a fly on the wall, and it felt like they were in a place they weren't supposed to be, and they absolutely loved it.

The trade magazine *The Hollywood Reporter* was owned by a woman named Tichi Wilkerson Kassel. And here you had *The Hollywood Reporter* and *Variety*. If you were in the entertainment business, you had to read them every morning. And Kassel loved us, and said, "You are really out there."

The Hollywood Reporter really helped us build this relationship with the industry. And the more they covered us, the executives of the studios, said, "Well if *The Hollywood Reporter* covers them, they must be important!" and so they paid attention. I think the first studio that jumped on board was Universal, and they gave us movie trailers. We ran them on the air and people loved it—the best two minutes of a $150 million movie.

When we would talk to the PR people, we would ask, "What's the biggest problem you have?"

And they said, "Well, we can't afford to advertise the movie more than a week before it comes out."

"Enlist the video crew on the movie set," we said. "Interview the director and the actors. You interview everybody there. Then give us the video, and we'll start covering the movie six months before it comes out. We'll help you build awareness and brand." Very typical marketing, but it wasn't being used in the entertainment business.

We started doing that, and then Disney called and said, "Hey, you're doing this stuff for Universal, how come you're not doing it for us?" Then all the studios began to realize that we were the friends of the industry. We were celebrating the entertainment industry, and then actors would come to us and say it looks like so much fun when I come to L.A., could I host? It was the Wayans brothers and Paula Abdul and everybody like that, and we were like, "Yes, sure," because we had this little studio and all we had to do was turn on the lights.

We would interrupt the show and go, "Hey, guess who just dropped in? Paula Abdul! Here you go Paula, here's the microphone. Just watch the teleprompter and introduce these clips." It was just so impromptu and so pirate. And people just loved it.

Alan and I always had this feeling that the Hollywood press treated entertainment too seriously. The business is not rocket science. You're not curing cancer. Hollywood is funny stuff. We were very irreverent. Then we came up with some ideas. I said to my programming folks, "I want to do a TV show that makes fun of TV shows." And they were looking at me saying, "Larry you can't do that. I mean, how can you make fun of TV shows when you're supposed to be covering them?" So we created *Talk Soup*.

We'd have Greg Kinnear stand in front of the teleprompter, and go, "Yesterday on *Jerry Springer*... now watch this clip!" And that show just took off. We used that show to be the place where we taught the audience what else we were doing. So you would hear Greg Kinnear on this crazy show. Then someone said, "How about Howard Stern? Why don't you do a story on him?" Alan and I met with Howard in the elevator in New York, and we went to his radio show. When we told everybody we wanted to put his show on TV, they said, "We thought you were crazy when you wanted to do *Talk Soup*! Radio died 40 years ago! Why would you want to put cameras in a radio station studio and show a radio show? That's like watching paint dry on the wall."

And we said, "You guys don't get it. This is the real *WKRP in Cincinnati*. It's a sitcom." It lasted seven years!

We expanded to fourteen countries. It was the fastest growing cable network in the U.S. Then people with money started coming out of the woodwork. "Why didn't you tell us this was what you wanted to do? We would have given you the money four years ago...!"

INFLUENCER

My definition of an influencer is somebody who has the ability to move people to do something. It could be something political, it could be something related to product, or participating in some form of media thing. People think that just because you have 20 million followers, you're an influencer. But it's become much more refined today. We're starting to understand that it's not just the number of people who follow you, it's the relationship. You could have fewer followers, but if they are actively engaged with you, that's real influence.

STRATEGIC INFLUENCER

In China, we always partner with other companies, because we don't believe as a U.S. company, we can navigate that market without having someone deeply involved in every aspect of it. We really look for partners who don't just bring money to the table, but who bring value in helping us navigate whatever the market is.

RELATIONSHIPS

The next level is relationship-based. First there's the level of being honest with each other. You have to develop a basis for trust, and that doesn't happen right away, particularly when you're dealing with a foreign country like China, where they just assume we've got some ulterior motive behind everything we do. I would say it took us three years in China before they began to realize that we really didn't have a political agenda. We were just about entertaining people and we had no political agenda. It took a while to build up, and it's a matter of being honest and transparent. It's probably one of the reasons we've been active in China for over a decade.

Most Western companies have failed because they've gone into the market and said, "This is the way we do it in Australia. We'll give you the program and you can subtitle it in Mandarin." We realized early on that Chinese people are very happy to be Chinese. So we decided we were going to produce in Mandarin, even though I didn't speak a word of it. We decided we were going to produce in their language for their people, and they appreciated that. We didn't come in there trying to change them, we just tried to entertain them and make them laugh.

CENTER OF INFLUENCE AND GIVING BACK

People have this idea of who I am and who I'm supposed to be. And then they think, "That can't be the guy. He's got that thick Brooklyn accent, he could be in the *Sopranos* or something." People have this expectation of you. People who know me just know that there are very few things I take seriously. One of the reasons I'm a little bit of a hermit in L.A. is because I would go out to meet someone, and invariably 10 people would approach me and say, I know you're really busy, but would you just read my script and tell me what you think? So I try to avoid things like that.

On the other hand, the pandemic has made me a little bit less of a hermit, which is ironic. I don't really look for notoriety. I like to remain behind the scenes. But my press person is always bothering me to do these interviews, and I've always shunned them, but now with the pandemic and having a lot of time, I don't have any excuses anymore.

I used to say, "I would love to do it, but I have meetings."

Now she says, "Larry, I *know* you don't have any meetings. You must do it." So I do more of it now. There's this thing on the internet called the Lunch Club. Every week I spend 45 minutes basically giving career advice to people. And I really enjoy that, because I'm getting to meet a lot of young hustler types, and they relish the idea to get 45 minutes with me. I love working with young folks.

DEEP DOWN HABITS

I've got a lot of energy. I'm up early in the morning to get things done. I worked for Nick Nicholas, who eventually became the chairman of Time Warner. He always said, "Be firm but fair." That's stuck with me forever. You can be demanding, but you've got to be fair. People have to know. I've kept that with me. People like working for me because they know no matter what happens, they will be treated and compensated fairly.

I used to watch the way Nick dealt with stuff, the way he dealt with people, and that really helped me a lot. People in the office would bring these ideas and memos, and he would just put them in his desk drawer. I asked why he did that, and he said, "If it was really important, they will come back." If they didn't come back, it wasn't all that important, and he would empty the drawer after thirty days. So an interpretation of that for me is, I would tell everybody, "Look, if you call me on the phone, maybe I'll get back to you in three days; but if you email me I promise I'll never go to sleep without answering every email." I've stuck with that for many years. I rarely answer the telephone for anybody.

FAST FORWARD TO TODAY

If I were starting again today, I would be doing something with the internet, requiring a lot less content to fill it and giving people what they want when they want it, on the device they want. I wouldn't start E! today as a TV network. It would be an app or web-based platform that people could consume as they wanted. It's just a shift in content delivery technology. You need to keep pace.

ONE DEFINING MOMENT

When he was 15, my son was diagnosed with terminal brain cancer. But fortunately, he turned it around, he's the miracle kid, and he's done incredibly well. But that was the point for me where I would examine everything, and start to question, how important is this really? It's not finding the meaning of life, it's finding what's important in life and what's not. It really leveled me out where in business I would get upset over something and I'd be frantic and then the next day I would ask, why did I get so crazy?

That experience with my son made me look at things that way. I'd say, "This wasn't a good day, but so what? Am I going to feel this way tomorrow, and just not get upset?" So now I'm very even. I don't have a lot of highs and lows, and that's probably one of the reasons I've been successful.

Larry Namer is an award-winning, entertainment industry veteran with over 50 years professional experience in film, television, live events and new media, Larry Namer was recently named Chief Operating Officer of FanVestor. He is a founding partner of Metan Global Entertainment, a venture created to develop and distribute entertainment content and media specifically for Chinese speaking audiences.

Mr. Namer is the Co-Founder of E! Entertainment Television, a company now valued at over $3.5 billion. He is the creator of several successful companies, including Comspan Communications that pioneered Western entertainment in the former Soviet Union and Steeplechase Media that served as the primary consultant to Microsoft's MiTV.

Email: ljn@ljnmedia.com
Websites: LJNMedia.com
Metanglobal.com
Fanvestor.com
BeautyKween.com

THANK YOU AND AUTHOR BIO

Thank you for reading my book! I hope it has helped you to chart your own path toward building an exceptional sphere of personal influence. I'd be delighted to hear from you! If you'd like more information about strategic based influence, about future business influence seminars, or about booking our organization for a speaking or training event, please contact us at info@successmasters.com.

GARY C. LANEY
CEO AND FOUNDER SUCCESS MASTERS

Gary is the CEO of Success Masters LLC, a holding company that has invested in business networking, online media, e-commerce and intellectual property.

An author, high-tech executive, serial entrepreneur, keynote speaker, professional trainer and startup investor, Gary has personally been involved in more than 20 businesses including a company that that went public where he ran world-wide sales. Most recently he was CEO and Co-Founder of Trustegrity, a fast growing, national professional networking company that was launched in 2012. Gary is known for his ability to turn-around businesses and to create dramatic revenue growth.

A dynamic speaker, Gary has been recognized as a top presenter, motivating tens of thousands of entrepreneurs, business professionals and sales people. Prior to his entrepreneurial run, Gary spent 25 years as an executive in corporate high-tech and commercial publishing. Gary has a Triple Major MBA from Northwestern/Kellogg in Finance, Marketing, and Policy. Gary and his wife Carla have six wonderful children made up of four daughters, two sons, and ten grandchildren.

Email: info@successmasters.com
LinkedIn: www.linkedin.com/in/garyclaney/

CPSIA information can be obtained
at www.ICGtesting.com
Printed in the USA
LVHW030353160721
692784LV00002B/149

9 781737 091592